Chris Searle

was born in Romford in 1944. He has taught in
Canada and the West Indies, and for several
years was an English teacher in a secondary
school in East London and an active member
of the National Union of Teachers. He is now
teaching in Mozambique.

He has compiled several poetry collections,
particularly anthologies of children's work:
Stepney Words (1971), *Fire Words* (1972), and
also a collection of pensioners' poems, *Elders*
(1973).

He has written books on English teaching, *The
Forsaken Lover: White Words and Black People*
(winner of the Martin Luther King Memorial
Prize, 1973), *This New Season,* and *Classrooms
of Resistance* (Writers & Readers 1975).

He has also written a children's story, *Ferndale
Fires,* a novel, *Poilu,* a collection of his own
poems, *Mainland,* and most recently four
stories, *The Black Man of Shadwell* (Writers &
Readers 1976).

He helped establish a local community press,
Reality Press, in East London, which has
published many books by local writers. He is
a member of the Writers & Readers Publishing
Cooperative.

The World in a Classroom

Compiled by

Chris Searle

Paving Stones

Along the streets of cities drear
The stones lie heavy: but I know
That prisoned under pavements here
The good brown earth is still below.

Beneath the stony lives of men
Grown hard and loveless, still I find
That whoso digs in faith again
Comes on a heart that's warm and kind.

From *Lansbury's Labour-Weekly* 1926

Writers and Readers Publishing Cooperative

Published 1977 by Writers and Readers Publishing Cooperative,
14 Talacre Road, London NW5 3PE

Typeset by Caroline MacKechnie

Printed and bound in Great Britain by Lowe & Brydone Ltd,
Thetford, Norfolk

Cover photograph by Mike Abrahams

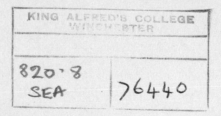

Contents

Preface 7

Introduction 9

Part One
Schools and Streets 17

Part Two
The World in a Classroom 33

Part Three
Hello Friend 59

Part Four
The Practice of Empathy 95

Part Five
The Embrace of History 179

Background Notes 229

Acknowledgements

The compilation of this book has been the result of two years of English teaching in a secondary school in Limehouse, East London. The children whose work is included were between the ages of twelve and fourteen.

This work by the children could never have been produced without the solid cooperative strength of a team of teachers dedicated to the same ends: the full development of the human potentialities of all our children, and all working class children the world over, in the context of the accompanying struggle for socialism. To the comrades of the classroom who formed our team of teachers this book is dedicated: to Irene Payne, Bob Brett, Tony Tarrant and Bill Foot — an ageless force of encouragement, criticism and strength. To Jean Bleach, who supported us, Juliet Buddle who was with us for a year, and Tom Mannion, Chris Pickett and the other teachers who lived with us. To Peter Andrews, who more than once defended us, and to all those friends and comrades who visited us or helped us: Russell Kenny, Andrew Salkey, Joan Jara, Peter Blackman, Peggy Seeger, Mohammed Haque, Ron McCormick, Lyle Alexander, Elaine Nicholson, Jack Warshaw, The Basement Writers, George Johannes of S.W.A.P.O., the Half Moon Theatre, Trevor Huddleston, Ivy Tribe, Terry McCarthy.

And the children, whose future is the future of the world.

Preface

It was for me a great privilege to be asked, a short time
ago, to speak at the school where the children, whose
writing goes to make up most of this book, are students.
A privilege because the subject chosen for the discussion
was South Africa and the violence in Soweto. A privilege
also because it was obvious from the response of the
children and their questions afterwards that the
background situation was well understood. This book —
most of it written by the children themselves, but with
a connecting commentary by their teacher — explains
how and why this particular school has this deep concern
for the issues of race and colour conflict. As Chris Searle
expresses it in his Introduction: 'The main purpose of
this book is to attack racism by urging teachers in our
schools to openly fight its causes and effects by engaging
children in such knowledge, argument and empathy in
the classroom that will combat and undermine its
poisonous influence.'

I do not pretend to share the political views of Chris
Searle and his colleagues at every point. Nor, I suspect,
do they share my religious philosophy and Christian
commitment. But we hold in common the view that
racism in all its forms and disguises is today the greatest
enemy to peace and the most destructive force threatening
our world. We also share the conviction that educators,
and especially teachers in those areas of our country
where 'immigrant' communities are strong, have an
absolute and over-riding responsibility in the matter.

It is so much easier to exclude from curricula the

7

subjects which, just because they are so urgent and so relevant, are also controversial and even divisive. It needs great energy, great dedication and great enthusiasm to generate the kind of concern amongst teenagers which will find such positive and creative expression as this book provides. I hope with all my heart that its message will be understood and acted upon before it is too late. We have 'only one Earth' — and it is a marvellous home for all of us if we can learn not to abuse it.

In the classrooms of our country, now that we are a plural, multi-cultural, multi-racial society, we have a great opportunity to fashion the community of the future. There is only one enemy to defeat: the racism that breeds fear instead of hope, violence instead of peace, hatred instead of love.

Let us make sure that the battle is joined and won before it is too late! And may this book bring encouragement to many — as it has to me.

Trevor Huddleston C.R.
Bishop of Stepney

Introduction

The lessons of our history,
Of immigrant and refugee —
Take them all in warm embrace,
Absorb them in our island race.

Jim Ward

My first point I will make pictorially, for behind and inside it lies the very substance of this book.

Opposite our school there is a public house, to which a group of teachers would often go after a day's work. On this one particular night as we entered, a drunken white woman was shouting racist insults at two Asian men who were quietly drinking at a corner table. Her abuse was clearly being enjoyed by various other white customers in the bar. We intervened, asking the woman to watch her tongue, and arguing with those around her who encouraged her. After the woman had, for the most part, subsided in her insults, we sat and drank with the Asian men.

They were father and son, Sikhs who had been in Britain for twenty years. They said that they had learned to live with this sort of incident, although they had noticed that the hostility had gained in passion and frequency lately. The son, a carpenter, was pleased to hear that we were teachers from the school over the road. He had been a pupil there himself fifteen years ago, and reeled off a list of familiar names of older teachers still at the school. He had been the only Indian boy in the school then, and he wore a turban in those days, he said, and although he had been the butt of some insulting comments and violence at first, he had generally got on very well with the other boys.

He told us of one particular incident. With his friends he was having a furtive playtime smoke in the toilets — the same roofless, playground toilets from which we still sometimes flushed out the smokers in morning break. A teacher on his playtime duty had approached the toilets unexpectedly, and the boys, reacting quickly, either doused their cigarettes in the urinal or nipped them out with their fingers and put them in their pockets. He had niftily wedged his cigarette in the fold of his turban at the back of his head. None of the boys thought that the teacher would stay long, but would only glance in, as was customary, and then move on to another part of the playground. This time however, he made a full interrogation. The Sikh boy, alongside his friends, protested his innocence, until the teacher saw the smoke rising from behind his turban. Realising his head would soon be on fire, the boy quickly whipped the turban from his head, stifled the flame, and faced the ire of his teacher. The other boys were lucky, and on that day at least, escaped undetected.

Coming from this man who had been used as the object of carping racist invective a few minutes earlier, and told with such humour, I could only marvel. An immigrant Indian boy, acting like an English schoolboy with other English schoolboys, enjoying audacity and mischief, and being found out like an English schoolboy — except with the props and garb of his Indian birth and culture. And yet now, sitting in a pub opposite the same school some fifteen years later, living in the same streets with the same neighbours, he was surrounded by suspicion and insult. And I remembered too that in my own class, a Sikh boy had not been to school for nearly three weeks. The reason? His father, following the stabbing to death a fortnight earlier of a turbaned youth in another part of London, was afraid to let his son out

10

of the house. I remembered too how a young Bangla Deshi boy in the same year had, with his entire family, been hounded out of his council flat by some of the white tenants in the same block, how his mother had lost a baby, suffered mental torture, how turds had been left on their doorstep, bricks thrown through their windows, how his father had been kicked and punched when he opened the door to an unknown caller, and how the boy himself had to run the gauntlet of local white youth on his daily walks to and from school.[1]

All this is Britain in 1976, and this is why this book has been compiled. For certainly, its main purpose is to attack racism by urging teachers in our schools openly to fight its causes and effects, by engaging our children in such knowledge, argument and empathy in the classroom as will combat and undermine its poisonous influence. I argue that the classroom presents to the teacher who is concerned actively to oppose racism, an imperative platform and debating room to counter the facile and inhuman ideas that organised racism has pushed into currency.

Four arguments are the basis of this compilation:

1 The present constitution of the population of British inner-city areas has been enormously enriched by the arrival (since the last war, and sometimes before) of children and their families as immigrants and refugees from all over the world. This gives teachers and schools an unprecedented opportunity to make knowledge of the world and its peoples immediate, practical and symbiotic in a way impossible before.

2 The classroom, and particularly the English class, must take its part in the battle of ideas that is being waged around the lives of our children outside school. This means that the activities of the classroom must openly and unequivocally generate the pro-human, anti-racist energies in the contest, and what is considered within the classroom must reflect the realities outside it. This

applies particularly to the task of countering racism, by involving children in debate and creative work which exposes and deals with racist ideas, and supports any initiative which they may take themselves against racism.

3 Both black and white children should be encouraged in the English classroom to extend themselves to the situations and struggles of other people all over the world through imaginative empathy and creative writing. Through this they will begin to understand that their own classroom is in fact a world in miniature, made up of children who despite their national or racial origin, are now undeniably a part of the British working class.

4 We must unashamedly develop, in the context of the classroom, a curriculum and body of knowledge that vindicates the national cultural traditions of British working people: a curriculum which now actively engages the 'new' British children in its historical embrace and in its present and future formation.

The work quoted throughout this book was written by twelve to fourteen year old children in an East London secondary school. The children came from mixed ability classes of English. At the time of writing, unemployment for school leavers in the area is 20%, and overall, 14%. From our classroom, my class and I overlook vast, dying dockyards and vacant building lots waiting for houses. Up the road to the east of the borough, Poplar Hospital has closed down — and other cuts in public health are promised. To the west towards the Tower of London, the Tower Hotel has opened in the dockyards of St. Katherine's Docks, with penthouse suites at £54 a night. The dock basin is filled with luxury yachts, making a new international pleasure marina. Warehouses and riverside houses have been converted into elegant studio flats for those outside the borough with the necessary wealth to buy them. Meanwhile, many of our children and their families still wait to be rehoused from sub-standard and appalling conditions. The Port of London Authority has declared its intention to close the last two remaining working docks in the borough, the West India and the Millwall docks. And this in an area which grew up because of the dockside industries and whose very heart and raison d'etre were the docks. Now the children see and experience around them an industrial graveyard.

Teachers themselves know these objective facts and how they affect the children they teach. They also know that their own livelihoods are threatened in this period of teacher redundancy, when their local union branch is already struggling to save jobs lost through the government's education cuts. The potential unemployment of their own pupils becomes implacably linked with the risks of their own redundancy. Thus teachers and pupils move within and share a common political reality as they work together in the classroom. This makes for an elision of consciousness which is both entirely objective and entirely political — and is completely removed from the bogus objectivity argued by the educational hierarchs. A new empathy is being forged between the pupil and the teacher as they work together — they are in, and of, the same class.

Sharing experience and common prospects, the teacher and child move towards a comradeship of the classroom, which is created in spite of the terrible gulf the bourgeois school imposes between the teacher and the working class child. For under capitalism, the school is a Janus. It is the institution of a State which condones the exploitation of an entire class, and promotes racism to divide its greatest enemy — which is that same class — for its own economic interest and survival. It is a part of the apparatus which seeks to provide a semi-literate and compliant labour force to man industry and public services. It turns out black and immigrant labour to perform some of the dirtiest, most tedious and badly-paid jobs in society. And yet within the School, which, as an institution of the State may purposefully underdevelop black and white working class minds, there is a growing power of resistance and commitment to transform the State and the School as a servant institution of the State.

This truth is as evident in the instance of the developing movement within schools against racism, as it is in the general rise in strength of teacher trade-unionism. It is also evident in the increasing demands of teachers to democratise the School structure; in the growth in control by teachers over the curriculum or body of knowledge considered in the School; and in the growth in political consciousness and unionisation of the school students themselves. For within a time of capitalist crisis, the School can be as pregnant with dynamism, change and resolution amongst its workforces as any other factory or workshop.

Thus the particular function of the progressive forces within the School of combating a false, pernicious or racist ideology, and a corrupt and decaying political system, must never be written off or under-rated. Simultaneously, the School must never be glorified or vindicated as the prime force for ending and removing that same corrupt political system. School, by itself, can never transform society. It is a battlefield of wills and ideas, of the moribund and the dynamic, of reaction and struggle, with a huge uncommitted, dormant mass of political power in between, which its progressive forces must win over. The School may ultimately serve the State, but it holds within it forces that can contribute to transforming the State.

A particular clash on this battlefield involved one Richard Edmonds, a declared racist and National Front candidate for Deptford, and a teacher at Tulse Hill School in South London — a school with a large majority of black children. After a long struggle involving teachers, parents and school students, the school branch of the National Union of Teachers taking organised trade union action involving systematic ostracism, has pressured Edmonds out of the school. So it is not sufficient to argue, as some do, that the School merely operates as a repressive State institution or a racist agency. Its function under capitalism may involve those things, but the internal energy and ferment caused by its progressive forces never allows it to operate completely in that way. The seeds of transformation are already planted within the School, and it cannot be by-passed, ignored or under-estimated in its actual and potential force.

For a teacher who is committed to the socialist transformation of society, and the transformation of the nature of the School itself, the classroom is a vital powerhouse. The teacher uses the cracks and contradictions of the School to deliver continuous body-blows to its function under capitalism. He or she rejects the State-licensed view of knowledge and replaces it with ideas which reflect and affirm the strengths and aspirations of their own class, which they come to realise is the working class. In schools right through our cities, that working class, including its teachers, is multi-racial and multi-cultural. Though their origins may lie in all the continents of the world, these teachers and pupils are absolutely a part of the British working class.

This book urges that racism needs to be confronted and argued against at every yard and corner of the school, and at any part of the neighbourhood where it spits its venom. We must ultimately push our attack on racism towards a view of the world which exists in spite of, and beyond the skin. The School, transformed and moved towards becoming a workshop of struggle, is potentially one of our strongest weapons and bulwarks against racism.

Part one

Schools and Streets

Survival of the Docks

London unemployment
Boomed up last year,
And now the closing of the docks
Has become a growing fear.

Now there are only two docks standing,
West India and Millwall —
It probably won't be long
Before those docks fall.

All the trade is going to other docks,
Tilbury, Felixstowe and Gravesend.
The London Docks have been deserted,
The dockers are going round the bend . . .

Philip Stanley

The Closing of the Docks

One day, I think it was about June 1976, me and Jimmy and
Shillinder were playing football in an old dockyard. We were
having a good kick-about when the ball went over the wall.

'Go and get it then,' I said to Shillinder.

'Cut out, you kicked it over!'

'Right, if you don't get that ball, I'll kick yer teeth down yer
throat!'

'No one can make me get that ball!'

'Right, you asked for it!'

BASH! BOOM! BAM! CRASH! SPLASH!

'That'll take care of 'im, now I suppose I'll have to go and get
the ———— ball!'

When I got over the wall, a man appeared as if by magic.

'Who-Who are you?' I said.

'I am the Ghost of Millwall Docks.'

'Wh-What do yer w-want?'

'I don't want anything, just to tell you that you are one of the
lucky ones who did not suffer when these docks closed down. You
don't need to worry about anything, but if you don't start bucking
your ideas up you will end up the same as me. I was a gonner.
When I first started work at Millwall Docks, I remember it was
very exciting, but now look at me, a gonner! But now I must go
back and suffer the pains.'

When he went, I rushed over the wall. When I was back in
school I tried to learn as much as possible, so I would not end up
like the Ghost of Millwall Docks.

Tony Smith

The objective conditions surrounding any school are what, ultimately, create the consciousness of its pupils. If those conditions involve: a high level of unemployment caused by the mass closures of local industry (in this case, the last remaining working docks in the area); a housing problem caused by the cutbacks in public spending and the continuing existence of large areas of sub-standard accommodation; a long waiting list for concentrated medical attention and hospital beds caused by government 'economies' and the closures of local hospitals and medical health facilities; and an educational ferment in schools caused by overlarge classes in the context of teacher redundancy and the slashing of the educational budget — then it is such conditions that will shape certain implications, underlying levels of thought and prevailing behaviour in the schools.

For the children and parents, suffering these genuine grievances and attacks on their standard of living and chances of happiness and human fulfilment, want to know, who or what is to blame? Why do I have to wait over two years for a simple operation on varicose veins? Why is my daughter complaining that she is not getting enough of her teacher's attention? Why have we waited so long to be re-housed? Why can't my son and daughter-in-law find anywhere to live in the neighbourhood? Why was there no job for me when I left school last year, and why, six months later, am I still on the dole? For however far we travel in this book, we must always return to these questions and the quality of the answers found to them, for it is such questions and answers that will ultimately determine the way our children and their parents think and act.

There are those, sometimes who move amongst us, who will try to apportion the cause and the blame for the enormities that working class people of all colours suffer, not to those guilty forces who own and control our economy and mode of production, but to our black and brown neighbours and comrades, who suffer as much,

and very often more than white working people. The
statement of a thirteen-year-old white boy writing in his
English lesson contrasts sharply with the bigoted view of
the *National Front Students' Association* quoted from a
leaflet handed out to London schoolchildren outside
their schools' gates in 1975:

School Students!

Are you tired of your school being wrecked by vandalism, which
the teachers are afraid or unable to check?
Are you tired of younger students being bullied or subjected to the
alien cult of mugging?
Are you tired of being held back in the classroom through being
pushed into the same classes as slower learners?
Are you tired of having lessons disrupted by a handful of trouble-
makers?
Are you tired of having to endure Social Studies or History lessons
where the teacher continually tries to run down Britain, while at
the same time Black kids have 'Black Studies' to give them more
self-respect and Black pride?
Are you tired of lessons where the teacher has to go at a snail's
pace, to allow immigrant kids who don't speak English a chance to
keep up?
Are you tired of having new teachers all the time, who are usually
inexperienced?
Are you tired of being sent home early, being deprived of valuable
exam lessons, because of a shortage of teachers?

If so, then the National Front Students' Association is the
organisation for you. The National Front is a national political
organisation dedicated to the welfare of the British people. We
say, 'Put Britain First'. We advocate the humane repatriation of
coloured immigrants and their families . . .

In England today, it is much harder for an English man, a Black
English man to get a job, because people reject them because of
their religion and their colour. If women are allowed to earn equal
pay like men, why can't Black men get jobs? Some boys in my
class are Black they come from other parts of the world. Just think
what their future will be like for them when the time comes, it
is bad enough for us. Their backgrounds may consist of a poor
family and they come over here to lead a new life, but what they
find is they are rejected, thrown out. Whether you are Black or

21

White, you still are Bone, Flesh and Blood, you still are a *Human*.
Grant Blackwell

There is no doubt that in a period of excessive hardship
and unemployment (when all working people are assailed
by government economies and attacks) the apparent
attraction, scope and efficacy of the racist arguments
increase. This is as true in the schools, and with parents'
attitudes to genuine problems in the schools, as it is in
unemployment, housing or health. One particular, easily-
identifiable group is forced to take on the role of the
scapegoat, to atone for all the real grievances of all
working class people, whether black, brown or white.
Exploiting the 'fear of the unknown' that white working
people may feel, these pernicious but calculating forces
suggest that beneath a turban or under a dark skin or
crinkled hair, are hostile and estranged hearts that are
determined to cause the predominantly 'white'
population gross and despicable harm.

Of course, racism has never worked to improve the
lives of white working class people. Behind its palliative
appeal lies its true function: to strengthen the grip of the
owners of production and to divide their greatest enemy,
which united is unassailable — the working class as a
whole. The racists serve only to weaken the white people
they claim they will emancipate. Their tack is a desperate
move piloted and promoted by the ruling class, in order
to keep their sinking craft afloat.

All around our school, on corrugated iron hoardings,
lamp-posts and derelict houses, as well as within the
lifts and corridors of the blocks of flats where our
children live, the racist slogans, stickers and posters have
been appearing. The currency of racism, turning on
unemployment and attacks on the welfare state and
education, is beginning to be passed around in a more
organised and pugnacious way. The media, the voice of
the establishment, too often reinforces these attacks. The

22

racist jokes of 'comedians'; the daily caricatures of black, Asian and Irish people; the emphasis on people's psyches of that same 'fear of the unknown', be it a houseful of illegal immigrants in 'Z Cars' or the submerged menace of 'Jaws' and its enormous commercial promotion, are all on the side of racism and all cohere to befuddle and prejudice the minds of white people against their own neighbours and workmates.[2]

Our children are growing up and going to school within this context. There is no hiding from them the poisonous ideas which may be circulating and infecting their homes and playgrounds, and causing them to re-think or reject their friendships and relationships. Our schools are pitched in the middle of this battlefield of ideas. As teachers, we must not sweep these distorted concepts under the desks simply because we despise them, or pretend that racist influence does not exist amongst our children, and sway some of them. Racism, at all stages, must be exposed, taken on, and dealt with. Such ideas thrive under cover, when they are not brought out into the open, argued against and despatched. They cannot prosper under genuine honesty and democracy, as they are irrational and finally nonsensical.

Any event in the school or in its neighbourhood that involves racism should be brought into the classroom and discussed and argued out. The English teacher is probably in the most favourable position within the framework of the school, to be able to promote this. The following play was written by two boys, both in the third year, one from India, one from St. Lucia. They were clearly worried about two of their white friends, who had been mouthing the slogans of a racist group.

Death Race

This is a play about two coloured people. One is Ted, he comes from the West Indies. The other is Shillinder, he comes from India. They are best friends, but they do not like Tony. He likes the National Front. His best friend is Jimmy, he likes a film called

Rollerball. Jimmy and Tony hate coloured people, black or brown, they hate you. Ted and Shillinder are going to a club about self-defence. Tony and Jimmy will live ten days after Shillinder and Ted get their black belts. We start the play down a dark street near the school.

Scene 1 *In The Club*
TED: Shillinder, we have got to do well to get our black belts.
SHILLINDER: When do we get 'em?
TED: In a couple of days' time.
SHILLINDER: Come on, let's go home, or to the disco near the school.
TED: Come on, let's go.
INSTRUCTOR: (*to Ted*) Wait Ted, you've got to have your test in the morning, and you Shillinder.

Scene 2 *On The Way Home*
TED: Here comes them two nazis.
SHILLINDER: Let's get 'em Ted.
TED: No, let them go. We can get into trouble and we've got to do our test in the morning.
TONY: Black cunts, black pigs, go back home!
SHILLINDER: You better shut your mouths snowflakes, before we do yer.
JIMMY: Come on then, come on then packy.
TED: We will meet you at Dod Street tomorrow night.
TONY: O.K.
JIMMY: You're going to get done!
SHILLINDER: Do you want a bet?
JIMMY: Yer.
SHILLINDER: How much?
JIMMY: You bring 50p and I'll bring 50p, and if you beat us up you get the 50p, but if we beat you up we get the 50p.
SHILLINDER: O.K. then.
TONY: Come on Jim, we'd better get home.
TED: Ah, your mama is going to tan your botty for you.
TONY: Shut up you nigger.
TED: You be quiet you ginger nut!
TONY: We'll see who's Ginger Nut tomorrow night.
TED: We will see, won't we?

Scene 3 *Back In The Club*
SHILLINDER: We will get our black belts today.
TED: Let's get on.
INSTRUCTOR (*after the test*) Right. Left kick first and then the right punch . . .
TED: We got our black belts!

SHILLINDER: Yes, we can do them tricks we learned in the test on the nazis.
INSTRUCTOR: You can come and get your black belts.

Scene 4 *Near Dod Street*
TONY: Do you think they will come?
JIMMY: No.
TONY: Here they come.
JIMMY: Right, get ready.
TONY: I don't feel like a fight.
JIMMY: Chickening out Tone?
TONY: No, course I'm not.
JIMMY: Well, get ready then.
SHILLINDER: Come on then Ted.
TED: Let's go!
JIMMY: PUNCH!!!
TED: Yous two asked for it now.
SHILLINDER: PUNCH!!! KICK!!!
(*Tony and Jimmy run down the street*)

This play was about two white boys who hated two coloured boys, two people that were the same age. The white boys thought that the coloured boys were weeds, but they were wrong.

THE END

Shillinder Singh and Ted John

If *Death Race* has a strong element of the fantastic about it (both boys had seen the film *Rollerball* during the same week), a real local incident captured the interest of three second year boys. Of the authors, one was a local white boy and the other two were black, one from a Guyanese and the other from a Jamaican family. They considered, through a short play, the response of a group of regular customers to a local publican instituting a 'colour bar'. The incident they based their play on actually happened, and finally the landlord of the *Railway Tavern*, a local pub at Mile End, was dismissed by the brewers and barred from managing any of their other houses. This followed the action of a group of local trade unionists and black ex-customers, who picketed the pub on several occasions and appealed to the Race Relations Board.

The Railway Tavern

ANDRE: Mark, let's go down to the pub.

M'ARK: Come on then Ozz. Let's go and meet our friend Charlie Abdu.

(*Later at the pub, the 'Railway Tavern'*)

ANDRE: Mark, he did say he'd meet us down here. He's not here.

MARK: Can I have a drink please, two pints of light ale.

LANDLORD: We don't serve people of the likes of you.

ANDRE: But that's ridiculous. I'm going, how about you Mark?

(*Andre throws down his glass*)

MARK: I'm not standing for this. Come on, let's get out of this ghetto and go down to the 'Prince of Wales'.

ANDRE: (*at the 'Prince of Wales'*) Hello lads, what you doing here? We've just found out there's a colour bar at the Railway Tavern.

MARK: Well, there's only one more decent pub round here and that's the 'Waterman's Arms'.

GEORGE: But first we have got to go down to the Railway Tavern and get things sorted out there. Come on lads!

(*We all go down the 'Railway Tavern'. Jerry, David, Andre, Mark, George, Peter, Tony, and John, including John's parrot*)

MARK: We'll stand outside and start a picket.

(*All of a sudden a window opens*)

ANDRE: George, you're wet! Jerry, you're soaked from head to toe.

GEORGE: Let's go down the Race Relations Board!

(*We came back a week later*)

MARK: Look, there's still the same landlord. Let's go and explain the position to Charrington's.

ANDRE: They said they're going to come on Monday.

(*We come on Monday*)

GEORGE: Look lads, there's a new landlord.

MARK: Come on lads, let's go in and have a beer.

ANDRE: Landlord, what happened to the other landlord?

NEW LANDLORD: He was no longer able to work for Charrington's or any other brewery.

(*So all the lads had a nice cool* CARLING BLACK LABEL)

Andre Waterman, Mark Philips, George Small

The teachers themselves, who had been on the pickets and helped to organise them, could give first hand information about the incident to the children, and this brought the children's interest more alive.[3]

At the same time, a Sikh boy in the second year was being victimised and abused by some of the elder boys in the school, who were kicking him and ridiculing his turban. The other boys in his class, white and black, were united in their indignation about the bullying of the Sikh boy, and as a group complained to the teachers about it, asking that the senior boys be punished. One boy, from a West African family, wrote a short acrostic poem to the pattern of the Sikh boy's name, which expressed clearly the collective attitude of the class. This poem was written out as a large poster and hung in a prominent place at the front of the classroom above the blackboard, for the rest of the year.

G urnam, Gurnam, sorry about your turban.
U nless we do something about the
pR ejudice in this school —
N ow the class has a petition,
A nd we have told all the school,
M any will not hit your turban!

Cherriffc Saine

If this short poem, in its own way, 'commemorated' a valuable initiative taken by the boys in defending their Sikh classmate against a racist attack, it also exemplifies the importance of using poetry, short story or drama as ways of keeping alive and making durable a significant and positive event within the school.

Later in the year, one of the white boys who had been so angry about the bullying of Gurnam by the senior boys, brought to school a racist sticker he had found on the wall of his flats. It depicted a group of advancing turbaned figures, with slit-eyed, shadowed faces wearing menacing scowls above a slogan suggesting that such figures were coming to take local white people's houses and jobs. The sticker tried to dehumanise Sikh people, picturing them only as a sinister threat. In the same week, Gurnam, who was improving fast in his writing and gaining much more confidence in his general expression, wrote a short autobiographical piece that was very moving in its honesty and starkness. This was read to the class, who were very affected, not only by its truth, but because it revealed its author as a person who already in his young life had passed through profound and unusual experiences that had spanned two continents. In its way, it was the boy's blow against bigots who were attempting to strangle his own humanity and that of his entire people. It was a claim for respect, fair treatment and equality.

India

My name is Gurnam Singh, I was born in England. My dad was born in India when England was half in India. My dad said that when they came from Pakistan to India, there was a war. My dad was saying everyone was running to get on the train, and then India won the war against Pakistan. So when my dad was 29 years old, he got married and then came to England. My mother had a baby, it was a boy who was my eldest brother. I had four sisters and three brothers.

When I was 1½ years old my mother gave me to my grandmother. My grandmother took me to India three times. The last time my grandmother was taking me to India, my mum said to my grandmother, 'I think I will not see my son again.' After two months when I was in India, there was a telegram came that my mother and my little sister died in a car crash. So my dad was in the crash. He could not talk. The doctors made a hole in his neck so he could eat and drink.

So my dad married someone else at last. She is my stepmother and she had two daughters. She is not good to us. She hurts us, and one day my stepmother hurt my sister. We could not do anything. She hurt us, and our dad takes no notice.

Gurnam Singh

When a second year white boy risked his life by diving into a freezing canal near the school (where they were playing in their dinner hour) in order to save his Indian friend who could not swim, it was a courageous act which called for similar 'commemoration' to stay in the minds of the other children in the school. The event was

followed up in English lessons, and many children wrote
poems and plays on its theme:

The Rescue

Ashok and Mark went to play by the river,
Mark said, 'It's so cold it makes me shiver.'
They threw stones into the river that was deep,
They stood on the bank that was high and steep.

But Ashok slipped and fell in.
Mark jumped in to save his friend —
If he had left him,
Ashok's life would have been at an end.

The water was cold in Limehouse cut,
Mark might have lost his own life, but
He still jumped in
To save his friend's life.

He took Ashok back to school,
They were both dripping wet —
But he saved a boy's life,
So he deserves the award that he'll get.

Denise Levey

Ashok and Mark

It happened down Limehouse Cut
When it was a very cold day,
When two boys wanted to get away,
All they did was wanted to play.

Mark and Ashok were
Throwing stones,
Then Ashok fell in
And could've broke his bones.

But Mark did not panic,
He just jumped in and helped,
Ashok would have drowned
If Mark hadn't heard him yelp.

He jumped in and saved him —
If he had gone under
He could have cut himself on a tin.

Mark dragged him out
And brought him back to school,

29

And Mr Mannion mentioned it
Next morning in the hall.

Lynn Torry

In 1975, after a Jamaican bus conductor in South London was killed by two passengers following a dispute about a fare for a dog, his union, the Transport and General Workers' Union, organised a massive and very dignified funeral. Many of the children, white and black, were moved by this, and these two poems, both by white children, were read out in assembly the day after the funeral.

Ronald Jones

Ronald Jones was a bus conductor,
He drove on a seventy-seven,
He can't anymore
Because he was punched on the floor,
But now he's up in heaven.

It was over a twopence fare
Over an alsation dog,
The passengers didn't help —
They were scared stiff like logs.

They punched him
And he fell back,
He smashed his head
On a bus seat rack.

Now the people
All went on strike
On the day of the funeral —
It proved he was liked.

Philip Stanley

Disgrace

The black helpful man
Who done all he can
For citizens today
Who are trying to get away.

It's a disgrace you know
To watch those poor buses go —

People begging you to go slow.
He'll never know what he'll miss,
From his wife a loving kiss.

His kids watch, wait and pray
For their poor daddy to come home today.
He saved and saved, poor Jones he did,
To see his wife and kids,
In sunny Jamaica where his family live.
They wish he was there,
And their love they could give.

Sharon Patten

The children were beginning to see throughout these incidents that they were all involved, that opposing racism, or understanding the life of a West Indian or an Asian immigrant was not merely the responsibility of black people, but of the working class generally. Ronald Jones, for example, was black, but he was also a working man, obstructed and killed while he was simply doing a day's work. In their own way, through their classroom work, the children were contributing to the struggle against racism and not merely being diverted by it. But they were also going beyond it to uniting, despite colour; to fight injustice as a synthesis of young workers who were not allowing their friendships and unity to be dismembered by poisonous ideas. For young people growing up with social and political injustice all around them, affecting each one of them, black or white, this sense of unity will be essential in fighting against those objective conditions that threaten them, and throw up the bigoted, racist forces that try to divide them.

D on't make the people unemployed,
O ne and a half million already unemployed,
N ever again we want it like the thirties,
T ry to fight to keep them open!

C an't we fight again?
L ove and brotherhood we now need,
O nly if you keep employed,
S houldn't the Port of London Authority
E ver try to help?

T ry to fight for our rights,
H eaven and Earth prevail,
E ast Enders did it before, so do it again!

D ocks needed to be worked,
O ver and under, work goes on,
C ouldn't we try to keep them,
K eep them well?
S ave some work for the East Enders!

Deborah Cordrey

32

Part two

The World in a Classroom

All the People Together Again

I had a strange dream last night and there were black people, white people, yellow people and all kinds of people. They were all talking and laughing together. Then a great big piece of paper was passing around the room and on the paper they signed their names and said they would never fight again. When the paper was all signed and a million copies made they all bowed down and shook their hands and prayed and prayed and prayed.

And in the streets below, the people were dancing round and round while guns and uniforms were scattered on the ground.

Tina Gilbert

This view of the world, which some might call child-like, others naive, Blakean or idealistic, is certainly becoming more and more of a possibility in our inner-city areas. It is true that children, white, black and brown, without the cancerous ideas of racism, live and work happily together, sharing each other's lives with generosity and empathy. A classroom that is insulated from outside racist pressures can present itself super-ficially as an island of harmony in an otherwise hostile neighbourhood. However, as teachers, we must not fool ourselves by the *apparently* harmonious surface atmosphere of some of our schools. It is not difficult for the administration of a well-managed school to paper over the deep divides of racism and pretend that the school is so good that it has quietly and efficiently smothered them. There are those headmasters and senior teachers who will quite categorically say in proud defence of their own school, 'We have no racialism here!' and then retreat to their own homes cushioned some-where in the suburbs where hardly a black face or a racist poster is to be seen. The point is not that the School should block out or merely cover up the racist ideas that may be circulating in the neighbourhood, and pretend that they don't exist in order to boost the prestige of the school's management, but that the school should effectively deal with these ideas, and counteract them with all its force of knowledge, argument and practical day-to-day classroom work. Teachers must work towards a genuine solidarity amongst our children by tackling nascent racism at the points where it emerges between them, and arguing against and refuting the ideas or compelling slogans that the children may have picked up from posters or the media coverage given to overtly racist groups that are trying to undermine the possibilities so beautifully expressed in the piece of writing that began this chapter. The teacher can allow himself no neutrality in the face of racism.

Certainly, our inner-city schools present opportunities to teachers that have been hitherto impossible. The enormous cultural richness that has been added to our schools by the arrival of children from all over the world, has given teachers a deep reservoir of experience, ideas and remembrances that have not existed in our schools before. For the local children, many of whom have rarely been out of the few streets or neighbourhoods around where they live and grow up (unless it be to traditional holiday resorts in Britain or the newer-style package in Spain) the children that have arrived in Britain as immigrants themselves, or who have stories that have been told them by their parents, have within them resources for classroom development and learning that any creative teacher would welcome. This pool of experience and knowledge must be tapped and savoured by the teacher and the other children, not only to give to individual children of foreign origins a sense of their own value, history and confidence, but because this knowledge is something entirely organic and first-hand, far better than text books or audio-visual aids. In this context education can become genuinely fraternal, learning about the world first-hand from your classmates who have been to places only heard and rumoured about, and have known these truths on their pulses. What to English children may be exotic dreams, or vague and 'dark' continents full of pygmies and cannibals where men swing off trees — the mythical and distorted views of Africa, Asia or the West Indies — come alive suddenly and intimately in all their reality. The truths being passed around in the classroom about the Third World by children that have known its realities, cut through the Americanised stereotypes that the established media promulgate and that colonialism has nourished for generations.

The utilisation of such experience by the teacher, married to creative work done in English classes, can produce, amongst almost any given body of children from our inner-city schools, what amounts to a micro-cosm. Certainly, East London, which has absorbed wave after wave of immigrants and refugees — from the Huguenots and Flemish weavers, through Russian Jews fleeing from Czarist pogroms, Irish dockers, African sailors, up to the predominantly Asian and Caribbean post-war influx, and other groups like Cypriots and East African Asians — is no stranger to this cosmopolitan concept. One twelve-year-old girl looked around her own class and saw this:

People come from different countries,
They have a different way of life,
From the wine of Cyprus
To the temples of Burma

To the countryside of Ireland
To the flowing streams of Scotland
Where the fish swim free,
And where many fishermen long to be

To Jamaica, the island in the sea,
They also make sugar to put in our tea,
And to St. Lucia's palm trees
That grow big and tall

To Sierra Leone, a land green with trees,
The forests are huge, with nothing but trees.

And to England, an island in the sea,

Where it's noisy in the city,
But in the country, it's as quiet as can be.

Denise Levey

It is clear that these children of the world are now specifically a part of the British working class, now becoming one of the most culturally rich and varied in the world. This is a fact which our schools should nourish and develop with pride. The potential for symbiosis of experience amongst our children, and the depth of their exchanges of separate views and knowledges of the world offer us new and expansive possibilities of a human solidarity stretching across continents and oceans.

My Life in the West Indies

My sister is 15, I am 13 years old. I lived in St. Lucia with my father and my mother and my sister. I called them father and mother. They were really my grandfather and my grandmother but I didn't know that. Then a letter came to St. Lucia saying, 'Your mother and father are in London, you can come and live with them now.'

I said, 'How come I've got another mother? I don't want to go to London.'

But my mother said, 'Well then, I will have to go to London and you will have to stay here.'

So I had to go.

I used to go to school in St. Lucia. We had to put on our school clothes and take a bag of food, yams and bananas, dasheen (dasheen is dug out of the ground. It has brown skin and is white in the middle like a potato). We took yellow yams, plantain, fish, and sometimes we took meat.

We had to walk a long, long way. Then we came to Aunty's house. We put our food bags down there, because we came there to eat. Then we went straight on to school. It was a big school, all green and yellow walls outside and nice and white inside. Lots of children went to that school. There were long, long benches to sit on and ordinary tables like the ones here.

We used to write in school but it was in a different language. Some people call it patois. It went like this.

'Comment-allez?' That means, 'How are you?'

'Dejeuner' means 'lunch', 'papier' means 'paper'.

'Il n'y a pas d'argent' means 'The purse is empty'.

'Un, deux, trois, quatre, cinq, six, sept, huit, neuf, dix.' That's one up to ten.

When it was play-time we all used to run out, down to the sea and dive and splash. We used to dive from boats. Sometimes we would catch fish, put them in the boat, then back home and my mother cleaned and cooked them. Sometimes we cooked them ourselves outside on a fire. We never cleaned those fish, just cooked them and ate the lot. They tasted very good. We made the fire with wood and matches. We usually caught rock-fish. I don't know the other name for them. My cousins had some rowing boats and we took turns to row out. Sometimes my father came with us. Once my father didn't catch any fish but I did. I caught one that was two feet long. At first my mother used to buy fish at the market, then I said to her, 'Instead of buying fish, you buy a hook for me please and I will catch plenty of fish, nice and fresh.'

So my mother bought a hook for me. After that we always had lots of fish all nice and fresh whenever we wanted it.

Sometimes, all of us, my father and my mother and my sister and me, all went for a picnic, high up in the forest. The forest goes up far, far, far up the mountain. We kill and eat things up there. We kill some birds that look like pigeons but they are a bit different. You have to watch out for snakes in the forest too. The dog-head snakes are the worst. There was a lake and a river in the forest, and we used to swim there too.

The forest comes right down near to our house and we make traps there all the time to catch birds and things. Our traps are like this. We get a big basket and prop it up with a stick. We tie a string to the stock and tie the other end of the string to the food. Food is the bait. Then when the bird comes to eat, he pulls the food, the food pulls the string, the string pulls the stick out, then the basket falls over the bird and he is trapped.

Once when I caught a bird in my basket it was caught on the wing and it couldn't fly so I just put it down there on the ground, but my cat had been waiting and watching and 'swoop', he was off with that bird.

Another time a mongoose had eaten my bird. When I got to the trap I saw half a bird, the mongoose had eaten the other half. I didn't want half a bird. Ugh! so I threw it away. When a mongoose finds your bird he will never go away. He will sit there all excited going hiss-ss-s, screak, squawk. Sometimes he can tip the trap over and catch your bird like he did that time to mine.

Mongeese are tricky animals. They can stand still for a long time and disguise (se dequit) themselves with the ground. They can steal chickens. They just stand still in the road looking for your chicken then they go 'arr-rk', and flash — they take it. Once I had two chickens, one big one and one small one. I put them down while I cleaned the chicken-coop. They ran to where the pigs were and when I looked, that big bird was already taken by the mongoose. I put the little chicken back into the coop and went to get food for him. When I came back the mongoose was running off with him too. I had a shot at that mongoose with a stick but he was too quick. They are like India rubber. I didn't have my catapult with me or I might have got him. They are very clever.

We sometimes made a trap for the mongoose. We usually put a banana in the trap because they like bananas. We bend down a branch of a tree like a spring, and put a book to keep it down to the ground, then we tie a loop of string to the branch near the hook. The banana has to hide the hook. At the back of the tree is a big net. We put some grass and stones about so as to hide it all. The mongoose takes the banana, out goes the hook, the loop is pulled round his neck, then the swing will roll him into the net. You should see him when he tries to get out of that net. Boy! Does he try!

We don't eat mongoose nor use his skin, and he is too cheeky to be a pet, but you cannot help but like him.

Gilbert Gonzague

Life in St. Lucia with my Grandma

When I was born in London, I was sent to the West Indies to my Grandma. I was still very young. Later on I grew older and got to learn the language. It was very hot and sunny in the country, because I lived in two houses, one in the country and one in the town. In the country we had a big, giant garden with vegetables, fruits, ripe bananas, plantains, red peppers, and we even owned sheep. Every day we had to go to school from the country to the town. It was about three miles to walk, but it didn't seem long because we played all kinds of games on the way. We used to nick coconuts on the way, and it got so hot that the sand on the road got hot and we would pull our trouser legs up, and the girls their skirts, and we paddled about in the water.

Every time before we went to bed we had to have a bath, and in the morning before school, and we would take nice, sweet, ripe, reddish, tasty mangoes to eat on the way. When we got into the town we put our school clothes on and went to school. School started at ten o'clock and finished at four. If you were late, it was best to stay out of school because you would get six of the best. When school was over we would go home in the town and my aunt would let me stay in the town. We lived right by the bay, it was Laborie Bay. It was hot, blue and lovely — we used to go to the seaside nearly every day and then go home to have some strawberry-flavoured ice from the fridge. The next day I would go up in the country to see my grandma again, it was fun. We got out of school at four, got to the country at five, went out to play at half-past five and then came back from play around ten. We used to wander out about a mile from our homes.

Me and my friends went to look for birds, and when we got home we had our dinner, went to our rooms, prayed, put our pyjamas on, went out and nicked some coconuts from the kitchen and went out to play in the night with the moon shining, and we went back at eleven p.m. Then we had a cup of chocolate and went to sleep. In the morning we got up, had a good wash, had our breakfast, went and knocked for our friends, went and kissed our grandma goodbye, and went off to school in the town. There used to be this little boy called Goodbye. He was about three years old and went around naked, and he swore at any person who went past him. But if you gave him a sweet he would eat it, and when he had finished he would start swearing at you like he did before.

Tony Amable

A Story of Jamaica

Although I have been in this country for nearly a year now, I can still remember over in Jamaica quite clearly. I remember the place where I used to live, it was very nice indeed. It isn't as nice as some of the flats in London. The sea was at a very beautiful place, it was called Port Royal. All my family went down there every Saturday. We used to bring a hamper full of mangoes, star apples and all sorts of other things. On Saturday, me and my sister used to go shopping to Saturday market. When we came back we would do some work in the house and have something to eat. Then we would go out to play for a little while. The sun was so hot that we only walked on the street with a little thin dress, and no socks, only a pair of shoes. The people down there were very nice indeed. I don't like the food a lot over here, but I liked it in Jamaica.

The place is a very big place, with a lot of people. There is beautiful scenery down Hope. Sometimes, in the holidays or when we came from school, we used to play running or Dandy-shandy. But most of all we would just sit outside the gate and talk to other people passing by.

Carol Johnson

In My Country

I was born in Sea View Farm in the country of Antigua. When I was a child we used to go out and play games like hide-and-seek etc. I used to live with my grandmother, she used to sometimes tell me 'Nansi stories. When I was about nine, I went to see my other nan. She lived in Old Road and she also treated me well. I visited my nan, but I slept with my uncle and his girlfriend. She had two children, Juliet and Charlesworth, but when Juliet was five she got killed. It happened when her nan was going to put the rubbish away. She had to cross the road, and when she was crossing, my little cousin was behind. It was a main road and they didn't have traffic lights, so as she was crossing the road, all of a sudden a car came and knocked her over. By the time she reached the hospital she was dead. We couldn't believe it because she was with us on Friday, and on Saturday she was killed. Anyway, we soon got over that.

The people in Antigua are very friendly and nice. Some of my favourite foods in Antigua are yam, dasheen, sweet potato, plantain and anchovies, with saltfish. My favourite fruits are mango, guava (semi-sweet). I always looked forward to August in Antigua because that is the time when we have the Carnival. The day before the Carnival, early in the morning, we call J'Ouvert Morning, and anyone who wants to can go and dance. I have never been to J'Ouvert Morning because I was always sleeping, to wake up for the next morning, which is Carnival day.

When I went to stay with my uncle, he lived next to the beach. All you had to do was cross the road and go on the other side. Where he lived was a coconut wharf, so there are still lots of coconut trees there. Also, my nan's brother had a sugar cane field, and when it is time to cut the sugar cane, I used to help him. The school that I went to was called Sea View Farm Primary School, it was a very good school. Every Friday the girls had to bring their dolls and bits of cloth and the teacher would show them how to make dolly dresses. I stayed at that school until I was eleven, then I had to come to England, where my mum and dad and the rest of the family was.

Pat Richards

Four Years in Jamaica

My name is Raymond Brandon, I was born in Jamaica. The
county was Clarendon, Orange Hill. When I was born, my sister
Christine was two years old. She had to look after me while my
Grandy and mum went to market at Old Harbour. They sold
chocolate, sugar and yams. She would come back next morning
at about 2 a.m. They slept at Little Men's house. When I was
one I helped my brother Gladstone cut the cane, then take it
to the house. Then David took it and put it on his lorry, then
he put it on his stall to sell it. One foot cost five cents.

I always played with my brother Gladstone, and Bobby, Tony
and Delroy, and we went to the river at Smithfield, on the cliff.
I dived off and landed safely in the water, but I watched my four
brothers dive and turn round three times before they splashed
into the water. The next morning Grandy and Mum went to
market. Then me, my brothers and their friends played detectives.
Before I went to the country I saw a man in the water. Bobby
and Delroy dived in and got him, but my brother Tony was a
doctor so saw him and cared for him. Then it was time to take
him to where he lived. But he was rich. He bought me a new bike,
and my brother got some things   he and my mum got a
thousand dollars from him. He came to this country, England,
with my mum. I was four years old. From that time I visited him
like an uncle. I called him 'Uncle Brian, the Rich Man'.

Raymond Brandon

My Childhood

I was born in 1963 on the seventeenth of July. In 1966, me, my
mum, aunt and two brothers went to Cyprus. We went by
aeroplane, my dad went there by ship. I was only three years
old, my one brother was two and my other brother was two
months old. When we went there, we did not have a house of our
own, so we went to live with grandmother. We were twelve
people in a house. In the summer my aunts slept in the front of
the house because it was really hot.

My small brother was christened in Cyprus. After two years
we had our own house, it was a restaurant as well. Our house was
at the end of our village, and it was quiet. There we planted wheat
and tobacco. When I went to school, I finished my first year and
I got an 'A'. My aunts used to come there every day. In the
summer we all used olives and cut the wheat.

In 1970 my mum and dad came to England, and me and my
brothers went to live with my grandmother. Every Saturday, me

and one of my aunts went down to our house to water the flowers and grape trees. We used to cut bunches and eat them while we watered the flowers. When we finished watering we put grape bunches in bags and went down my grandmother's house. My small brother was born in 1971 in England, and my uncle took him to Cyprus because my aunt said she would look after him. When we went to cut tobacco, sometimes we went there at 4 o'clock. We started school at half-past seven and finished at half-past twelve. On Thursday we came home in the afternoon, and went to school on Saturday.

One summer holiday I went down my aunt's house for two weeks. Her village is near our village. At my uncle's wedding I was a bridesmaid and carried a big white candle. My brother with my grandfather used to take the sheep sometimes down to the sea, and sometimes up the mountain near our village.

In 1974 when the Turks came, we left Cyprus and came to England. We did not want to come, and we cried.

Maria Georgi

Early Life in the War in Cyprus

I was born in 1961 in Kandou village. When I was three years old, the war came up in Cyprus. I mean it was in 1963. The same things were happening to our village in 1974. My village was between two Greek countries. At that time, when the war came, all the Greek people closed the roads. They closed the roads for us because they thought we couldn't find bread, or anything else to eat. These things couldn't happen any longer, at last we were going to die. How long could we stay hungry? Before the war started, my dad did all our shopping, but our shopping didn't last any longer. I can remember very well that one morning when I woke up I was very hungry. Then I told my mother, 'Can you do something for me to eat, because I am very hungry?' But my mum didn't do anything because we didn't have nothing to eat. When I told my mum that I wanted something to eat, she started to cry. I didn't get any idea why she was crying, but when I saw her crying, I asked her, 'Why are you crying mum?' She didn't say anything, because she didn't want to tell me about our home. After half an hour she told me that we hadn't got anything in our home to eat. We had got only tea, but we hadn't got sugar or milk. After that, she made tea for me without sugar and milk in it. I drank that tea, but it wasn't good with no sugar or milk in it.

These things happened to us for more than two weeks. We couldn't find anything to eat. My mum and dad could stay hungry, but I couldn't. I was always crying because I wanted to eat something. When I said that I was hungry, my mum started crying because she didn't have anything to give me to eat. Everybody got the same things, in that they didn't get anything to eat. After that, one night we turned the radio on and it was saying the news. We heard that the Turkish soldiers were coming with their jets to Cyprus to drop bombs in every Greek part of the country. But before the Turkish soldiers came, the Greek people and soldiers went to each Turkish area and they killed all the people.

It was nearly our turn, I mean the Greek soldiers were going to come and kill us too. But they wouldn't come because the Turkish soldiers came to Cyprus and they started to drop bombs into the Greek parts of the country. When they saw that, they stopped the fighting. Then the fighting stopped in all the Turkish areas. One day they came to visit our village too, and when they came I ran to say to them 'welcome!' I was very happy that time, because we won our freedom. I mean we were free. I can remember very well that when they came to our village, one of the Turkish soldiers held me in his arms, and then I told him, 'God Bless You, because we are free now!'

So my early life in the war in Cyprus is finished.

Ulfet Hailil

When I was seven years old I was living in Cyprus, and the city I was in is Larnaca. It was quite big, but there was one thing that everybody hated. It was the Turkish, because they had half of Larnaca. There were soldiers everywhere.

Then one day on the radio, it said 'Makarios is dead!' But it was a fake. So the Turkish came and invaded Cyprus. It was like this: when Archbishop Makarios is dead, the Turkish could take over because a long time ago Cyprus was a part of Turkey, and one day they will take over Cyprus.

When we heard this, we ran for shelter, and the Turkish aeroplanes came and bombed Larnaca. But they did not stand a chance, so they went to Nicosia and took half of Nicosia, and still they have Nicosia. But one day we will find our freedom.

David Goodman

Burma

I was born in Burma, in a town called Sirium. My mum is English, because my Grandad was in the Army. And my Dad is Burmese. I came to England when I was seven years old, that was in 1971.

I have been in England for five years.

Burma is a very hot country. Sometimes when it rains, we go outside and play with the rain. Every year we have a water festival when people throw water over each other. When I was young I remember we used to have a flower shop. My cousin Martin helped with it and people would come and buy from the shop. I can't remember what the flowers looked like, but we used to wrap them with newspaper.

I lived in a city called Rangoon. There was a market right in front of my house. Every morning my aunt went to the market. A mile away there is a lake where people can go to picnic, and near the lake there is a church. When we played games, we played in the night because it was cooler. The games we played were all like English games — like hide and seek, run outs and lots more that I can't remember. My mum sent me to an English school, she had to pay for it. I cannot speak Burmese, my own language, but I can understand it.

We left Burma because everything was getting very expensive, and my Nana came to England. So we followed her. Before we was going to England we was going to Australia. Then my Dad could have come with us. But because we came to England he could not come, because he did not have a British passport. My Dad works for the British Embassy in Rangoon.

Corrina Mendes

My Childhood in Barbados

I was born in Barbados in 1962, and I lived with my parents in Silver Sands, Christchurch, near Niles Corner. My mother and father left me when I was a year old, and after that I went to live with my grandparents. They were very kind people to live with. They looked after me as their child and gave me a home and everything that I needed. As I grew older and older, I was about to go to school at St. Christopher's Girls'. When I was about the age of nine, I was looking after the sheep and the cows every day, and every morning before I went to school, my brothers and I had to take the animals out on the pasture to graze, and in the evening after school we would bring them home and feed them and give them water to drink.

When Sunday came it was time for Church, and you can't or don't want to go. When seven o'clock came you had to be ready early in the morning for Church. When Church was over and you reached home and had eaten, then back to Church at four o'clock, but this time it was time for Sunday School. I was confirmed at the age of twelve. When Sunday School was over, it was time for the animals to come home, and then it was time to play. There were happy times.

Pauline Pilgrim

I was born in 1962 in Kampala in Uganda, on the 30th of June. It used to be sunny and hot there. It hardly used to rain. We didn't live in a very big house, but it was nice and kept us cool. In Kampala there used to be a big market every week. I only liked one thing about my country. We used to have freedom to run all over the place in the country.

When I was five years old, I went to school, with my mother. It was only for three hours a day. My mother picked me up every day and took me there. I have five sisters and one brother, but one of my sisters died. My mother and father weren't very rich in Uganda, we had to pay for school. There was a lot of value to money. My mum and dad had to pay three pounds each for every one of us except my two small sisters, because they didn't go to school.

My mum didn't go to work, she stayed home and did the housework. My dad worked in a big factory with lorries. He used to drive lorries to all different towns and places.

Bin a Kakkad

Guyana

When I went to Guyana I was ten years of age. When I got there it was very hot. There my uncle came and picked me up and we went to my grandmother's house. While I was in the car I saw sugar cane, coconut trees, mango trees, and rice growing. As soon as I got there, I looked around and went off across the sand to the other kids. I made some friends, then I had to go in. I went to my Uncle's. There they had a porch. We and my cousin were chasing a lizard, then we went out into the back and I killed two snakes and had some sugar cane.

I went to the Courentyne district in the night. I was sick and went by car, and it took us two hours. When we got there it looked more civilised and there were a lot of coolies. Most of the people had Datsuns — they were big Japanese cars. When I came back the next day I went to Georgetown. That was more like a city. My Aunt lived in this house, and my brother mucked up the typewriter and my dad had to fix it.

We went home the next day, and that night we said Goodbye and took our plane home.

Andre Waterman

Gibraltar

My nan comes from Gibraltar, making my dad Gibraltarian. That makes me half Gibraltarian. Last year I went there, for the first time. It was much hotter than here, and when it is, the sea gets very rough and I have nearly drowned. I have an uncle and an aunt and four cousins. Every Sunday, and most days of the week we would go to the beach and stay there all day. On Sundays all the family would come. Uncle Alex and me would go snorkeling on the reef with spear guns and catch octopuses.

The reef is fantastic and you float on the surface four feet from the reef and the fish come within a yard of you as if they want to be caught. While I was there I went to St Michael's Cave. It is a hollow limestone cavity in the rock down by the water. There are all stalagmites and stalactites there. We also went to the tunnels dug by the revolutionaries in the Civil War. The tunnels go deep into the rock and there are many storage rooms dug in hard rock.

Tony Brown

Memories of my Childhood

I record my memories of childhood between the ages of 4—7. The environment of where I lived was very varied. The country that I was born was Kashmir — which is North of Pakistan and South of China. I lived in a small city called Sialkot.

I remember once going somewhere with my brother on his bike. He was very good at riding his bike. Sometimes we went riding up as far as we could up a very steep road. Once his rear brakes were not working, so he had to use his front breaks temporarily. When we were coming down that road he slowed down. We very quickly got to the bottom of the road and we had to make a left turn, so he suddenly put the brake on and the bike went spinning through the air and CRASH!!! into a bus. I fell on top of him and he fell on the bus and the bike got both of us. We got into trouble — but managed to get out without our parents knowing; if they did we would have been half killed.

Anyway, around where we lived were some mountains where we often went for picnics — they were the Himalayas, a few miles off. There was a cool blue lake in the mountains, which was very popular for swimming. The mountain tops had snow on them, while on the ground it was baking. That puzzled me for a long time.

There was also a very busy bridge that was solid and had three large arches to let the water flow and the ships and boats pass.

I used to have little habits like collecting insects in a small jar and seeing for how long they could live. I also collected different sorts of stones which my mother thought was disgusting and she wanted to throw them away. Once she did throw them away. I was angry, but controlled it just in case she would beat me to death.

One of our neighbours was a nice man who used to wake up early and have a regular walk for exercise, then he would do weightlifting and running later on. Once there was a competition on the grass, a few houses away from us, to see who was the strongest man around. The man in charge set a weight on the barbell; (I think it was about 290 pounds). Many strong men tried but couldn't lift it very much. So I ran to my friend, Iruf was his name, who came and had the bar above his head without any problem. Despite the fact that he was extremely strong, he was extremely modest and helpful too.

When Iruf found that I was interested in this sort of stuff, he told me that he would take me with him every morning for a walk. I agreed. I went like this for a long time and I used to have a cool shower and a cold one during the day.

In my city wrestling was a very popular sport. It was always on a Saturday morning, and people would always turn up. There were many bouts. There were wrestlers that were quite heavy — with an average weight of probably 14 stones — while some were light and some of a medium weight. The bouts would be between anyone — no matter what their weight was. The game would have no rounds as they do here. The contest would be won by the person who could make the other person submit. Iruf did wrestling bouts sometimes, but wasn't very good at it and usually lost — he still enjoyed it. I would always go and watch him wrestle.

Anyway, I had started school at the age of 6 and was in class 1. Next year I would be in class 2, if I failed in the exam I would have to stay in the same class. Gradually at the age of 16 I would be in class 10, which is equivalent to 'O' Level and 14 would be approximately equivalent to 'A' level. This system is used widely in that area even now — it has been a very successful method. The work wasn't very hard in the 1st Year and I walked over the simple exam and went into class 2. In this year I had to do a lot of memorising. In schools, in that country, memorising is considered as part of education. We had to memorise whole chapters, which seemed impossible — but after lots of times, reading it again and again, it seemed very easy. My friend was better than me at work, but often he forgot to do the homework. So he used to get the cane. By the way, the teachers obtained the canes from some trees between the two buildings, the branches of the trees were very pliable, so that's why they used them as canes — the cane was hit on the back of the hand.

There were two buildings to the school — most schools were the same or similar. One building was the mosque, (it was a sort of church), in which we could go and do memorising, reading or praying. One of the teachers was a molvi, (a sort of priest), who used to take us for reading. He had a walking stick and sometimes used it for corporal punishment.

The school used to begin at 8 am in the summer and 9 am in the winter. The school used to finish at 2 pm all the year round. Gradually the finishing time of school would increase in a few years. This school was primary — going up to the 5th class (age 11). There was no break or dinnertime. The lessons were not split up — we had to do a bit of each subject. The teacher would decide when we had enough of one subject, then we had a rest between subject changes. The holidays over there were not as many as over here.

There were many things over there that could be used to pass the time; the most popular were these: fishing, watching wrestling, playing ludo — probably the most popular game, and watching horse racing — there are no bets on the horses.

Fishing used to be done in a nearby canal, which had clean water, and people swam in it also. One way of catching fish was by a bowl which was covered by cloth with a hole in the middle and food inside. The water was chest high, and the bowl is placed on the canal bottom. The fish used to go in for food and soon got crowded. In a few minutes the person would slowly move towards it and put his hand on the hole and pull it out — this was a very efficient way of catching fish. The other method was by swinging a sort of wire as far as possible. The fish would be attracted to the food on the hook thus fish are caught. The least common was by a proper fishing tackle. Anyway I came here when I was about 7 I learnt to speak English in about 2 years — also I speak Urdu and Punjabi very well and can read Arabic, nowadays a bit of French too.

Tariq Mahmood

Life in Bangladesh

I am Ouhidur Choudry, and I come from Bangladesh. I lived in a village called Chorisoppur in Sylhet. I was born on June 1st, 1963. After 2 years after I was born, I remember my mother telling me about when I was sitting in front of our house. It was like in a field, when a snake came which I was trying to catch. But luckily my mother saw the snake and pulled me away. Then the snake in fear ran away.

Later, when I was about three, I visited England. When I came to this country I felt happy, with lots of friends (and some of them I can't mention). When I was about five I went back to our country and lived in the village with my grandma. I made so much fun living with my grandma. Every day we had to have a bath before going to school. When I went back to Bangladesh I could not walk barefooted.

After a while I went to our old village where there was the civil war between East Pakistan, (now Bangladesh) versus West Pakistan (now Pakistan). I was not sure of escaping from the soldiers of Pakistan as soon as the war was starting. Our country-men began to call our country 'Bangladesh'. We could not walk in towns like Sylhet after 4 o'clock because there was a curfew by the Pakistan soldiers. It was known that Bengalis would be shot after that time. They even killed Bengalis anyway. I always wanted to see the Pakistani soldiers. One day we saw some smoke, it was from a bomb dropped by a bomber. A few days later at home, our house was shot at by a fighter plane. Then lots of Pakistani soldiers were killed by lads as young as me, or older than me. The easy way the lads attracted soldiers of Pakistan was to shout, 'Joy Bangla, Bangla joy!' (meaning 'Long live Bangla!'). When the soldiers came and asked the lads 'who said that?' or 'shut that up!' they said, 'A group of people going that-a-way.' When the soldiers moved away from them they started shooting them, getting guns from their belts or throwing grenades. They were trained to do that and I hoped to join them, but I never. After the war, I went to the town and lived there until we again came to this country in November 1972.

Ouhidur Choudry

My Childhood Life in Bangladesh

I was born in Bangladesh, in a town called Sothogram. It is in Comilla which is in Bangladesh. I went to Hong Kong and stayed there for five years and then we came back to our village, where there was my uncle and aunty and grandma and grandpa. But my father had found a nicer house with fields all around. There are more than twenty fields all around it, and my father bought it for 40,000 takas (or rupees; there are thirty takas to a pound). It was one of the biggest houses, with most fields, in our village. It is one mile from Sothogram Bazaar. It has ten mango trees and eight jackfruit trees, 25 banana trees, 2 apple trees, 2 orange trees, 6 coconut trees, 4 lemon trees and last of all 50 date trees, and one borry tree. The date trees are one metre apart, so you can imagine how big it is. Everyday I used to go to school at 8 o'clock and come home for dinner at One o'clock, go back to school and then come home at 5 o'clock and have a little snack. Then I'd go to school, which teaches you about religion for two hours.

I come back home at seven o'clock, then bring my schoolbooks and memorise all the lessons for the next day, and if you forget it, or talk in the lesson, you get 20 of the best. The only weekend holiday was Sunday, not like in this country at all, every Saturday and Sunday. At nine o'clock we have our dinner, and then start memorising our religious studies. Then we go to sleep until 11 o'clock. On Sunday we go to the bazaar or we go swimming or play football or even practise archery.

At the age of ten I came to England.

Ashfaq Kazi

My name is Siu. I came from Hong Kong in 1974. I lived with my family in Leeds. My father had his own restaurant in Leeds, but he didn't like it much so he came to London.

I was born somewhere in Hong Kong. It was nice in Hong Kong 13 years ago, there was no killing or robbing. But today in Hong Kong is horrible. Every day in newspapers you can see lots of news about killing. Sometimes when they kill a person they even chop the body in pieces.

It is busy in Hong Kong, lots of cars, buses and lorries. It just looks the same as in London. There are lots of buildings too. The highest building in Hong Kong I think is about 52 floors. Three quarters of the buildings in Hong Kong are shops and factories. Not many people live in Hong Kong, they only work in the city. They live in the New Territories. New Territories is some part of China, not far away from Hong Kong. A river is between them, and there is an undersea tunnel from the New Territories to Hong Kong. It was built about two years ago because lots of people who work in Hong Kong every morning have got to go over the river by boats. It takes 25 minutes. But when the tunnel was built they could go by bus or they got their own car.

The children who live in Hong Kong start their primary school

when they are three years old. Then after two years they go to
the Middle School for six years, then High School for five years.
The teachers give lots of homework for children to do in Hong
Kong, and in some schools they have tests every day. It's too hard
for a child only nine or ten years old. So sometimes some of the
children run away from home, because of too much work to do.
In England we have Cooking, needlework or woodwork, but in
Hong Kong we don't have any. We sit on the chair all day long.

Siu Mui Tang

My Lifetime in Nigeria

All I can remember is that I started school in 1967 at the age of
five years old. They didn't use to judge by your age, but your
hand had to go over your head and then it has to pass your ears.

We got canes as well as we do in London. But if you wanted
to send your own children to an English school, you can and they
speak English there, and the behaviour there is like the ones
here. But when I was going to school I had my food in the
morning, with Nigeria pancake made out of corn flour. Then
when you are in the classroom you must listen very much
because you get exams every end of the month. Early in the
morning we had to stand up when the teacher comes in and we
had to be very quiet. Then we are asked our tables, up to twelve
times tables from when you about the age of eight years old.
You must get it or if you don't you have to stand up till it comes
to your go again, and then if you get it you will sit down and be
quiet.

If you are not clever you will repeat a class probably twice
or even thrice. If you pass you will go to the next year. And
everyone is forced to wear school uniform up to the sixth year,
and every morning you will have a check up, with them looking
at your hands to see if they are clean. They check your teeth,
and your shirt to find out whether it is clean.

Alaba Opesan

Ghana

A big building, almost square, with rooms all around,
Followed by a big open roof, with gravel ground.

At the corner of the square was a big black tank,
We used to go down to the river to fetch clear water
Which we would use for washing clothes —
We covered it with a plank.

For ironing, we filled it with hot charcoal,
And when it was hot we used it — it works, but it was a bit slow.

The girls used to do all the house work,
And the boys went down to the farm and pick cocoa to dry,
It was fun, but it was hard work.

I lived near the school, so it wasn't hard to get there.
We didn't have to know the time
Because the church bell rung when it was time to go.

Sometimes we used to go with our feet bare —
And when I was eight, I came to London, here.

Andrew Ohene

On one occasion at school with the children, Peter
Blackman, a black Barbadian poet, now retired after
many years of working for British Rail, a man who had
originally come to Britain looking for work in the
thirties, came to read some of his poetry and talk to the
children about language.[4] He finished off his reading with
an extract from his magnificent long poem, 'My Song is
for All Men'. This was published as a pamphlet by
Lawrence and Wishart in 1952, and very quickly sold
thousands of copies amongst the trade union movement.
Like the composition of the class he was talking to,
Peter Blackman's poem stretched right across the world,
breaking down national and ethnic walls. We had
duplicated the last section of the poem, which the
children followed in front of them as the poet read out
loud:

In these and with these I remember the ordinary man in any
    street or village
Who ever held out to me the hand of a brother
I grasp this hand wherever I find it in Perth Paris Prague New York
    Buenos Aires Pekin
This hand piled flowers in my praise red roses in Prague
All the earth's blooms gathered in Moscow
I hold with particular tenderness the hand of a German woman
Fled from the Nazis because she saw herself demeaned in their
    thinking about me

Look this is a white hand it is my hand I am the black man

I hear strong voices calling me brother from the rough horse-hair
    tents of Mongolia
In Korea the rivers and mountains leap with the cry of their
    welcome
My heart sings in the lilt of the tear-twisted caress from the
    mountains and far lands of China
I gather like greeting from the red roughened hands of the
    steelmen of Sheffield
My smile is the smile of the miner descending the coalpits of
    Rhondda
I am by the side of the stevedore heaving bales in the shipyards of
    Antwerp
I reach around earth to embrace the Australian docker
For his handclasp assures me victory over subtly plotted deception
These are my strength my force their varied conceivings
My calm that in them my living may never decay

And since I am of Africa all that is Africa comes with me
Striding hot storm we come tenting our courage and hope
With the hope and the courage of the men of America Europe
    Australia and all the sea islands
The good men the true men the strong men the working men
Whose sweat is their daily bread whose strength is their class

Scientists craftsmen teachers painters poets philosophers come
We shall work till our power invested together create a new world
Till there be no longer famine in India
Till the Yangtse flood no more
Till we plant gardens in Gobi
Till we gather each year the harvest of the Sahara
Till our force bright as the atom blasts the evil oppression which
    cripples all our creations

And so, I rest the little blond German child gently against me
I trace the years with him
I rest the little black African child gently against me
He and the German boy trace the years with me
I rest the little Kamchatchuan child gently against me
I rest the little Georgian child gently against me
She and the little Japanese boy trace the years with me
Let our love hold them till bright as the atom together
Their power blasts the evil oppression which cripples all our
    creation
Till man cover the earth with his glory as the waters cover the
    sea.

As soon as the poet had finished, and had left the room and was on his way home, a white girl in the class was writing this:

Nations

Black, white, yellow,
Whatever they may be,
A little child will always be
Welcome to sit on my knee.

A word that can be hurtful to them
Is 'nigger', 'honkey' or 'chink'.
A word they need
Is a kind and loving word,
    FRIEND

Their language is different
Their features are different,
But the one thing
We will all be the same,
    A HUMAN

Karen Durrell

This was followed by other pieces written by local white children in the same spirit, the spirit of Peter Blackman's poem and a spirit that must be upheld and vindicated for the sake of all our children.

The World in the Classroom

In my classroom there's all nations from all over the world some from Jamaica, some from Hong Kong. I don't really care, they're all friends to me. From the hot countries to the cold countries and from black to white, we're all friends in our classroom. Our class can prove to all prejudiced people all over the world that people from different nations can live together. My background is a cold place called Britain. It is cold in the winter and quiet in the summer but not hot like in the other countries of America, India, Africa. The only difference between our countries is colour and language, and that's nothing really, we are all human and we can all show friendship and love for each other, and not war and hate between our colours.

Tommy Robertson

People in the classroom from all different places,
India, Africa, England and Japan.
All tied up like laces
In one big clan.

People in the classroom all need a friend,
All need someone to work with,
So there'll be an end to wars and battles,
So that we can live.

Anthony Power

Nothing is wrong with colour,
A colour is a colour.
Nothing is wrong with a human,
A human is a human.

Nothing is wrong with an Australian,
African and an Englishman.
But people are hurting each other,
Just by saying a few words
Like 'white honkey, spottie ossie and nigger',

People are kind and say,
'Hi Brother, watcha pal, and hello'.
That's the words we should say,
And it will all be settled.

Michael Smith

And Sezin, a Turkish Cypriot girl who was a newcomer
to the school from a refugee camp in Cyprus, wrote
without bitterness, in sheer generosity:

People in Need

The world is lovely,
And life is lonely,
Like the road with no end.

Somebody richer or poorer,
Poorer ones need food and money,
Richer ones need friends.

I want everybody to live together,
They never get angry
At each other, forever.

People need a long life
For their future,
They want to live happy
On this world.

The voice says:
'Everybody, everybody
Can you hear me?
I want to live all together
On this world.'

Sezin Mustafa

Part three
Hello Friend

When Peggy Seeger, the American folksinger, visited our school to sing to the children in April 1976, one of her songs in particular seemed to have immediate significance for our children. She explained that she had been inspired to write this song after seeing a group of West Indian people standing in the rain by a bus stop in Wolverhampton, Enoch Powell's parliamentary constituency:

Hello Friend

Hello friend, I see you're a stranger, where do you come from?
Hello friend — something in your face reminds me of the sun,
But the northern light is thin against the darkness of your skin,
HELLO FRIEND, I'M GLAD THAT YOU COULD COME.

When you talk, I hear the echo of the places you have been.
When you walk, colours all around you, fluttering in the wind,
When I listen to your song, I feel you really do belong,
AM I THE STRANGER, THE ONE WHO'S JUST COME IN?

I think I know what made you come here, but what makes you
    want to stay?
Will you go, if the weather and the welcome seem too cold and
    grey?
Do you feel you'll never find all the warmth you left behind?
NEVER MIND — I HOPE YOU WANT TO STAY.

Did you find new friends to help you? Can you earn a living
    here?
Do you mind the smoke and grime around you and the warning
    loud and clear — ?
Or did your troubles just begin with the colour of your skin?
NEVER MIND — I'M GLAD TO SEE YOU HERE!

Did you come to climb a mountain and end up in a hole?
Have you won the right to join our people signing on the dole?
Can you be happy here amid suspicion and the fear?
OR WILL YOU RUN AND NEVER MORE RETURN?

Hello friend — all of us are strangers in this Green and pleasant
    land,
Once again, battle ranks are forming and we need a brother's
    hand,
Yours the fear and ours the shame, but our goal is just the same
IN THE END, THIS WILL BE OUR NATIVE LAND.

Peggy Seeger (Copyright Ewan McColl Ltd)

We studied the song in our classes after Peggy's visit, and often sang it with the children. Its thoughts and arguments stayed very close to us through the rest of the school year. For during May and June 1976 it was obvious that racism on a vicious scale was being fomented locally and nationally. Powell was pouring out his sadistic prophecies of a 'dark and darkening future', using all his benighted imagery of the unknown to stir up the fears of working people. The national press was building resentment against a hapless group of Malawi Asians who had unwittingly been placed by the insufficiently financed local services in an expensive hotel on their arrival in Britain. At Southall, a Sikh youth had been murdered outside a cinema. Two local Asian students of Queen Mary College, Mile End, East London had been stabbed to death near their hall of residence in Woodford, and a local Sikh building worker, Rawal Singh, had been attacked in the street twice — his neck badly gashed on the second occasion — and only a few streets away from our school. In Newham, the borough immediately to our east, after a racist demagogue from the 'British National Party' had declared at a street rally that after the death of the Sikh boy in Southall it was 'one down, a million to go', a local white youth had also been killed after a violent incident. In the same borough, Asian women were being attacked while shopping by white youths and their saris set afire.

In this ferment, the venomous lies and myths of the organised racists were getting through to the passions of some of our children. After the death of the white boy in Newham, a white girl at the school wrote this, reproducing all the scapegoat-isms and violent myths about local Asians that are the false armament of fascism. All her anger and indignation was being projected against people of her own class:

The Immigrant

They come over here to laze about,
They never work, but are always on the dole, the dirty louts.
They stink and pong and never wash,
But have a cat lick or a slosh.
They buy up all our shops and buy up the banks,
And they wonder why we hate them.
They killed a white boy, I forget his name,
A quiet kid, very tame.
His mother cried, his father promised
That he will get revenge
Against those BLOODY PACKS!

It was imperative that in this context we should
consciously begin to organise our lessons to counteract
this false knowledge. Of course, we had the statistics
to refute the gross hyperboles and lies of the national
press in their distorted and frenzied approach to Asian
immigrants, but it was also fundamental that our
children should understand that they — or most of them
— came from families that had once been immigrant
families. Two centuries ago, this very East London where
we now lived and learned, had been mostly meadowland
and marsh, with the occasional farm, cottage, lime pit,
wharf or hamlet. The port of the East End where we
lived had only really grown as an industrial area through
the influence of the docks in Poplar and Millwall, which
had been constructed in the nineteenth century. Its
population too was built up almost entirely of workers'
families coming in successive waves of immigration from
the English countryside, Scotland, Ireland, Europe, and
the British Empire and Commonwealth. We discovered
that we were all from immigrant families, teachers as
well as students: that at some time in all our family
histories, our ancestors (or we ourselves) had been
uprooted or moved, compulsorily or voluntarily, and
come to live in East London. Some had come for work,

some for safety, some for stability. We found poems
which expressed this truth simply and clearly. First, there
was this one by Arthur Clegg:

The English — Are They Human?

I'm Celtic and Saxon, a Norman, a Dane
a bronze smith from Africa, India, Spain
    a megalith mason
from the Middle Sea basin
    Continents, oceans
and wonderful notions
mix in my structure and seethe in each vein.

Forebears from Asia who tamed the wild horse
slaves for my ancestor, Roman and Norse;
    a Frenchman, a Fleming
    Dutch from Terschelling
    Irish from Dublin
    Slavonic from Lublin,
African seamen who served under Nelson,
Jews, Czechs and others fleeing from Belsen,
    descendant of Legion from every region,
    a myriad mixture — English, of course.

And a Hackney railwayman, Jim Ward, had written this
song to the tune and chorus of a song associated with
the Caribbean,'Island in the Sun':

Who are the English?

Many, many years ago,
As our history goes to show,
Invaders came to this island,
Today he's called an Englishman.

Chorus:
Angles, Saxons, Jutes and Scots,
Normans, Danes and Huguenots,
Irish and Jew with races new,
Take them all, and *they are you.*

Angles, Saxons, Jutes and Scots,
Vikings, Danes and they begot
From them came the English tongue
Handed down to daughter and son.

Normans came from Normandy,
Huguenots from Brittany,
From them all a nation grew,
Take them all and they are you.

Centuries passed, our nation grew
Enriched by Irish, and the Jew,
With their craft and industry,
Love of life and liberty.

Chaucer, Shakespeare, Dickens too,
Wrote for many, not the few.
They wrote for the common man
And proud to be an Englishman.
As we saw the war recede,
Production was our greatest need,
Labour from old colonies
Help to man our industries,

Enoch Powell can't save his face
If he ever tries to trace,
He will find to his disgrace
The English are a bastard race.

The lessons of our history,
Of immigrant and refugee,
Took them all in warm embrace,
Absorb them in our island race.

We tried to remove the irrational stigma attached to
the word 'immigrant' by explaining how the population
of East London, as Jim Ward's song emphasises, was
built up, and exists now, as a conglomeration of
immigrant peoples. We followed by reproducing some of
the pieces in the previous chapter, of immigrant children
telling their own stories, and thus ploughing back the
children's own experiences to them. Soon other children
who had actually lived through the process of immigration were writing prolifically and unashamedly, giving
us more plays, stories and poems that encompassed the
world and revealed through the microcosmic energy we
had in the classroom, the difficulties and prejudices that
their families had sometimes faced. We were finding that
honest writing was breeding honest writing.

An Immigrant's Story

I was born in Hong Kong on the 21st of January, 1963, and I
came to England when I was about 11 years old in 1974. It was
nice in Hong Kong. I lived in a big house, with a big garden in front
of it. Every day I went to school at 8.30 a.m. and back home at
12.30 p.m., or sometimes I started school at 1.00 p.m. and
finished at 4.30 p.m. The lessons that I had were not the same as
I had in England. We didn't have needlework, woodwork or games.
We sat on the chair from the start of the lesson to the end of
school time, and we also had lots of homework to do. If we
didn't finish it on time we would get the cane from the form
teacher or from the headmaster.

In 1969 my father came to England. He stayed in England for
a few years and then he had his own restaurant in Leeds. So he
sent my mother and our five brothers and sister to England. My
mother came first, and then after a few months we came. We
lived somewhere in Leeds, and it was a nice house there. The first
week that I arrived in Leeds, everything was strange to me, but I
knew I must get used to it if the days come past. Anyway, it
didn't come true. Every time that I wanted to go out somewhere,
on the way I heard lots of things. The white people or coloured
people — they keep on calling me 'Chinese', 'chin chon' and even
sometimes they hit me. At that time I couldn't do anything at
all. I didn't know English, and I didn't like to fight. And so in
the first two months if I didn't have to go out, then I just stayed
at home and read books. My parents always asked me why I
didn't go out to play. So I told them the reasons, and my father
told me something about him when he came to England.

'In the first few weeks,' he said, 'before you came, I usually
used to work in a restaurant sometimes in London when it was
a holiday. I and my friend always went somewhere and sometimes
I heard some English said to me, and because I didn't know
English and didn't understand what they said, I asked my friend.
He told me, then I started laughing. My friend asked me why, and
I answered. I said that I was laughing at myself. If next time
someone said these words to me again and they know I don't
understand, what will they do? My friend didn't say anything,
and I was laughing all the way to the place where we wanted
to go.'

Siu Miu Tang

An Immigrant's Story

Before I came to this country, life was very hard in Kenya. When
my elder sister was born, my mum and dad had no money, only

a few shillings which they could buy bread with. We had no friends or relatives. It was lonely, as my mother told me what had happened in the past. I would almost cry. As my mum said, we had a table in the middle of a room in an African village which had a few slices of bread which we would get from the baker down the road. We would be, that is my mother and father, lying on the floor because at that time we did not have money to buy anything. We would sit there for hours till we were hungry, that is very hungry. When we were hungry we ate a slice of bread which was hard and not very nice to eat.

My mother used to cry a lot, and my dad used to go and look for work and come home about two in the morning. By the end of the week there would be no money in the house, so things would become hard again. Because what money my dad got went to buy all the good things for my elder sister. This is all true. After a long time I had another sister and a brother who were older than me, then another sister younger than me, then two twins, brother and sister.

Things got even better then. We had a farm and chickens. I remember a lot because I know we had a great time, a lot of fun. Especially when we went to picnics near the streams and the river falls. When my two youngest brothers and sister were one year old, we decided to come to London.

Salim Kassam

I n 1963, when I was two in Ghana,
M y mother came here to England.
M aybe it was because of her colour that three white boys
    nicked her purse,
I t was hard to find work at first —
G hana High Commission Bank is where she worked,
R eally it's because she had lots of friends there.
A t that moment, my mum was expecting —
N ations of all kinds must learn to live together —
T hen in 1970 I came over to join her.

I n my brown skin I walked the streets,
M emories flash by of my time at home,
M isery in this place called East London,
I nsults shouted after me everywhere I go,
G roups of white kids gang up on you,
R unning here and there hiding,
A nyone I see, my heartbeat grows louder.
N eglected by other people —
T errible things are done to immigrants.

Andrew Ohene

20th July 1974

It was one Monday morning, the date was 15th of July, 1974. When we woke up, we turned the radio on and it was saying the news. Suddenly we heard that somebody had killed Makarios. When everybody heard that Makarios was dead, all the Greek people started to fight each other. But on the 16th of July we heard that he was still alive. After that, all the people started to get ready for the fighting. But before that the Greek people closed the roads for us. We couldn't go anywhere.

On 20th of July the Turkish armies came to Cyprus. In the afternoon, it was 4 p.m., the Greek soldiers attacked the Turkish people and then the big war came up in Cyprus. I mean between the Greeks and the Turks.

The players' names are: HALIL, ULFET, VASFIYE, SEZIN, REMZIYE, MEHMET, AZIZ, NIKO, ANDREA, TIANNI.

Act 1

HALIL: Hurry up and go in, and shut the windows and door.

REMZIYE: Why, what's the matter?

HALIL: Because the Greek soldiers have attacked the Turkish areas.

REMZIYE: Who told you?

HALIL: Mehmet came from Limassol and he told us that they attacked the Turkish people.

(*then Mehmet came in*)

MEHMET: Hello! What are you doing?

REMZIYE: Come in Mehmet. Tell us what happened in Limassol.

MEHMET: Well, they started fighting. But first of all Greek soldiers threw a bomb through the Turkish side.

(*Remziye started to cry*)

REMZIYE: Oh my God! What have we done?

ULFET: What is the matter mum? Why are you crying? Come on, tell us.

REMZIYE: No, I can't tell you.

SEZIN: Come on Auntie tell us. What's the matter? (*Ulfet and Sezin hold together*) Come on, tell us what's happened.

ULFET: You tell us dad, what's the matter? and why is mummy crying?

HALIL: Nothing.

Act 2

(*suddenly Aziz came in*)

AZIZ: The Greek soldiers have attacked our village!

(*When he was talking to us the gun noises interrupted him. Then we understood that the Greek soldiers had attacked us. When*

Vasfiye heard the gun noises coming to us, she started to cry.
Suddenly Ulfet came in)

ULFET: What's wrong Vasfiye?

VASFIYE: Nothing.

ULFET: Why are you crying?

VASFIYE: Because I am afraid of the Greek soldiers.

SEZIN: Don't be so afraid, they can't do nothing to us.

VASFIYE: I know that they can't do nothing to us, but I am still
    too afraid of them.

(Suddenly the Greek soldiers came and they knocked at the door.
Remziye went to see who was knocking at the door. When she
opened the door, she saw all Greek soldiers in front of her and she
shouted to the others than the Greek soldiers had come to their
home. One of the Greek soldiers began to talk)

NIKO: Don't move! If you move we are going to kill you.

ANDREA: We came here to have a look to see if you have got any
    guns or something like that.

TIANNI: Have you any young men in your home?

REMZIYE: No, there aren't any young men in our home.

NIKO: Where have they gone?

REMZIYE: We don't know where they have gone. They left home
    last night and they didn't come back.

(After that we heard that all the men went to the Episkopi camp.
That camp was called 'Happy Valley' [Mutlu Vadi]. But we didn't
have any idea about our family. So one day a man came to our
village from the camp and my uncle had sent us a letter with him.
In that letter my uncle wrote to us that 'You must come to the
camp with him.' Then my Auntie called us)

REMZIYE: Ulfet, Sezin, come here, I've got some good news for
    you.

ULFET: Where are you mum?

REMZIYE: I am in the sitting room.

SEZIN: Hello Auntie, what is the news about?

REMZIYE: Look, your dad sent us a letter, and he said that we
    must go there with this man, and we must take our British
    passport with us too.

ULFET: All right, I agree. What do you think Sezin?

SEZIN: All right, I agree too. That's a good idea.

REMZIYE: Come on then, let's get ready.

(so we went to the 'Happy Valley' camp)

Act 3

When we went to the camp, we saw our family and all the other
people. We were very happy when we saw my dad and all my
family in the tent. We were fifteen people in it, because my

grandad and grandma lived with my dad, and aunties and uncles too. We hadn't got any clothes to change what we had got on. We hadn't got food.

In one week we didn't eat anything. We carried water with buckets and bottles. And we had no bath for fifteen days. We lived there for six months in tents. Somebody went to England. After six months we went to Turkey with Turkish planes. So then we went back to Cyprus and stayed in my cousin's house. Then we came to England.

Maybe one day we will go back to Cyprus. I came here for school. Now I am going to school, and I am very happy now.

Ulfet Halil and Sezin Mustafa

I am an immigrant. I came from India. When I left India I came here by aeroplane. I was too afraid in the aeroplane because I had never been in one before. When I got to England it looked very different to me than India. My brother came to the airport to take me home. I didn't like it for the first few days, and my brother began to teach me English at home. I didn't go out to play, I stayed at home and watched the television. And after a few months I began to speak a little English, and I came to school and learned English and all the other lessons.

When I came here from India it was like I couldn't believe my eyes, and why I really came here is for to learn English and live here and work with the English people. And I want to be a doctor in this country, not for my own country, but for this country. And it is not like the white people to call me paki. They are very good to me and if I am good to them, they are very good to me. And other people come here from Pakistan, Jamaica and all countries to work here. About two hundred years ago this country had not enough people, so they had to invite them from other countries. In East London, there was nothing there and people came from other countries and drove the buses and built the houses, and they lived here and worked here.

Hanif Driver

And children from Scotland and Ireland were also remembering their own families' migrations:

A Scot's Story

I am Scottish, I was born in Glasgow. When I was one my mum

had another baby and she already had three before: my brother Robert, then my sister Ellen, then my sister Margaret. So when my other brother was born we moved to a place called Barrow-field, still in Glasgow. When I was about ten, I got into a lot of trouble with gangs — breaking into places and that. And there was this man in our street who had funny hair and people said he hadn't changed his wallpaper since he moved into the place. We called him Gollywog because of his hair and we (my friend and 1) always used to smash his windows with stones. One night we smashed all his front windows and I went myself round the back on a railway, and smashed his back windows. People told me to stop it and I just said, 'Shut up, you nosey old bag!' and still threw stones at the windows. Next morning my mum told me off. She couldn't hit me because she was in bed sick, and couldn't get up. My mum had to pay for all the windows that were smashed. My dad couldn't do anything either, because he was here in London looking for a job.

I was eleven when I came down here. It was only me and my brothers that came down. My mum and sisters and two brothers stayed up in Glasgow. When I came down here I thought there would be hardly any people living here. I was wrong. I hadn't seen so many coloured people in all my life. In Glasgow I had only seen about two blacks and about twenty Asians. Any time that I had seen a coloured, black or Asian, I called them 'Headhunter', 'cannibal' — things like that.

When I first came down to London I wanted to see all the famous things, go down Piccadilly. But there was no time for it because I was always going places with my dad. When I was on my own, I was thinking of Glasgow — all the friends I was missing. Then suddenly I remembered what I did to that man's windows. I felt sorry for him but that wouldn't do any good. I was thinking of all the games I played with my friends. Games like dodgie-ball. The way you played it was for everyone to get into a circle — about seven people at the most, standing up with our legs open. Someone would bounce the ball in the middle of us and say 'dodgie ball, dodgie ball, one, two, three'. Whoever's legs it went through were on it. When he threw it, people had to dodge it. It's the same as 'E ball'. Other games we played were 'kick the can', hide and seek and tig. The way you played tig was any amount of people could play and they would chase you and hold onto you and say your name. They would say '2, 4, 6, 8, 10 William Faulds on it', and I would have to help the boy who caught me to catch the rest.

William Faulds

I am an Immigrant

They call me Potato Merchant,
They call me Paddy,
They call me spud man.
I am proud to be Irish,
I would hate to be English.
They call me what they want
But they are mongrels themselves.

Tony McLaughlin

Paddy

Go home Paddy go home now
We do not want you hanging around
Can't you see what you could do
You I.R.A. bastard you're fit for the loo.

'Heh Irish' they call, and then spit in my eye
'Go home bastard, go home now'
Then they kick me to the ground
The pigs only do it for spite.

I have been here all my life
Born, bred, lived in Stepney
I do not know why I am called a name
Everybody is the same.

Gary Quirke

For the last writer, his Irishness was a generation away. Other children whose parents had been immigrants, empathised with their parents' experiences when they had first arrived. Some of these sons and daughters were now confronting, through their writing, the ignorance and bigotry that their parents had to face, and that now the Asians in their own classes were facing every day in the streets around the school.

T he family came over to England.
H aving left Westmoreland, they say to themselves,
E ven the houses are different.'

I am Mrs Reid.
M any people here, but not like the West Indies,
M any factories too, but no lovely palm trees.

I am an immigrant, so they all say.

G oing places? Not much.

R ound and round I go, always ending back at the start.

A ny work for a poor black immigrant?

'N o.'

T hey don't give us a chance.

Avia Reid

My Dad from Sierra Leone

Before my dad came to England, he was on a ship. He was working on it when a metal bar fell on his big toe. Then times were hard, so he came to England by ship. On the ship he met my mum. Then they got to England and got married. Then he was asked to work in Dagenham with the Ford carmaking. That meant he had to work night duty, so he didn't take the job because he was scared in case something happened to my mum.

Then he got a job as a man who stacks the wood in a wood factory. He gets £59 a week. Then my mum and dad had an argument and got divorced. And now my mum has moved, but my dad is till living in Mathews House.

One day when I came home from school, I said to my dad, 'Tell me about the laws in Sierra Leone.' He said that if they got a man who was a thief, they would put him in a barrel and bang nails in it, and roll him down the hills into water. Then they took him out and kicked him. Then my dad told me a lot of stories, but they were true, what he told me. One day, when he was a little boy, he was on the golf pitch and a man got him. So he took a stone and threw it and busted the man's head, so that man didn't go anywhere near him again. He and his mates knew where a mango tree was, and they went there every day. When the gold workers had sandwiches, they got a banana and put a bit of gold in the bread and heated it. Then they brought it back out and changed it for some money.

Tony Ellis

An Immigrant's Story

I was living in Stoke Newington before coming to East London (Tower Hamlets) and moved into a women's aid centre. Everybody was staring at us, not making us feel at all welcome. They kept calling us 'Blackie, this isn't your country, go back to the jungle and swing on the tree.' But what surprises me more is that some of the blacks were saying it to me also. My mum's friend told them to look between their legs and they would find a bigger jungle.

We did not get much abuse from people, which to me was very surprising. When we was moving, I didn't want to, because I thought that everyone would start on me and call me all the names they could think of. But I don't think I needed to worry because it wasn't at all bad and I was surprised to see the amount of friends I made.

My mum likes it here and so does my brother, he and my mum have also made a lot of friends. There are still some people who hate us but we don't mind. My dad one day had a fight with one because a man called him a Blackie and broke the piping and told the foreman to sack him. So my dad hit him in the face and the man hit him back. But the man was taller than my dad and did not know that my dad knew Judo, and he ended up getting the worse. And from that time no one in the firm touched him. There has been a few scraps but they always get blown over in a day.

Sonia, with an Irish father, at first wrote about her family:

I was born and bred in England. My mother was born in Newcastle but came to London when she was very young. My father was born in Ireland and lived there until he was fifteen. He then came to England and grew up here. People say that because he has lived here for 27 years, he has lost his accent. My friends, when they come to our house, cannot understand him so I have to sort of translate as if he came from Holland, Greece or Belgium.

He liked to tell me what life was like in Ireland. There was not any fighting in Belfast then, but in other parts of Ireland. People thought the fighting would never come to Belfast. A few months ago, my father's mother and brother both died in Belfast. He recently went over to Belfast for one week. After his brother's funeral he came back, then on the Saturday morning he got a phone call saying his mother had died of a broken heart. He then had to go over to Belfast again for the funeral.

Sonia Quinn

Then she imagined herself as her father, stepping back a generation, yet forward in her understanding. She suggested at the end of her piece that prejudice may eventually be endured and assimilated, but that it leaves a skin of insensitivity around the receiver, who may often pass it on to the next and most recent immigrants, thus creating more false divisions amongst immigrant peoples.

While I was in Ireland I had plenty of friends. When I was 15 I came to England by ship and I lived with my sister Anne in the East End of London. At the age of 16 I went to join the navy. Men in the force called me 'Paddy' and used to tell jokes about the Irish, which I thought very annoying. When I left the navy I found a flat in East London. I used to walk into pubs and be welcomed by people I did not know. Later on, after talking, I found out that they were my father's friends and that they heard that his son and daughter had come over to England. I used to talk to them a lot, and found out quite a bit about my father, who, when I was little, had gone to England and died there.

After a couple of years I got married and became the father of five children, but one boy died, whose name was Anthony. My children's names were Maria, Anthony, Sonia, Suzette and Francis. My wife's name was Josephine. When I sat down in the living room I used to think about when I first came over and how people talked about the Irish. I feel a bit silly about ignoring the Irish jokes, but now I am more sensible and always laugh at them. I have never minded being called 'Paddy' or any Irish name because at least I am not called 'Nigger', 'Ching Chong' or any other name. I suppose it's because I'm white and Ireland is a part of England.

Sonia Quinn

Another girl used an acrostic form to muse about her West Indian immigrant father, whose identity for a long time was kept secret from her. Writing the poem seemed to help her to strip away a mystery surrounding her own, most personal identity.

M y father came from Montserrat,
O nce I knew him as a stranger.
N o one told me he was my father,
IT troubled me so much about this man.
 S ome time ago, when I was about two

HE came and told my mum to tell me,
R ight away, which she didn't like to.
WR ong or right, she should have told me,
A s soon as I understood her.
T he time came, and she told me when I was nine.

The attitudes which many of our children, black and
white, showed towards the Pakistanis and Bangla Deshis
— the most recent groups of immigrants to East London
— were being polluted and dynamized by rumour, myth,
prejudice and political opportunism. It was crucial that
the children should realise and understand the historical
continuity of immigration in their own neighbourhood,
and how their own families had contributed to it themselves. Now these 'new' people from Pakistan and Bangla
Desh were only an extension of that same continuity.
We were trying to demonstrate to them that a national
population arises through the migrations of different
peoples to a particular, common place, and national
culture results from the combined and cohesive development of the traditions, languages and specific life
struggles of those different peoples. The question of Work
was also paramount. The Sikhs were becoming prominent
as the building workers and bricklayers in sites throughout the East End, just as the Irish had been famous as
dockers and stevedores, and the West Indians as transport
workers on the buses and trains. Now Pakistani and
Bangla Deshi garment workers and haberdashers were
the main workforce in what had previously been a
predominantly Jewish industry. These Asian newcomers
were keeping an important East End industry in the area,
whereas other local industry had moved out of the area
in the profiteering search for cheaper labour. The shirts,
skirts and blouses which many of us wore were made by
Asian garment workers here in East London in the
workshops of Whitechapel and Spitalfields, often in
appalling sweatshop conditions. This was a truth which
many of our children, particularly those infected by

racist ideas, found difficult to accept. But it was our task as teachers continually to put these facts before them, to assault and destroy the vicious mythology that put white child, or black and white child, against brown.

Again we went back into past and recent history to find precedents for what was happening on local streets now, to Asian people. One girl imagined herself as an Irish farmworker in the eighteen-forties, forced by the Potato Blight to emigrate to England and work building the docks in the East End. For many of our white children, their forebears would have known experiences such as these. And yet it was now some of these same children, and their parents and elder brothers and sisters, who were making life insufferable for local Asian immigrants. In this context, it was imperative that they evoked the histories of their own families.

The Potato Blight

I come from Ireland. In 1840 in Ireland there was a disease which rotted all the potatoes that grew. Me and my family were poor and were very hungry. One morning I saw a poster which said 'Come to England and help build the docks.' I was very tempted because it was the only offer that I could find for a bit of money to buy food.

I told my wife about it, we discussed it and we finally decided that we would come to England. In Ireland I was a farm worker. I went to work for one more week on the farm, then we came to England on a little old boat which was crowded with people, but it had to do because I didn't have any more money to get a decent boat to travel on.

We left all the people we knew behind in Ireland, our relatives and friends. When we arrived in England we found it very hard to rent a room, but in the end we found one. The following morning I went to the docks to find a job, and my wife went out looking for somewhere where we could live. I got a job digging the docks, but the wages were 3d an hour. I knew it was terrible, such hard labour for such terrible pay, but I had to take it or starve. When I got home my wife had found a place where we could live. It was a little tenement. She said it was terrible but she took it because the rent was too high in the room we were living in.

I told my wife it was all right to take it, but we couldn't have gone on paying the rent for it with the wages I am earning. My daughter and son had to get jobs so that we wouldn't starve. My daughter found a job in a clothing factory and my son became a mudlark. He had to go through the mud of the River Thames when the tide went out, and see if any ships had dropped anything over the side — things like coal, iron and other things. Then he would sell them.

None of us had good jobs and earned good wages, but in our situation we couldn't be fussy about what jobs we wanted and how much wages. It wasn't easy living in London. Me and my family were always getting picked on because we weren't English and because of our Irish accent. My daughter came home from work in a right state. All the girls had started on her for nothing just because she was Irish. We all got called names like Paddy, Murphy, or Spud Face. But we had to go on.

Mandy Ince

Another girl imagined herself as a Jewish immigrant, taking on the historical persecution of her people:

Jewish

I come from Israel and I am a Jew,
People call us names, we just shout, 'The same to you!'
We're never rude to our parents, we'd never dream of that,
The children used to say, 'Eat that, it's like you — a rat.'
We go to the synagogue before breakfast,
We break bread before we eat,
My mother lights the candle
Covering her head with a piece of embroidered sheet.
When my brother was thirteen he had a barmitzvah,
He had to sing from a scroll
Which the Rabbi put before him.
They put money in a bag
Labelled with a tag —
A hundred pounds he did collect,
Now he's labelled as a man.

How many years were we tortured in Germany?
How many years were we hurt?
People did not know, people did not care.
The Germans, tall and fair,
Shot us standing against the wall,
Lurking over us, long and tall.

That's the history of the Jews.

Julie Veale

And Louis, a Barbadian boy, took himself back to the postwar years when London Transport were recruiting in his island, and in Trinidad and Jamaica, for transport workers to come to Britain to work on the buses and the London Underground:

I Come From the West Indies

I am a young man, I live in the city in Barbados. I am looking for a working life. I have left high school — looking all around. WAIT . . .
LOOK — there's a job:
'A chance of a lifetime. Come to England, We got the work, You get the change, Work on the buses and trains, We pay the fare, So come inside.'
This could be the chance I've been waiting for. I must go in.
'Good afternoon. I see you have something in the window.' 'Yes, would you like to go?' 'Yes. This might be the chance of a lifetime.' 'It could be. What's your name?' 'Louis — Louis Browne '
'Louise Browne?' 'Yes.' 'How old are you?' 'Twenty years old.' 'Have you a mum and dad?' 'Yes.' 'Why would you like to go to England?' 'To get a job, so I can buy a house and things like that. You know.'
'Yes — settle down in England.' 'Yes — you know what I mean.' 'When would you like to go?' 'What do you mean?' 'You can go every three weeks. The next departure is next week.' 'Can I tell you tomorrow?' 'Yes, that will be all right.' 'Well, I'd best be going home now. I have a lot of talking over to do with my mum and dad. Bye.'
'Bye.'
Next week I could be in England. That's if mum and dad don't say nothing — it's best if I don't say nothing until tonight. (He walks up the pathway.)
'Mum, I'm home.' 'Afternoon Louis. Did you find a job?' 'Whooo — well yes, but I'll tell you later what job.' (At tea that night he told them.)
'Louis, you said you'd tell us later. I think we have been waiting long enough.'
'Well, I was walking in the city and I saw a poster saying "Come to England and have a chance of a lifetime". So I went in, and the man said it was free to go, and there was jobs, and I could go by next week. Tell me mum and dad, what do you think?' (The two

people sat there, no longer wanting something to eat.)

'Son, you have to take things into account. Like you have never been to England — how do you know you will like it there?'

'Mum, that's a chance I will have to take. This could be the chance I have been waiting for.'

'But who says they are going to like you there?' 'Mum, look at it this way. I'm young, and I want to have a good chance in life — and this is a chance of meeting people, seeing the world, getting a good job.'

'But you have no friends over there and people say England cold. You have never been in a cold country in your life.'

'I can keep warm, I know I can.' 'You says you can! Anyway, it up to you.' (Mum gets up and walks out of the room.)

'Son, you know your mother's getting old and you're the only one left. Your sister went when she was twenty years old and now you're going.'

'Well, I have to go. I'll come back to see you, send you money — it will be all right, you see.'

'Well, if you say so. Anyway I'm going for a walk. It's best you think it over. It's your life, not mine.' (He gets up and walks through the door.)

'Well, it's up to me now. If I says yes, it will be it, if it's no, no it will be. Anyway, I've had enough for one day, I'm going to bed.' (He gets up and walks to the bathroom, washes up and goes into his room.)

'Mum, going to bed now.'

'Goodnight, son.' 'Goodnight.' (He gets in bed and soon he was fast to sleep, then he goes into a *dream.*)

Louis Browne

The risks the immigrant takes, his leaving of his family and cutting loose from the old life that Louis had expressed, were now close to the experiences of the 'new' Bangla Deshi immigrant. These were put directly to the children when we invited an elder brother of two Bangla Deshi boys in the school to speak to our classes. He was a student at a local polytechnic, and had himself been attacked on a bus by youths affected by racist ideas, and even in his own home.[6] He told the children about these incidents, and revealed to them the thoughts and fears of a Bangla Deshi immigrant living in East London. His visit was followed by a spate of imaginative pieces by the children, who were now directing their empathy — which for many became a substitute for their irrational hatred — towards the Asian immigrant. A Jamaican boy took the speaker's theme and embellished it with his own details.

The Bangla Deshi

I was an immigrant to England because I never agreed with the government when East Pakistan changed to Bangla Desh, if I had never come over here I would have been put in jail. When I came over here, I came through the barrier and they said, 'Have you a mother and a father?' And I said, 'Yes, I have, why? Is it any of your business?' Then he said, 'Why did you come over here in this country? We have got enough of you Asians and Niggers.' I never answered. Then he let me through and I saw my brothers and sisters and mother and father.

They would not let you into England unless you had a good trade. The next day on the news it said that they only let 5% of Asians come over to this country and they had nowhere to go so the council made them live on the street. Then I was on the bus reading the 'Daily Mail' and a white man said, 'You paks should not come over here, soon you all will take over England.' I never took any notice, I just carried on reading my paper until I came to my stop.

I was an electrical engineer, I fixed all electrical things like freezers, fridges, hoovers, washing machines, etc. Then on the way home some youths came up to me for some money and I said I never had any change. So they said, 'If you have no change then give us all your money.' So I said, 'No.' They beat me up while people were watching them running down the street. The people just stood there like the statues in Trafalgar Square.

George Small

A girl imagined the despair of such an immigrant, this time from India:

The Immigrant

I come from India,
It's a country large and sunny.
But I hate it here in England,
Because gangs of white kids beat me up and steal my money.

My dad got a job,
But he was only paid a couple of bob.
The kids used to look at me and call me names,
So I watch them from the window playing their games.

If I was in India, I would be out with a friend.
But I just sit in my bedroom and wait for the day to end.
I hope I can get back to India one day,
I can't get used to living this way.

My mum says it will get better,
But I don't know when.
If I get back to India,
I'll make sure I never come back here again.

Denise Levey

Two boys, one a local white boy, the other the son of
Guyanese immigrants, combined on a story which carried
a forceful lesson.

Beaten Up

One day Ozzie and I was walking down Brick Lane when we said
'Look, there's a pakky over there, let's go and do him.' We started
to walk over to him and I said, 'Gis a fag.'

'Sorry, but I have only two to last me through the day.'

'We don't care how many you bloody got, we want them now.'

'No.'

'Oi Ozz, I think he wants some aggro, so let's give him some.'

We both started laying it on thick. Then Mark kicked him in the
chop and I kicked him in the groin. He started crying out for help,
but no one came to his rescue, there were some white people
watching but they did not help, they just laughed at him crying.
We just walked away as if it was nothing while he was still crying.

About a week later we were going down the Chinese for some
nosh when the man who we gave licks come round the corner. He
was with his tribe. He shouted out, 'Look, there are those
Englishmen who beat me up.'

All of a sudden they came hurling with sticks and bottles, and
they really gave us digs! As they were running a bottle came
flying and hit Mark in the kisser — WHACK!

Before long an ambulance was on the spot and we were both
rushed to hospital. I had eighteen stitches in the head and Mark
had to have twenty-five under the kisser. This must have
knocked some sense into us, because now we know what it feels

like to be beaten up bad.

Mark Phillips and Andre Waterman

Other pieces empathised with Southern European immigrants:

Immigrant Story

When I arrived in Poplar they called me 'greasy dago'. Poplar was too cold for me. I wish I was in Italy because at least I had some friends there. In Poplar it rains too much. It is cold almost every day. All my clothes have to be thrown away because all my old clothes were clothes for hot weather. But now I've got to buy warm clothes for the rainy and cold days. I don't like any of the people in Poplar because they call me all bad names. I know because my Dad understands English — but I am learning quickly. I learn most of the dirty language. I don't like going down to the shop because I don't know the names of the food and sometimes I think they charge too much but I can't say anything because I don't know what to say to the shopkeeper in English. So I just go home unhappy, like always. I try to make friends but they just take it out on me.

DO PEOPLE THINK I AM FROM OUTER SPACE? I AM JUST HUMAN, NOT A MUT.

I AM HUMAN.

John Osborne

Is It Home? By an Immigrant

When I came over here from Cyprus I did not like England at all. We, that's my family and I, had to come here because of the fighting between the Turks and the Greeks. The Turkish dropped bombs on us, and other terrible things. But when our country was at peace, everyone was very happy in our country. People in England do not like us because of the smell of our food, and also they dislike us because we kill pigeons and make pigeon pie out of them. But I do not see why this is wrong as they eat chickens and turkey as well as all the other meat that they eat. We also have a yellow kind of skin, which the whites do not like, and they separate us by saying 'You're yellow, you don't belong here, get back to where you came from!'

Sometimes I wish I was back in Cyprus, then I would not be disliked. At least, when I was in Cyprus I had some friends. But now that I'm in England I have no friends. I stay in at night and watch the T.V. and even on T.V. the English show how prejudiced they are against us being a different race. Sometimes I sit alone and wonder why people do these things. We're all humans, why are people so unreasonable? I wish I knew.

Dawn Tizzard

Three white girls wrote with real compassion about newcomers from the West Indies and Bangla Desh. Tracey's piece showed how it should be, and opened the huge possibilities of generosity and hospitality amongst East London working people.

I mmigrants come from all round,
M any a new country they have found,
M aking a living out of a few pence —
I n London for foreigners life is dense,
G oing out and getting beaten up,
R ound the East End they live in slums.
A nyone abuses them
N ever do they reply — be
T ender to everyone, including you and I.

Karen Durrell

The Immigrant

My name is Ohidur Kazi and I was born in a little village in Bangla Desh. My mother and father had a shop in the village and they sold animals. I didn't go to school much like my big brother and sister, I stayed at home and helped in the shop.

My mother and father had been having discussions about emigrating to England because the war was getting nearer the village and the business would go bankrupt. So I must have been about eight, and my parents said, 'We are going to England to live.'

We went by plane and the winds were very light once we reached England. Then when we got over here we were shown to our house, and when we were going in, all the people were staring at us as if they had never seen any Bangla Desh people before. Then, a couple of hours later the lady from next door came in and asked if we would like a cup of tea. And I went to school over here and got on O.K. and made a lot of friends, and my mother and father got work and settled down O.K.

Tracey Hatcher

The Immigrant

I came from the West Indies when I was young,
But the people here don't speak in our tongue.
I was only eight when I came to this place
But the people here laugh at my face.
I started to think of my friends back at home,
And here I am now with no friends, all alone.
Sometimes I think I will make some friends here,
But then I think 'no' and soon shed a tear.
I'm happy at home being with my folks,
But I can't go out here and talk with the girls and the blokes.

Cheryl Wakenell

Another white boy saw himself as an immigrant from
Australia, as one of his classmates was. He followed this
up by becoming one of the Bangla Deshis that the
Australian boy had befriended.

The Immigrant

I came from Australia to England. When I got here it was alright,
but when I went to school, they called me names. They took the
mick out of the way I talked and called me a kangaroo. There was
some pakistanis who were treated in the same way. I didn't have
any friends so I tried to make friends with these Pakistanis, but
there was one problem — they couldn't understand me, so it
wasn't worth trying to make friends with them. But after a few
weeks they started going to a language class so they could learn
the English language.

We made friends, and every night after school we were beaten
up. So one night we got together and waited to be bullied. One of
the Pakistanis started fighting back and I joined in. We beat them.
The next day we went in and they didn't say anything and they
didn't pick on us.

I came from Bangla Desh. Before I came to England it was hard to
find work in Bangla Desh. When I came I was looking for a more
exciting future, but all I found was misery, because when I came
people were protesting to chuck us back to our own country. I
didn't know, and when I came it was a big shock to see people
hating people.

I was taken in a coach away from all the trouble makers. When
I saw all the people I felt like getting back on the plane and going

back, but I stayed. I didn't know any areas but I was told I had to go to my relations. I had a piece of paper saying where they lived. When I was looking for the street I asked a man. He didn't say anything. Then two men came to me and they said, 'Go back, we don't want you here.' I tried to walk past them but I was just hit over the head.

John Outen

We duplicated, and read together in class, a story in the local paper, the *East London Advertiser,* of the cowardly attack on a local Sikh building worker, Rawal Singh, which happened in the close vicinity of the school. He had been attacked twice, and on the second attack the thugs had tried to cut his throat. His wife had been with him, and she had run up the street shouting for help.[7] A Jamaican boy wrote a convincing account of this incident, projecting himself into the victim's consciousness:

My name is Mr Rawal Singh, age 41. I was on my way home from work at about 7 o'clock at night, when I started hearing laughing and giggling at the side of me. I turned round quickly, but could see nothing except a long wall, about my height. I took no notice and kept on walking. Then suddenly I heard about two or three bottles hit the ground beside me, and the laughing and giggling got louder and louder. I started running, then I fell to the ground with a painful throbbing in my head. Then a warm liquid ran down slowly onto my face with a senseless, and after a while painless kicking in my back.

I felt a warm and cuddly pillow on the back of my head and warm blankets around me. I was lying in a hospital bed with my head in a doze. I could only see a fading vision of what looked to be my wife Rajindar. I tried to tell what had happened, but I only muttered in my doze.

I had come out three weeks later with stitches over my left eye. I was walking down that same street, Bow Common Lane, with my wife about a week and a half later. I thought that the thugs would never attack twice, but I spoke too soon. I heard the same laughing and giggling again, but bricks were thrown at us this time, and then the thugs attacked. I told Rajindar to run, she got away alright, unhurt. The thugs jumped on my back and started to jump and kick, and I only managed to knock one thug off while the other one held my arms behind my back and another was in front of me with a knife, coming towards me with it. I tried to struggle backwards but was helpless. I saw his eyes stare into mine and I knew it was the end for me. I saw my childhood in front of me, catching me up, at that very moment leafing through my memories like a book. And then a doze came over me. I felt that same warm liquid again, but on my neck and chest. My mind filled with swirling figures, I could not make them out. I looked up and saw the thugs, and saw that they were Pakistanis as well as myself. I saw them all looking down at me laughing, and then it went black.

Keith Randall

Sonia, the girl who had previously written about her Irish father's immigrant experiences in East London, now became Rawal Singh's wife, caught in disillusionment and confusion after the attacks on her husband.

The Pain I Felt

After my husband's second beating I was in a terrible state. After my husband had been treated at St. Andrew's Hospital I still couldn't get it out of my mind. I would look out of the window and mutter swear words about the white men that beat up my husband. He would say to me, It's all over now, they won't do it again, but I knew in my mind that now they have done it twice, there's no end to it.

I sometimes thought, did my husband really know how I felt? I couldn't bear it. At nights I would cry, and my husband said I shouted, 'White bastards' in my sleep. I had a pain that throbbed every time I walked past a white person or even thought about them. It was dreadful.

Sonia Quinn

We hoped that we had moved on the children's knowledge of the immigrant peoples in their own neighbourhood, and the experience of immigration itself, through these imaginative exercises. We were trying to show them that the word 'immigration' was not the dirty word which the racists had made it; and to be an 'immigrant' was not to be dehumanised or reified into a 'thing' despite the way the national press tended to use the word. The immigrant children themselves in their writing had showed us that they, and their families, were normal working people who tried to enjoy childhood, earn a living, look after their families and achieve human respect, like anyone else living in East London. These children, despite and beyond Race, were all in the same class, and we carried no shame for attempting to develop their compassion and generosity across the artificial lines of Race, and nourish their friendships with other children of different coloured skins. Certainly we wanted to develop in them a basic understanding of the history that they and their parents and forebears had created themselves in the composition of their most unifying factor — their class.

We, as teachers, fighting at school against the ideas that put white against black and were being commonly spread and sometimes accepted in the neighbourhood — the same neighbourhood where these children would probably spend the greater part of their lives — could not hope to completely drive out racism from their minds. But we could edge them forward, get them thinking, prompt them to feel and know the living experiences of oppressed and harrassed immigrants, give them a basis for rejecting and resisting the poison that was running through the veins of their streets and estates. All these could be real and dynamic harbingers, if continued and nurtured, to changes of attitude and action. Certainly some of the children, like Philip, were drawing school and streets together, and developing an insightful overview of the material we were considering in the classroom.

Immigrants

The Asians are coming,
The Irish are here,

The West Indians are settled
But racialism's still clear.

Scuffling between races,
Stabbings lead to death —
The Asians and English people
Will soon have a fight with the Irishman as the ref.

The Asians will start leaving —
A victory for the National Front,
Then the West Indians will be picked on,
They won't be free to grunt!

There won't be anyone left in the country
If just the English are here,
Then who will do all the work?
The coloured races? No fear!

What has happened to England?
Not a person to be seen.
The National Front have kicked themselves out,
And the immigrants think about it in their dreams.

Philip Stanley

We concluded our work on 'The Immigrant' by
considering the migrant labourers of Europe. John
Berger's *A Seventh Man* provided a magnificent and
deeply empathetic account of the lives of these workers.
We projected slides made from Jean Mohr's photographs
in the book, and read from Berger's text. Although this
work offered a more oblique view of immigration as far
as Britain was concerned, the point was not lost on our
children that with Britain's E.E.C. membership and the
pattern of her immigration laws, the 'guest worker'
immigrant, with no civil rights or rights of permanent
sojourn — was becoming more of a possibility in this
country. We asked the children to imagine themselves
as migrant labourers leaving Turkey, Yugoslavia or
Spain. We found all the names we needed amongst our
own children in the classroom — and Philip remembered
the name of a Yugoslav international footballer to give
his protagonist a name. Again the fraternal message

from children whose origins linked the continents of the world was clear and compassionate: from Ghana, Bangla Desh, Spain and East London.

Drajon, The Migrant Labourer

He left Yugoslavia,
Prosperity he tasted,
He headed for Germany
With a smile on his face.

Munich was his destination,
He wanted to work with cars,
To find some good friends,
To drink in the bars.

But when he got there
The sight was so sick,
Ten to a room
And the maggots were thick.

Eating with other people
He did not like,
Sleeping with them,
Oh what a fright!

His wages were low,
His humour was poor,
He wants to go back
To kick his front door.

His posters are high
Up on the wall,
But he's made a mistake,
He feels a big fool.

Back he will go,
He hates the Express,
They're all cramped together,
He just wants a rest.

He will go abroad again,
He has no work here.
Good bye to his family
For another long year.

Philip Stanley

The Migrant Labourer

It was 6 a.m., I was saying goodbye, although I did not really
think I would. My family were sad, my friends were sad, but it's
no use staying in this dry, unproducing village. There's no hope
for me, there's nothing here — just waste, dry ground. So I've
made up my mind to go. The bus will be here at 6.20 a.m., and
then I shall be driven off from my homeland, leaving sad and happy
memories. My mother handed me a package of food and my
passport. I looked at my mother, she was all I had. I threw my
arms around her. 'Goodbye Feyza,' she whispered in my ear as the
bus sounded in the distance. I fled from my mother with tears
pouring down my face, I climbed onto the bus. I turned and saw
my mother waving at me. I brushed the tears from my face, not
knowing if I would see her again.

The Journey

The bus jumped up and down the dry ground. I had stopped
crying by now. My heart was bitter with pain and sadness. I was
on a dirty, dusty seat with three other men and two women.
One's name was Emine, she was about 18, the same age as me.
She was with her sister-in-law whose name was Sezin. Sezin was
sad but Emine was cheerful, she made me cheer up. I forgot my
bitterness and pain and talked to Emine. Emine only had her
father and sister-in-law left. Her brother and mother were dead.
I told Emine about my family. At first she hung her head down
into her hands, and then said,

'Never mind, we have to leave our sadness behind and look to
the future now.'

'Yes,' I said, looking up to the roof of the bus.

Then the bus jerked forward and came to a halt. Everybody
moved slowly off the coach, scuffling their feet in the complete
silence. Some of the women cried. It made me feel like crying,
but Emine did not let me with her cheerful face, even though
neither of us knew what was in this future for us or anyone else.

We stretched our legs and poured some tea from a small flask.
It was now 8.25 and the Orient Express was due at 8.40 a.m.
I could not eat any breakfast because my stomach was very
uneasy, but Emine was soon tucking into a sausage of salami.
I wondered what she was thinking about, she looked pretty happy.
Sezin was staring into the darkness of the hills. She was probably
looking for the train. For a moment I sat on the dark ground and
wondered if my mother was okay. I also thought about where I
was going. Would I get a good job and good money too? Then
Emine tapped me on the shoulder. 'The train's here,' she

whispered in my ear. I got up from the ground and brushed the dust from my trousers. Steam echoed from the train. Everybody climbed on, trying to find a seat. The train was packed, people were everywhere. I finally held on tight to my luggage and managed to get on, followed by Emine and Sezin. We didn't get a seat, we just hung on to the bar across the roof of the train.

Dawn Tizzard

The Migrant Labourer

The people leave their home
To a place which is unknown.

They go to a room to be checked,
From toes up to the neck.

Just because the colour of our skin is brown,
In the human scale we're going down and down.

Down there in the mines, it is so hot,
I feel like giving myself a clot,

For involving myself in such a mess,
And while the pay is less and less.

Ashfaq Kazi

The Farewell

It was nine o'clock a.m. It was time for Manolo to go. Everyone on the street who knew him was waiting outside their house to say farewell. But the time came, and Manolo stepped outside his house. Then followed his mother, crying her eyes out. Then stepped out his father, with his face as bright as the sun. Then came his nan, crying. Then his grandfather, then came his brother and sister. Then it was very quiet.

All of a sudden there was a speech. Manolo said,

'Goodbye my lovely people, goodbye La Linea and goodbye Spain.'

Then there was a bucket of tears on the floor, everybody was crying, and as Manolo walked down the street everybody was saying farewell and 'hope you come back soon'. As he got to the end of the street, his best friend Antonio jumped out in front of him. He gave Manolo a letter which went like this:

'Dear Manolo, we all love you very much, and here is a bag full of clobber you might need.'

There was a watch, some German marks and an alarm clock to wake him up in the morning. Then at the end of the letter it said, 'We hope you like it in Germany. Love from all the people in the town,' (because there is only about one hundred and ninety-odd people and he knew nearly all of them).

Luis Johnson

Farewell

Farewell my friends, I have to go!
I am going, hoping to make my money grow.

A new life I have to face,
My heart beats at an unbelievable pace.

Arrived at Munich on a stuffy train,
I worry about my family, but it only leads to pain.

Lined up for a fitness check — am I fit?
Branded by a number, put to work in the pit.

Don't get much pay, we're just migrant labourers,
I am lonely, I don't know the language of my neighbours.

I am going back home and the result is none.
'Was it good?' they ask, I just said 'it wasn't much fun'.

Andrew Ohene

Part four

The Practice of Empathy

In this section, my intention is to demonstrate empathy in action in the classroom; as a weapon to weaken and destroy racist ideas. In our English classes, the teachers, working as a team, took certain contemporary and historical situations in Europe, America and the Third World, and encouraged the children to re-live these through their imaginations. We urged them to write in the first person as much as possible and to communicate a sense of witness and participation in their writing that would actually take them through the situations they were describing. In doing this, the children were in the process of becoming, through their power of imaginative empathy, a nomad in Oman, a Chicano farmworker in California, a Maroon in Jamaica, an imprisoned anti-fascist in Spain, a black shoe-shine boy in Johannesburg. The scope of the material — expansive as it certainly was — only reflected the spectrum of races and nationalities that made up the composition of the classroom, and was an attempt to create a dynamic curriculum that would demonstrate to the children the tremendous wealth of knowledge and culture to be found both inside them, and outside in the entirety of the world which they reflected.

If we were striving to cross the barriers of nationalism in our classroom work we were also attempting, through the catalytic power of the imagination, to overcome colour. It was just as important for a white child to project his mind into being black in South Africa, or into Desmond Trotter's cell in Dominica, as for a black child from Africa or the Caribbean. The children were not slow to recognise that it was their class that ultimately united them with other oppressed people all over the world, and not necessarily their colour. Working together in the classroom, there was no embarrassment or coercion involved in a white child becoming, through his power of empathy, an Arab, an African or a West Indian, or a Pakistani boy becoming a Portuguese disc-jockey, or an African boy becoming a

Mexican-American grape picker. As a teacher, it was difficult not to be continually moved into thinking that the world had no boundaries for these children, that their fraternal power was immeasurable, and that the social love they generated and which bound them in unity, was the most vibrant force for the future of a world they spanned themselves.

The stimulus material presented by the teachers, teaching as a team, was also used in a spirit of unity. We combined classes sometimes so that more than one teacher could join in discussions with the children. We used the same theme material, prepared teaching resources together and had joint 'theme lessons' with combined classes when we had a film to show or new material to be presented. This fraternal attitude and methodology adopted by the teachers in the classroom, apart from giving each other strength and support, often relaxed the children and infected them with a similar collective spirit.

Oman

We dealt with the situation in Oman very early in our 'theme' as it was a powerful example of knowledge that was 'hidden' from the children, and not to be found in the media that were their normal sources of information. Here was the British Royal Air Force operating in this oil-rich sultanate, supporting the regime of Sultan Qabus, a corrupt and reactionary ruler who tolerates no trade unions or democratic rights for the Omani people, whose jails hold over 800 political prisoners, and who on a recent return trip to England (the Sultan had trained at the Royal Military College, Sandhurst) had spent £18,000 in Harrod's on perfume 'for his bath'. He had built at least three new palaces for himself in Oman, a £5 million royal guesthouse and a special royal air terminal, and had ordered built a £20 million town named 'Qabus City', where the cheapest house would cost £20,000. British building companies like Taylor Woodrow (who had recently made enormous profits over the construction of the Tower Hotel in East London, near our school), and Costain's were gaining great business from Qabus, and Wimpey were building a £5 million military base in the northern interior of Oman. In addition, Qabus had announced plans to open a Hitler Museum in the Bavarian mountains where he had bought Hitler's former estate.

To help protect and bolster the Sultan and such British economic interest against the liberation fighters in Oman, the R.A.F. were aiding a military campaign which included the burning of villages and crops, the poisoning of wells and waterholes and the strafing of populated areas and herds from the air, particularly in the southern province of Dhofar. Although a Labour Member of Parliament had called this war in Oman 'another Vietnam' and there was such a strong military presence of British forces in the country, there had been what almost amounted to a Press blocking of the war in the so-called 'popular' papers, in favour of the usual female nudity, gossip pages and commercial stunts.

Certainly the children were getting no news of this war, which was being operated by the same British military forces that would be hustling them for recruitment in a few years' time. It was important that they should know, not only these facts and events, but the scope of the violence that British aircraft — paid for by their parents' tax contributions — were committing on the Omani people who were fighting for justice and equity in their own country. In poems and stories, the children transported themselves to Oman with great conviction, and the events held particular significance and interest for two Bangla Deshi boys.

A Super Story About Oman

I am a nomad, my name is Abdul Ullah. I live in Oman. It is dangerous to live in my country because there is no water which you could find. You have to look for a water hole, in which you can get some water. But now there is a war going on between the Sultan and all the poor people. Now it is hard for me to live because the R.A.F. think that the opposition use my tent as a shelter, so they bomb on my tent and on the waterhole where I get my water. It is impossible to live without water. So I have to make myself a new tent, and move on. But they keep bombing the waterholes. Our King Sultan is a meanie, because he makes so much money but won't give some to the poor people or spread them over the country for good occasion. I might as well join against the Sultan, I am so angry because they keep bombing on my shelter. Even they shoot from the sky with their planes. It took me a long time to afford a new camel and a new tent. It is a hard life being a nomad, peasant or a fisherman in Oman. This is really dangerous.

Ouhidur Choudhry

My name is Ahmed Ali, I am a nomad. One day, as I was putting my tent I heard a great roar. I knew at once what was happening. Then I had an idea. I took all my spare goat skins and covered the waterhole, and I put some camel skin on top of my tent. Then I hid myself under some trees which were growing near the waterhole. Then I saw some R.A.F.s dropping bombs. I was lucky none of the bombs exploded. Well, I then covered the bombs with goat skin and camel skins, then I went to the Sultan's palace.

The guard stopped me and he asked me why I was there. I told him that the sultan wants some water. Then the guard let me pass and I went into the palace. There I took a chisel and hit the bomb, which exploded. It was so loud that the other bombs exploded. But the Sultan was lucky, for he was visiting England at that time. But his palace was blown to millions of pieces!

Ashfaq Kazi

In Oman

I live in the desert
In my tent,
I really have to
Because it's free rent.

In the desert
Where it's so dry,
You can't have a chat,
No people go by.

Sultan Qabus
Spends all the money,
He don't care,
He thinks it's funny.

There's a war overhead,
We will fight —
Yes, that's what I said.

They'll kill us off
One by one,
They'll leave us dying
To rot in the sun.

But still we'll fight,
Fight day and night,
We'll fight, fight, fight,
Till old Qabus sees we're right

Lynn Torry

Freedom

In Oman you get a tan —
Go where the bright lights are.
But at night planes in flight
Going to water holes,
Plowing them out from under your nose.

Eighteen thousand pounds spent in Harrods,
Just by one rich arab.

Freedom fighters, freedom fighters,
Come and see what Qabus is doing
To people like you and me!
Killing in their own homes,
With babies at their knee.

But one day he will be dead —
That's when we can rest in our beds.

Peter Smith

In Oman

Me and my cattle were going for miles and miles, we were looking
for a water hole. I wasn't sure if I saw one, because it could
have been a mirage, but as I got nearer I could smell the blossom,
and I unpacked all my things. I took all my animals to some grass
and water and then I went for a drink. Then I heard some noise,
like an engine. I looked up and I saw some jet planes heading
straight for us, and the cows were making a stampede into the
sand. They all ran into the desert and got shot. So I went and ran,
and some of the animals got up. And my wife was shouting at
the top of her voice and all the children were crying and the
animals were dying and the hot sand was flying around everywhere.

Jimmy Doyle

In Oman

I had just stepped off my camel onto the soft, boiling sand. I threw
my belongings down and fell to sleep. I was awakened by such a
terrific storm blowing away all my things. I got up and chased
after my things until they were all gathered up. I set to work fixing
up a tent in the right place, and then I had a few pieces of fruit to
eat. I covered my camel up with a big piece of cloth to keep him
warm, because if he would die in the night, I would have to walk
miles without knowing where I was going. I tied up my belongings
so that they would not blow away and then I went into the tent.
As I lay down, covering myself with a sheet, I thought how the
Sultan lived. Plenty of food, water, clothes, money and everything,
while poor peasants and fishermen have to grow and hunt for
food, water and clothes.

I soon got to sleep, but was awakened by a shooting noise and
banging noise. I got up and looked out of the tent. I looked up at
the dark sky and saw lighted planes with huge, lighted balls
falling down. I could not figure out what they were until one of
the balls landed near my tent. As soon as it hit the ground, sand
was blowing here and there. I knew by then that it was a bomb,
and immediately set to work gathering my things up. I climbed
onto my camel, and we started to move very slowly. I stared up
at the sky remembering what my people said, 'We must fight for
our living!' was the last words they said.

Sonia Quinn

Spain and Portugal

During the first weeks of the school year, 1975—76,
Spain, and the rest of Europe were in ferment over the
convictions and death sentences passed on a group of
young Spanish anti-fascists. They were to die by the
medieval instrument, the garotte, until, at the twelfth
hour, the Spanish government, under massive international pressure, gave way and changed the method of
execution to death by firing squad. The two convicted
women who were pregnant, had their sentences post-
poned until after they had given birth to their babies.
There was a huge wave of protest at these executions
throughout the British trade union movement, and they
were only the beginning of a momentous few months
for Spain, culminating in the death of Franco.

For many of our children, Spain was only a place in
Europe where people went on holidays, and where many
of them had been themselves, to Majorca, the Costa
Brava or Benidorm. Their experience of Spain had been
the package tour, which had insulated them from the
real conditions of living and working in a fascist state.
We thought it imperative to use the events surrounding
the executions of the anti-fascists to educate the
children about the recent history and contemporary
conditions of working people in Spain. We showed them,
in small groups, the entire film of *To Die in Madrid,*
which gave them the background of the Spanish Civil
War and Franco's rise to power. Then we read some
prison poems by Spanish trade unionists, imprisoned for
mere trade union activity, which had been printed,
together with prison sketches, in a book published by
Amnesty International called *From Burgos Jail.*[8] We
discussed the repressive conditions imposed upon
Spanish working people by Franco's police, and one boy,
whose family was Spanish, confirmed this by recounting
a very graphic incident in which his father had been

chased and beaten up by the Civil Guard, before he had come to live in England.

At the time of these events, a book was being published in Britain called *From a Spanish Jail,* written by an imprisoned Spanish radical, Eva Forest. In her diary and letters from Yeserias Prison in Madrid, Eva Forest's insights about the nature and potential of the Imagination were clearly related to the empathy our children were showing towards the imprisoned anti-fascists. Amongst the poems quoted, apart from two by local white children, one is by an Antiguan girl, one by a Jamaican girl, one by a Ghanaian boy, another by an Indian boy, and the final one by a St. Lucian boy. It was as if they were all meeting in this Spanish jail, adding real confirmation to Eva Forest's words, which came to be a close expression of our own methods and practice in the classroom.

. . . I suddenly saw very clearly what imagination means to me. 'Imagination is what is possible.'

It seems to me now that the Imagination is a kind of motor — that it moves, and it moves other things. It is what collects up the accumulation of past experience, and changes it into new forms and 'dynamizes' it and propels it into the future.

. . . If my data from the past and the present are accurate, and correspond to the reality, then my imagination will be building upon a really solid base, and will be intervening in reality in a rational way; therefore it will be a continuation of advancing knowledge.

(Eva Forest, *From a Spanish Jail*, Penguin Books, 1975, pp.27—36)

Condemned to Die

Five prisoners condemned to die,
On the 26th September they will die,
Not by the garotte, but by the firing squad,
Not by the executioner but by the firing mob.

They fight against Franco and his Civil Guard,
They fight with courage and they fight very hard.

Some are the Basques and some are the F.R.A.P.
They think Franco and his government are a load of crap.

Now two more women are condemned to die,
They won't escape from prison, they won't try,
They both are pregnant, so they moved the sentence on,
As soon as they give birth they'll be killed —
    That's not very long.

Now Franco is hated throughout the land,
From mud, rock and marshes to bright, yellow sand.
When Franco dies, the Spanish people will cheer,
Singing 'Franco is dead' with their mouths full of beer.

Phillip Stanley

Condemned to Die in Spain

I sit here all alone
In a freezing cold cell,
Looking around at bare walls,
When will they come and get me
    have they forgot?
Leaving me in a place to rot.

Will they kill me, or execute me,
My poor baby as well?
We will be put in the garotte well,
And be strangled to death.

My poor child is suffering
For what I have done.
Shall I kill him myself,
So no pain will come?

Theresa Braithwaite

The Prisons in Spain

Spain — think of all those unlucky people
Suffering all the time,
Their husbands, fathers, brothers too
Sitting in prison in smothering grime.

Conception and Maria
Are expecting this year,
Their babies saved them
From a terrible fear.

People go to Spain every year
To rest and sight-see.
But the people in prison stay where they are,
And all are not in glee.

If you are in prison
You will all get the same,
But just be grateful
You are not in Spain.

Sharon Randall

In Prison

In prison it is like you are in your grave,
Wondering of how many more days.
I should not be upset,
I was only tortured to tell a lie,
To stop me getting killed.

When my child is born
I would be worn out by that garotte.
I only told a lie
To stop getting tortured.

I was very wrong to say that,
But I had to stop getting tortured.
When I am in prison
I forget all about the world outside —
Just think of my child,
She would be without a mother.

Pat Richards

F   ranco is a Fascist,
R   ich people say we should have a fascist king,
A   nd, 'we support Franco!'
N   ever will he put Spain back as it was.
C   ome and help the Spanish take Franco out of the country,
O   ver all these years the Spanish people are angry with Franco.

Shillinder Singh

C   ondemned to die in a miserable cell
O   ut of the way of civilisation,
N   early time for my death, I pray for help,
D   eath is something I fear most of all,

E ven I have forgotten what flowers look like.
M emories of my happiness don't exist in my mind.
N ever have I experienced such misery,
E ven the warmth in me has escaped,
D on't see anything interesting in here,

T omorrow I shall die,
O n this moment I am having my last dinner.

D ying in this cell makes me shiver
I feel like smashing that garotte.
E ven now they are coming for me, I must go.

Andrew Ohene

C ondemned to die in Spain,
O h my God, it's bad in Spain!
N ever seeing your wife or the trees and sky, just sitting in the
    dark —
D arkness is the only thing you're going to see,
E very time sitting, looking at the garotte,
M iserable and frightened you are
N ever will you see the sky again,
E very time you hear the guards marching up and down
D ying burns inside your brain.

Tony Amable

The events in Portugal of 24th April, 1974, were both
an antidote to the repression in Spain, and showed the
children an alternative to the people's subjection,
happening simultaneously in a neighbouring country.
One of our teachers had been to Portugal, bringing back
posters, souvenirs, anecdotes and reminiscences of events
there since the April revolution, and also some recordings
of songs currently popular in Portugal. These included
the song 'Grandola', which had particular significance.
On the night of the Revolution, a disc-jockey
sympathetic to the Armed Forces Movement had played
this song over the air of Radio Renascensa in Lisbon as
the signal for the soldiers to move into the city, arrest
the dictator Caetano, and set democracy in Portugal in
motion, spreading the streets with red carnations for the

people. The disc jockey's name was Jose Vasconcelos, and at 12.25 a.m. that morning, he played the record which began with these words:

Grandola vila morena,
Terra da Fraternidade,
O povo e quem mais ordena
Dentro de ti, o cidade . . .

(Grandola, sun-soaked town,
Land of Fraternity,
O people who rule
Within you, o city . . .)

We re-enacted Vasconcelos' thoughts and movements in the studio, trying to regenerate the narrative excitement of the incident. We played the record to the children, trying to engage them in re-living those early morning moments, the thoughts going through the disc-jockey's mind, and the joyous reaction of a people now free of fascism. The long passage by Tariq, a Pakistani boy, convincingly entered the mind of Vasconcelos, and the acrostic from Cheryl, from a West Indian family, radiated a feeling of massive exhilaration and freedom, which contrasted so immensely with the real sense of confinement the children had communicated in their poems from a Spanish jail.

The Red Carnation

T he red carnation stood high,
H igh up for our banner.
E veryone cheered for the triumph it brought us.

R ed, red is the colour for
E veryone, true joy, red is the colour.
D own with Caetano and his kind, because red is the colour for
    happiness and joy!

C arnations are things you take for granted,
A nd things you see every day. But
R ed is the colour of the carnation that brought us
N either sadness or tears,

A fter the greatness of our freedom from such unkind
T reatment and poverty —
I nnocent people dying from hunger,
O h, how they suffered.
N ever had there been such happiness in the land, Red is the
    colour for joy!

Cheryl Holder

Jose Vasconcelos — The Thoughts He Had

The date was 20th April 1974 and I was a regular late night radio
broadcaster. I had been working for over three years in the studio
of Radio Renascensca. The country wasn't in very good order and
there were killings and shootings in the city, Lisbon. The P.I.D.E.
(Caetano's secret police) used to kill and beat people, and probably
take the person along to torture him, all this was done secretly.
Once I was also attacked by the police, in the evening, but I
showed them my identity card and they just went away without
a word. So from then on I knew how the people were suffering —
because it almost happened to me but I narrowly escaped them.
I was a kind of patriot and although I wasn't particularly rich, I
wanted to be similar to the citizens of Portugal. Before that
incident I liked Caetano and am in favour of all the rich people
because they were the ones who put me in such a high position.
Then I realized that they all were wrong and they were terrifying
the lives of ordinary, innocent citizens of Portugal.

    I used to think a lot about the situation and how to help the
people and how to right the wrong. I used to walk around during
the day and have a look around at the people. I was soon known
by people and they used to talk to me and I used to talk to them.

    Then one day as I was walking a group of young men suddenly
pulled me into an alley through which no one passed. They told
me that they were going to take over the country soon, and have
tanks, guns and other ammunition. I couldn't believe my ears
when they said that, but they seemed very determined and therefore it was true and was going to happen. The day was 25th April
on which the Revolution was.

    For the first few days I worried and thought a lot about my
wife and kids and what would happen to them if I failed and what
would happen to me. I sometimes thought why me, Why me? They
could have picked out of the millions of people. I stopped
thinking about that in order that I wouldn't lose my sense, and
calmed myself by thinking I am the only one that can help millions
of innocent people. So I said to myself 'Succeed or die.' I

remembered those words all through the days and I also became determined and desperate for freedom. Then I started thinking what would happen to me if I and all the people won freedom. I thought probably my heart would burst with joy. At this time I was laughing and chuckling happily to myself. The onlookers just said words of disgust to me for laughing for nothing and said 'You lazy daydreamer. Dreaming for nothing at such a crisis in this country. Good for nothing.'

It was the 25th today and it was 9 p.m., and the message sent would be by the song, Grandola, and the Revolution would begin, at midnight. I was the Key to the revolution and if the message wasn't sent everything would be spoilt and we would have to wait for years again. (Later.) There are five minutes to go until midnight. The last song is on. I am nervous and jumpy. I am quiet and would easily panic if anything went wrong. There are two minutes left now, my eyes are opening wide, my muscles tensing, every now and then automatically, my heart is throbbing and pumping fast, my fingers are trembling. One minute to go. I can hear my heart loud and clearly and felt as if it would stop any second. I was very tense and hot. My hands are trembling and sweating. My forehead muscles are lifting my eyebrows as the record finishes and the next one comes on automatically. I wipe my sweat and try to be serious as the record begins.

Now I can hear gun fire and suddenly I am confident and I know and feel we will succeed.

Tariq Mahmood

The day of the Disc Jockey

1 I play records on the radio,
   But today is a special day
   Because when I play 'Grandola'
   It will set the revolution on its way.

2 The people don't get much money, they are very poor.
   And all the people who work on the land are scared to ask for
       more
   But soon the soldiers will be here
   And when they arrive, everyone will cheer.

3 The soldiers are coming to Lisbon fast
   And the dictators rule will be over at last
   There will be better days
   With better pay, for everyone soon.

110

4 The soldiers came into town
And gave everyone carnations
And they got control over everything
even the radio stations.

5 The people jump on the soldiers' tank,
Soon they will have some money to put in the bank.
The soldiers say 'people of Portugal now you are free'.
So everyone sing with me —
                                        'Avante'.

Denise Levey

The Caribbean

For many of our children of West Indian origins, their
childhood had been a London childhood, and their
knowledge of the Caribbean restricted to the nostalgia of
their parents, and their own dreams of leaving a cold,
polluted European capital and returning to a vague
paradisical island that was their own, or their parents'
heritage. Other children, who were more recent
immigrants, knew differently about the realities of
Caribbean life, whether they were from a small island or
from a large, sprawling tropical city like Kingston or
Port of Spain, with their slum and shanty areas as well
as their large, colonial houses, savannahs and botanic
gardens.

Some Caribbean children who had spent most of their
lives in London, wrote acrostics about the islands of their
origin, which revealed the vague, idealistic view.

J amaica, Jamaica, oh what a country.
A ny where you go
M any people cheer for happiness.
A ctive people everywhere,
I   f you could see it, you would stare.
C oconuts, ripe mangoes too —
A re you a Jamaica girl?

Juerline Ingram

111

S unny island is St. Lucia,
T o the world it brings pleasure and beauty.

L ucia, Lucia is what we want to hear,
U nwanted smells are nowhere near.
C ome to this island and you will see
I n St. Lucia the lovely fruit,
A nd you will love to swim in our lovely sea.

Ted John

Another boy, whose father was from Gambia, had a
similar idea of that West African country:

G ambia is a nice place, not at all like East Dry River.
A ll it has is nice towns and palm trees, it is a
M uch better place than England. The people eat
B ananas and live in harmony.
I would really like to live there,
A nd the people stick together.

Cherriffe Saine

The idea of 'eating bananas and living in harmony',
with its enticing, sentimental view of a utopian existence,
was very common in the wish-fulfilling ideas that many
of our second-generation West Indian children held
about the Caribbean. This concept tended to complement
the tourist propaganda promoted through the media to
potential English travellers, to entice them to spend their
holidays in the 'sunny' or 'tranquil' 'paradise' of a West
Indian island, where they would be served lush fruits and
rum punches by smiling natives to the sound of steel
bands and calypsoes. An Antiguan girl wrote:

Antigua

Antigua is a beautiful place,
Mixed with all the human race.
And lots and lots of sunny days,
The water is warm and blue,
There you can't catch the 'flu.

There are lots of coconut trees
Where you can get the lovely breeze.
The sweet-smelling buttercups filled the air,
When the smell fills the air —
Everyone gets a fair share of what's going on.

The land is very beautiful
With friendly people all around.
There you can't miss the steel band sound
During the Carnival seasons.
You have to go for good reasons,
To hear the calypso music in the Carnival season.

Pat Richards

Such a view sets aside the realities in the Caribbean of
unemployment, poor wages, bad housing, and the other
results of European and North American 'investment'
and neo-colonialism, that are as real as the tropical sun,
coconut trees and soft sand beaches.

It was important, not to reinforce utopian mythology,
but to break through to the reality of the social and
political situation in the West Indies by considering
historical and contemporary events there, both in a small
island and in an urban context.

The latter was tackled by reading Errol John's play,
set in Trinidad, 'Moon on a Rainbow Shawl'. This tells
of a group of citizens of Port of Spain who live in a slum
area, East Dry River, and who are trapped there by a
cycle of poverty and despair. The play ends with the main
character, Ephraim, a trolley-bus driver, escaping by
emigration to Britain. His motives for this, and the
position of all the characters raises the question of why
so many West Indian people, including the parents of
some of our children, have become immigrants into
Britain over the last thirty years. The boy who wrote the
'Gambia' acrostic immediately wrote another short piece
after reading the play, which suggested he had understood something of its theme, and another West African

boy wrote another acrostic, about East Dry River which certainly worked to deflate the 'paradisical' myth about the Caribbean.

Trinidad Boy

A Trinidad boy has no joy,
He stands by the bay, day by day,
You might say, 'where does he live?'
But he will just turn away in disgrace.

I wish I could get away,
But I know I'll have to stay
Even though I cannot pay —
There is nowhere else to stay.

A dirty shack in a dingy yard,
But all the same I am barred
From the outside world.

Cherriffe Saine

I n East Dry River it is full of slums,
N early two years I've lived here.

E ver since, I've lived to regret it,
A lways painting the wall so the damp won't show,
S tripping off wallpaper and putting new ones back —
T his ent the life for me, I've got to go.

D irt everywhere, houses made of tin,
R ain is scarce so food is hard.
Y es, I know what to do run away, but where?

R un where? Anywhere I go might be the same,
I f you come to our district to see the slums, you'll understand.
V illage on top of the hill, looking down on Trinidad,
E verybody here is poor, except for the landlord,
R iver small as anything runs down the back of our little village.

Andrew Ohene

A Jamaican girl took the conflict in the play between a mother and daughter, and applied it to her own life in London.

Trinidad Story

I was living in Trinidad and I was trying to get into High School.
But things weren't going well with my family. Maybe it was
because the houses we were living in weren't quite what we were
used to.

Well, the story starts when my mother was in the kitchen and
was calling me.

MUM: Pat, Pat.
PAT: Yes mum?
MUM: Did you hear me calling you?
PAT: No mum, I was in my room playing records, and I didn't
hear.
MUM: Well, I am coming out of the kitchen now, so you can come
and wash the dishes and clear up the kitchen too.
PAT: Anytime I'm doing something, you must want me.
MUM: Playing records is doing something for you? It's not going
to learn you anything before you take up books and read.

I didn't know what was going on. All of a sudden my mum had
changed, she seemed to be cruel to me now and again. I would
never get a chance to go out with my own age. Then I tackled her
about me going out. She kept on shouting at me until there were
tears in my eyes.

PAT: Mum, why can't I go out with my own age?
MUM: (*shouting*) Don't talk to me about going out! You have
got work to do in the house because you are my oldest girl and
I need you.
DAD: ESM, what's for dinner?
MUM: Salt fish and green bananas with yam and dumpling.
DAD: Pat, go and put the kettle on and make me a cup of coffee.
PAT: Yes dad.

Well, things are going on fine, my mum and I are getting on fine
now. She lets me out now and again.

Avia Reid

We went back, in our classes, to the period of slavery
in the West Indies,[9] and although by using Julius
Lester's *To Be a Slave* we emphasised the brutal oppression of the middle passage and the years of slavery —
a Jamaican girl wrote this —

I who work the sugar cane all day,
N ight and day, cutting away all day,

T errible scars I do bear, lashes of the whip,
H atred builds inside of me, I wish to break away,
E ngaged to work on the sugar cane fields,

D reading the end of the day for lashes they do give,
A gony arises, still we work on the sugar cane,
Y es, forced to plant and harvest the crop,
S ighing for relief at the end of the day.

O nward we work, onward we fight,
F earing the lash of the whip, no one knows the task.

S leep we have none, no rest, why Lord?
I who mourn for freedom to come,
A nger we have learned to control —
V ictory is our aim, out of this world,
E ngaged as an animal to work,
R emembering how we used to live,
Y earning for those days to come back again.

Cherie Brown

we also concentrated on the ways the slaves actively
resisted slavery. We studied extracts from *The Fighting
Maroons of Jamaica,* by Carey Robinson, and later
invited the Jamaican poet and novelist, Andrew Salkey, [10]
to school to talk about the maroons. With this background, the children wrote poems and stories about the
exploits of the maroon leaders, Cudjoe and Quao, and
both black and white children managed this with
conviction. The folk heroes of the Jamaican people were
beginning to have value and significance for British
children also.

Free, As a Runaway Slave

I was born as a slave owned by white masters. My mother and
father were also slaves, but were sold, so I'm alone. But after ten
years of being a slave I heard about the Maroons. They attack
plantations, take more slaves and cattle and ammunition, and
disappear. That night I prayed they would attack this plantation
and I'd go happily and join the Maroons. Well, all the slaves were
talking and our masters were asleep when a loud outburst rang
through the plantation. It was Cudjoe's gang of Maroons. I ran out

116

of the mud hut, proud, happy, and joined the gang. More and more slaves joined in, we raided everything and I left with them. We travelled quietly into a hiding place. It was where my Papa had talked about — the Cockpit Country. I talked happily with Cudjoe, a thick, strong-fleshed man, huge and powerful and black. My misery had ended, I was a runaway slave, black, but proud.

Every night I prayed thanks to the Lord for freeing me from such pain and misery, I was free in Maroon Town and Accompong Town. This was our land, we were no longer slaves. I'm still mourning the loss of my parents, still in the arms of slavery. But I'll always love them, and remember what my father taught me. Every nightfall we'd raid a different plantation and kill, steal and gather more slaves, and then go back to our haven. My life was out of danger, Cudjoe was a great man.

The Cockpit Country, in the western part of Jamaica, is full of many tiny-formed hills, winding, twisting narrow valleys which give us safe hiding. Most of the slaves who had joined Cudjoe's gang were from the 'Gold Coast', from Ghana in West Africa. Since 1655, Cudjoe has been a man of great pride and courage, strength and wisdom, and we have all learned to respect and honour him. Well, bye and bye, years go by and the British Government started to worry us and hunt us down. We were all prepared, Cudjoe said to us all:

'Now is the time for me to decide whether we stop here in Petty River Bottom and fight the army, or run and leave it behind.'

But instead of us running, the army ran. They knew how powerful Cudjoe was so they made a treaty with him. If he stopped raiding farms and plantations, they would leave us in peace in the Cockpit Country. The treaty was signed in the year 1739. We rejoiced, and built our own farms.
Cherie Brown

T he Maroons are proud fighters,
H ere in Jamaica we fight for freedom,
E very second of being a slave makes me mad.

M isery upon us, terror upon our children,
A rriving in this country which we don't know about,
R un away!' my heart tells me, 'run for freedom!'
O ff I went, I went to Petty River Bottom,
O ur leader Cudjoe he fought hard, now he's free.
N ever have I been so happy since I came here,
S worn to fight and free other slaves, so that they may end their
    misery!

Andrew Ohene

117

A man called Cudjoe, that's his name.

M an, aint he strong, and he knows it too!
A man of courage, that he is.
N othing can stop him from getting his people free!

C an anyone get him?
A t the moment, no.
L ives in the Cockpits,
L ying with his brothers —
E ven the English can't find him now,
D own to their deaths they will go!

C udjoe is the man to free his people,
U ndo the things which they don't want.
D igging his way through the jungle,
J umping out of sight.
O ver here, over there, over everywhere,
E ven the people know that Cudjoe will help.

Avia Reid

Life as a Maroon

It's quite an easy life now, all we have to do is rob a farm or a
plantation. I'm with Quao the Invisible Warrior. He's not really an
invisible warrior, he robs the white people, runs back into the
jungle, and hides in a cave behind a waterfall. When the soldiers
come, they can't find us, that's why they call our leader 'the
invisible warrior'. When we do a raid, we sometimes free some
slaves, and if they want, they can come and join us. Our base is
Nanny Town, that's where we all live. Once, some soldiers came
to destroy the town. We all left the huts, and when the soldiers
came, Quao led them away, and after a few hours they all started
falling like flies in the heat. They walked for miles and miles until
they came to a river, and then we ambushed them.

Now there's talk of a treaty, but I don't like it. The reason is,
I don't trust them English one bit. All they think about is their
slaves and making us all slaves again.

Tommy Robertson

We continued by dealing with a post-slavery event in
Jamaica, the Morant Bay Rebellion of 1865. The
'emancipated' slaves, living in extreme poverty, hunger
and mass unemployment since the decline in sugar
exports, rose against their British plantation owners and

colonial government. Their leaders were two black men, George William Gordon and Paul Bogle.[11] A white English girl wrote:

The Morant Bay Rebellion

Since England's been growing sugar beet
There has not been much food to eat.
But every time we ask for more,
They tell us to go away then they shut the door.

Till Paul Bogle said, 'this aint right,
Pick up your sticks and stones men, we're going to fight!'
There was fighting in Morant Bay,
With Paul Bogle leading the way.

The men's hearts were full of fear
As the police and troops drew near,
But with their sticks and stones in their hands
They headed back to the land.

Bogle was hanged, along with Gordon, his friend,
So the Morant Bay Rebellion came to an end.
But Jamaican people remember him wherever they may be,
Because he helped his people to become free.

Denise Levey

A Jamaican girl brought the emphatic sense of 'witness' and authenticity we were trying to encourage amongst the children, to this acrostic.

A n eyewitness,
N othing I could do,

E verybody screaming for food,
Y elling and banging
E ach and every one of us,
W ishing we could get our hands on them.
I f only we could!
T hey took in our friend Paul Bogle,
N ever did he return,
E ven when we were banging, pleading for our friend.
S top it! Stop it!
S hall we ever see him again?

Juerline Ingram

From this historical emphasis, we moved to the present, and to a small island, Dominica, in the Windwards. There in Roseau, the capital of the island, a young man was in jail, awaiting death by hanging. He was Desmond Trotter, who had been sentenced to death despite an iron-hard alibi on extraordinarily flimsy evidence which was later refuted, for the murder of a white American tourist, John Jirasek, during the 1974 Carnival in Dominica. The conspiracy and frame-up against Trotter, mounted by the government of Prime Minister Patrick John in Dominica, and reinforced by the Geest and Cadbury-Schweppes monopolies which own most of the banana, cocoa and citrus plantations of the island, was not unrelated to Trotter's attempt, as a trade unionist and organiser of the unemployed, to help his own people in Dominica. There, half the adult male population was unemployed, and the wages of those workers who were employed by the monopolists were derisory. The Government had passed a law a few months before, stating that 'dreads' like Trotter and his comrade Roy Mason who wore their hair in long plaits, could be shot on sight by the local police. We followed the case through those papers that were interested in reporting the story, until Trotter was reprieved through international pressure in April, 1976.[12]

These two poems, by white children, expressed a high level of understanding of the situation in Dominica, and the reasons for Desmond Trotter's struggle.

What a Life!

What a life!
It's not much of a life for a man like me,
I work all day and get a small fee —
I work for Cadbury's getting cocoa beans,
O what a life!

The wage I get in your money is about 50p
But in our money only a dollar a day.
I am a dread and I like my hair,
But the government say it shouldn't be there.
I have to be at work dead on the dot —
If I have my hair like it is
I will be shot on the spot!
What a life!

Mark Phillips

Lost in a mass of slaves,
Some live in mud huts and caves,
We are making money for men who are white —
That's why Roy Mason and Desmond Trotter fight,
A good education the two of them have,
They could go out and earn good money,
But they did what you may think is funny
They have stayed with their people to lead them on,
And try to get rid of Patrick John.

In a prison cell
The police are making his life hell.
A concrete floor for his bed
And some bad injuries on his head
Men and women all over the world
Have heard his case,
And they are arguing about him
All over the place.

Karen Durrell

These insights were reinforced by other poems by West
Indian children that we displayed all around the classroom on large posters. Here, a St. Lucian boy and a
girl from a Barbadian family make their pleas for
Trotter's life. Sonia's poem is a free adaptation of a
sentimental song associated with the West Indies.

121

D ominica is the place where he was born,
E very day he studied very hard —
S ummer, winter, through the rain,
M onday, Tuesday, it's time to go.
O n November 1st 1974 he was arrested,
N o one knows if he killed John Jirasek,
D esmond is sentenced to hang by the neck.

T ormenting the rastas and the dreads,
R otten police with rotten heads —
O how they beat the dreads,
T o and fro with their plaited heads,
T o the towns to preach their word.
E verybody campaign with us,
R eady to fight and give us your trust!

Ted John

Desmond Trotter was no rotter,
He helped the people well,
But all the police put him in a cell.

Poor Desmond Trotter, he was no rotter —
Oh Desmond Trotter, you'll never be a rotter,
Back in Dominica where yellow bananas grow
Desmond Trotter's heart will always glow.

Poor Desmond Trotter was never a rotter —
Oh Desmond Trotter, you'll never be a rotter,
Yellow bird from high in banana tree,
Yellow bird let Trotter free!

Sonia Christie

Lastly, the short play that follows was written and
acted out by a group of twelve-year-old girls, including
a St. Lucian and a girl of Burmese origins. It shows a
remarkably acute insight into the kind of likely secret
manoeuvres would were behind Trotter's conviction and
sentence, as well as the economic forces working behind
the veneer. The girls had written a short play exposing
neo-colonialism, and had certainly become more than
aware of the paradise lost, or never achieved, in the
Caribbean, for the mass of the people living there. They
were beginning to see that the islands' working people,
like Trotter, were fighting against the same evils that they

faced themselves: unemployment, bad wages, outside control of their lives, economic exploitation — and for the same justice and equality that were their own rights, sitting writing in their classroom in East London, an ocean away.

Desmond Trotter

Desmond Trotter *Corrina Mendes*
Roy Mason *Ruth Stone*
Patrick John *Julie Veale*
Guard & Friend *Mandy Ince*
Antiguan Girl *Jean Samuels*
Schweppes Man *Denise Levey*

Scene 1 *In the cell of Desmond Trotter and Roy Mason*
GUARD: (*kicks Roy Mason*) Get up you lazy dreads, and sit up while I am talking to you. Roy Mason, you are being freed at one o'clock, but if I had my ways you would be hung. I don't know, they let criminals out these days.
ROY MASON. We're not criminals, we are only trying to help get more money for workers.
GUARD: Well if you're not criminals, what are you doing here then?
ROY MASON: Is Desmond being freed?
GUARD: No, he's staying here.
ROY MASON: Oh well, can I have a few more minutes with my friend?
GUARD: Sure, you aint being freed till one o'clock.
ROY MASON: Wake up Desmond, Desmond wake up! (*shoving him*)
DESMOND: What's the matter?
ROY MASON: Listen Desmond, for I have only got a few minutes till one o'clock. I have been freed.
DESMOND: Have I been freed?
ROY MASON: No, I'm afraid you're not being freed.
DESMOND: You know why I haven't been freed, because they're trying to make it look like I killed him.
ROY MASON: Ah well, so long.
DESMOND: Still carry on with our plans, won't you?
ROY MASON: Yes, I will.
GUARD: Roy Mason, come with me!

Scene 2 *In Patrick John's office*
PATRICK JOHN: Talk girl, talk! You know you saw Desmond Trotter kill that American man.

ANTIGUAN GIRL: I never, I never saw Desmond or whatever his name is killing that American. I only came over here to see the Carnival.

PATRICK JOHN: That's where the killing took place, at the Carnival. Tell the truth, you did witness this killing.

ANTIGUAN GIRL: Oh leave me alone, I swear it, I saw nothing.

PATRICK JOHN: Hopeless, just hopeless. Guard.

GUARD: Yes sir.

PATRICK JOHN: Take her back to her cell. I have an appointment with Mr Moore from Cadbury Schweppes any minute now.

(knock, knock)

PATRICK JOHN: Come in!

CADBURY-SCHWEPPES MAN: Good morning Mr John, I have your money.

PATRICK JOHN: How much?

CADBURY-SCHWEPPES MAN: £250.

PATRICK JOHN: Getting better!

CADBURY-SCHWEPPES MAN: We have made good profits this week, that's why! Well, if that's all Mr John, I shall be off.

PATRICK JOHN: Oh there is just one more thing. We are having a bit of bother.

CADBURY-SCHWEPPES MAN: Oh, what?

PATRICK JOHN: Well, you know Desmond Trotter and Roy Mason?

CADBURY-SCHWEPPES MAN: We shall have to watch them two!

PATRICK JOHN: Yes.

CADBURY-SCHWEPPES MAN: Well, if that's all, I will be going now until next week.

PATRICK JOHN: Goodbye Mr Moore, see you next week.

Chile, and Victor Jara

Manifesto

I don't sing for love of singing
or to show off my voice
but for the statements
made by my honest guitar
for its heart is of the earth
and like the dove it goes flying . . .
tenderly as holy water
blessing the brave and the dying
so my song has found a purpose
as Violetta Parra would say.

Yes, my guitar is a worker
shining and smelling of spring
my guitar is not for killers
greedy for money and power
but for the people who labour
so that the future may flower.
For a song takes on a meaning
when its own heartbeat is strong
sung by a man who will die singing
truthfully singing his song.

I don't sing for adulation
or so that strangers may weep.
I sing for a far strip of country
narrow but endlessly deep.
In the earth in which we begin
In the earth in which we end
Brave songs will give birth
To a song which will always be new

Victor Jara

In dealing with such serious and complex material as we
were using with second and third year children, we
continually needed to infuse fact with narrative, to give
the material thread and plot. This is one reason why, for
example, the stories of Cudjoe, Quao, Morant Bay or
Desmond Trotter had been well received by the children.
Their narrative, 'story' quality and strength had been
strongly marked. When we came to deal with the
situation in Latin America, and life under one of the
several military dictatorships on that continent, the
narrative element was again important for the facts of the
situation to be accepted by the children, from the
material we presented.

It was necessary, although hardly pleasurable, to
present the facts of life in a fascist state to the children
and to make clear the historical and contemporary links

between fascism and racism. With emergent fascist and racist groups springing up in Britain, goaded on by unemployment and government cuts in public services, it was imperative that we introduced such facts. The consequences of such groups gaining power were already in evidence in countries like Chile, Brazil or Uruguay. The story we took for our theme was the story of Victor Jara, the son of Chilean peasants, who became a popular folk singer, guitarist and recording artist during the years of Allende's government of Popular Unity in Chile, before the fascist coup in September, 1973. His story was simple and heroic: a folk artist, who, as a Jamaican boy expressed it in his poem, 'knew how the people's heart beat'. He was arrested and put inside Santiago Stadium, an improvised prison, by the military junta, as soon as they took power and had killed Allende. There, he sang and played his guitar for his six thousand fellow prisoners, and was tortured by the guards who broke his hands with their gun butts, and later killed, when in spite of his broken bones, he carried on singing to the other prisoners.

We read and studied Victor's lyrics, in translation from the Spanish, and the children were clearly moved by their simple poetry and profundity. We played the songs from the 'Manifesto' long playing record, reading the translations as they were playing. We also read, in unison as a choral poem, Adrian Mitchell's ballad, 'Victor Jara of Chile',[13] which tells, very starkly, the story of Victor's life and death. The background to Victor's story was reinforced by showing a film of the 'World in Action' television programme made in Chile a few weeks after the coup, which documents clearly the torture and repression of trade unionists and supporters of Allende and Popular Unity. As the children wrote about Chile and Victor, with his own words and music playing in the background, their own writing, it seemed, had been affected by Victor's uncomplicated and poignant use of words.

In the Stadium

The blood drips on the ground
The men of Chile are waiting to be
Pounded on like flies.
Poor Victor Jara, what a good man,
He had such gentle hands.

He had great joy to play the guitar and sing,
But he had a thing to help people in need
And to make them happy when sad.
Poor Victor Jara, what a good man,
He had such gentle hands.

They killed his hands for life,
And played with their knives on his gentle hands.
Poor Victor Jara, what a good man,
He had such gentle hands.

Karen Hallett

Santiago Football Stadium

The blood dripped from Victor Jara's hands,
Those prison guards broke every bone in both his hands,
So he couldn't play the guitar which sounded so grand,
But he went on singing like a strong man.

Victor's singing was so beautiful
He kept all 5,000 men's spirits up,
And then the guards heard him
And that was Victor's lot,
They killed him in one shot.

The Americans built tanks in Chile,
So Allende and Victor put a stop to that money
Leaving their country.
They helped to make the poor a bit rich,
By taking the land from the rich.

Mandy Ince

Death of an Innocent Man

In a mass of frightened men
Locked up together,
A sudden sound of fear now and then,
All huddled together —
Depressed and feeling down,

When Victor starts to sing
He restored their spirits.
So the generals tortured him
And shot him down,
But these wicked men got scared
In case the prisoners resisted them
When they heard the voice of
Their peasant friend
   VICTOR JARA

Karen Durrell

I know how the people's heart beat
When I sing on my record,
But I don't think my voice is as good as that,
But I support, I have a gift for singing.

But when my guitar is just as good as my singing.
When I think of the wind flowing by
Making each leaf drop off in the Autumn . . .

Patrick Martin

Victor Jara

Victor Jara,
Victor Jara's hands
They are like gold,
Made like the hands of God.
They're not cold,
But they're hot,
Hot of playing the guitar in the sun.
It is not hard work,
To him it is joy and fun.

Victor Jara,
Victor Jara's hands
They played so well,
But after a while, he was in a cell.
As he sang a song
Which is full of happiness, and strong,
There came a general
And took him and busted his bones.

Ashfaq Kazi

Victor Jara

Victor Jara was a very good man,
He did not steer a plane or drive a van —
Instead, he played his guitar all his life through,
Writing about the people of Chile and the military coup.

Victor Jara was a peasant, helped his father on his farm.
He worked hard in the rough and he did not break an arm,
He worked for Allende, helping him win a campaign,
He helped him in the sun and in the rain.

The generals heard about Jara and decided to seek him out,
They were now sick of Jara and would kill him, without any doubt,
They caught up with him, but didn't have any jail,
So they took him to Santiago Football Stadium and they refused
    him bail.

There he played his guitar to his mates, it was very sweet,
Then the guards broke his hands, so he could not repeat.
That was a dreadful thing to do —
They shot him in a firing squad, and broke his wife's heart in two.

Philip Stanley

The children's writing seemed to be so full of insight,
and compassion for Victor and the people of Chile, that
we invited Joan Jara, Victor's widow, to school, so that
the children could show her their writing. Joan, who was
English-born, had escaped to London with her children
from certain arrest and torture in Chile. She came and
read our children's work, in their files and on the classroom walls, showed a very moving slide and tape sequence
about Victor's life and answered their questions about
her husband, and the present situation in Chile.[14] Before
she left, the children copied out all their work on Victor
for her, and Julie, a twelve-year-old girl, read out loud
to her across the classroom this poem.

Victor Jara's Hands

Victor Jara's hands played music like angels' hands,
He played the strings like silver bands,
Until one day it came to be
That a new government came and the old did flee.

He was captured and placed in a cell,
As they pushed him he fell.
And he played his guitar,
Yes he played his guitar.

He sang about the freedom that he once had,
The golden leaves
On winter trees,
Cold springs and streams flow by,
And the animals so shy.
And he played his guitar,
Yes he played his guitar.

Then the guards came and took him,
And tortured him until his hands were no good.
And he could not play his guitar,
No he could not play his guitar.

So instead he did sing till night time fell,
And his cell began to smell.
So they took him again,
And with his hands behind, so for himself he could not fend.

They hit him so hard that he screamed,
And they shot him next day at dawn.
But he still sings and plays in the heart of his wife,
Yes he still sings and plays in the heart of his wife.

Julie Veale

The children had seen clearly through Victor's story, how fascism hates and strives to frustrate music, poetry, love and freedom, how it kills the beauty it cannot distort and control. Their sensitivity and affection for Joan Jara was as strong as their understanding of Victor's struggle, and the agony of his people.

Victor Jara's Wife

Victor Jara's wife
Would have lost her life
If she had stayed in that cruel land.
But she got out of Chile and was England bound.

People said he was a hero
But he only did what was right.
So when people say that to me,
I say, 'all he did was fight'.

At night I leave the light on,
Waiting for him to come in.
But deep inside me I know
That he'll never walk through that door again.

It's hard being a widow
When you're only young,
Our life together
Had only just begun.

I keep his records to remind me
Of the man I loved so dear,
And every day I play his records,
The ones I loved to hear.

Denise Levey

America:
Chicanos and Sioux

One of the main emphases of racist activity is to stereotype and create myths and insulting humour about the
particular racial group under attack. These myths and
prejudices are then embraced by the 'regular' bourgeois
media and become a species of false, vicious folklore and
degenerate humour which create fears, ignorance,
superstition and walls between people of different
complexions or cultures. Thus Pakistanis become only
sinister and methodical welfare state scroungers, the Irish
are simply 'as thick as two short planks', West Indians
animalistic, non-intellectual 'coons', and Jews become
either financial wizards or misers. At the present moment
the 'National Front' is proudly compiling a book of
racist jokes and advertising amongst their readership for
any contributions, in their campaign to dehumanise any
racial group that is not white.

We decided to attack racist stereotyping by objectify-
ing the process, and studying some of its victims in, what

is self-advertised as the heart of the 'civilised' and 'democratic' world: the United States of America. Certainly the 'cowboys and indians' myth is still one of the strongest and most commercial myths peddled at British children of all colours. It depends utterly on the underlying idea that the American white man is superior in strength, intellect, morality, religion and culture to the American Indian, and has a right to effect the gradual genocide of a subjected people. As such it is a racist myth, and gives unequivocal support to the idea of the domination of white culture and white power, a process in history which has dealt blow upon blow to the American Indian people.

In the same way, the 'Mexican Pete' image of the Mexican, either raving 'bandito' or sun-soaking layabout leaning against a cactus bush with his sombrero over his face, has helped to shut off the Mexican-American or Chicano people from a rightful share of social and economic power in the U.S.A. His caricature in chewing gum or chocolate bar advertisements is again evidence of the commercialisation and profiteering behind the myth, at the expense of the reality, the work, the struggle and the humanity.

Our task was to undermine the venal mythology about these people, and attempt to show our children who had been repeatedly exposed to these myths, the reality of subjected but struggling people fighting against the domination of historical bigotries and caricatures backed up by economic forces. At the time that we were tackling the subject, the United Farm Workers Union of America, multi-racial but composed predominantly of Chicano people, was vigorously extending its campaign for the boycott of Californian grapes into Britain. The struggle of the United Farm Workers to secure contracts for their members for the picking of grapes on Californian farms was not against the wealthy growers themselves, but against the racist and corrupt American transport union, the Teamsters, which had been expelled from the A.F.L.-

C.I.O., (the American equivalent of the Trades Union Congress) for corruption. Its President, Fitzsimmons, had made an arrangement with the growers behind the backs of the A.F.L.-C.I.O. and the United Farm Workers. The Teamsters and growers had thus cemented a racist axis against the United Farm Workers, and the local police were acting as paid servants to this axis, harrassing farm workers, breaking up their picket lines and supporting the scab teamsters, who were intent on breaking the farm workers' strike.

We discussed the lives of migrant labourers in California, the conditions that the chicanos were enduring — the farm labour camps, the constant danger from poisonous pesticides, the child labour and lack of proper education and health facilities and the racism from the Teamsters that forced Cesar Chavez and other farm workers to found the United Farm Workers. The children were beginning to get behind the caricatures, and through their empathy, sensing the reality.

Going Through Hell!

We poor grape pickers go through Hell,
To keep our employers safe and well.
Will we live until we're old?
We must keep on going, we must be bold.

We can't hide from the sun,
But from the locusts we'll run.
The pesticides give us a rash,
They'll kill our lungs, our lives they will smash.

My mother and father are too weak to pick,
My father's going strange, the work's making him thick.
I look forward to the day when I come to a stop,
My life has been a misery, the life of a flop.

Philip Stanley

133

Suffering in the Field

I am a migrant, Pedro is my name.
I work in the fields although I am lame.
While the sun is burning on
I stay and pick all day long.
The dirt is flying everywhere,
The beetles and locusts give you a scare.
Sand in your eyes, back aching all day,
Working so hard for so little pay,
Burning and scorching, our face filled with sweat,
Waiting until . . . what might come next.
As the days pass by, the work is harder,
No food for my mother or my father.
Soon at last it will all be over
And the strike will be dead and gone.
The people will have a better wage
And we'll live again for years to come.
For years we suffered
But we'll soon be on our feet.
The strike will make it better,
And we'll have enough for our keep!

Sonia Quinn

Poisoned by Pesticides

My father works on a grape plantation where we all live in a
stinking farm labour camp, in which in the summer you bake like
a roast dinner and in winter freeze like ice lollies. I do not go to
school, so I help picking grapes. One day I was out picking grapes
and my arm started irritating, so I started scratching it every time
I went out picking grapes. The irritation got greater and greater,
and after about a week I started breathing heavily and feeling
dizzy. I had a terrible fever, and my mother and father thought
I was going to die, but I was one of the lucky ones. I was no
longer allowed to work on the plantation. Many other families had
lost small children and we all agreed that something serious must
be done.

We all thought that the best thing for us to do was to form
our United Farm Workers' Union and go on strike. Because if we
went on strike the plantation owners would lose out on money.
You may think that we would, but we put all our money and

belongings together and we made a large tin barrack which we would all live in. It was made of the tin from our own huts. We weren't getting on all that well really, but we didn't let them know. All we wanted was for the pesticides to be abolished. After six months the plantation owners gave in and we got the pesticides abolished, and on top of that, a little more pay.

Mark Phillips

The Life of a Migrant

I remember one day when I was playing with my friend, and my mother called me over to help carry the heavy box of grapes. It was really getting on my nerves. Then me and my friend decided to run away at the night time, and we slept through the day. Then one day we were playing in the fields and we fell asleep. I woke up before my friend and I got a drink of water, and when I went back I could see this tractor coming. It was going towards my friend and there was me and the tractor racing towards her. But the tractor was going to kill her. Then I heard a scream. It was my friend. She had been killed in cold blood. I went back to my mother and she asked where my friend was. When I told her she told me off for running away, but she was still glad to see me. She asked me why I ran away. I said it was because we didn't go to school for our education, and we were always going to different farms. And I always had to carry heavy boxes and it was hurting my back. That is why I ran away.

Tracey Hatcher

We duplicated and read some poems written by Californian chicano farm workers that had been published in the United Farm Workers' journal, 'El Malcriado'. These were full of moving descriptions of the lives of migrant farm workers, still the poorest workers in the U.S.A., still not covered by national Labour legislation, still with over 800,000 children under 16 working full-time in the fields, and with the workers' life expectancy 49 years.[15] We learned how and why the new union had to be formed, how it fought against the racism of the bosses and the teamsters, and how it organised its strikes. We hired the magnificent film of the 1973 strike and boycott, 'Fighting For Our Lives' from the United Farm Workers' representative in London.

This was a tremendous visual lesson in Trades Union organisation and solidarity, and I have rarely seen a film make such a profound collective effect on school-children. It documented clearly the attacks on the farmworkers by the police, the growers' cronies and the scab union, and the fortitude and courage of the strikers themselves. At the end of the film we sang Woody Guthrie's 'Deportee'[16] from duplicated sheets, to follow Joan Baez' graveside singing of the song at the funeral of Juan de la Cruz, one of the farm workers killed during the strike. For days afterwards, the children were declaring loud around the school 'Viva la huelga!' ('Long live the strike!'). A group of boys, one English white, one Indian and one St. Lucian, went straight into the school hall after seeing the film, and wrote and acted out this short play, borrowing as much from Chavez and the United Farm Workers as it did from 'Kojak'.

Strike

Act 1 *The Picket Line*
CHAVEZ: How many want to join our union?
FRANK (Teamster): There aint gonna be no union.
PEDRO: There aint no law about having a union.
FRANK: There is now pussy cat. Get them boys!
CHICANOS: ARH! ARG! OUCH!
ROB (Teamster): Get this one Joe.
JOE (Teamster): Got him Rob.
ROB: Got the knife?
JOE: Yeh man.
CHICANO: ARG!
JOE: You've killed him Rob!
ROB: Let's get out of here!
(*Siren*)
Song (Teamsters):
Get more teamsters
They're on the attack.
Watch out! Watch out! Watch out!
'Cos the chicanos are back.

Act 2 *At the market in San Francisco*
CHICANOS: VIVA LA HUELGA! (*five times*)
FRANK: I hope you know you're blocking the sidewalk?

136

CHAVEZ: So what man?
FRANK: I'm sorry baby, you're under arrest.
CHAVEZ: VIVA LA HUELGA!
CHICANOS: WE SHALL NOT BE MOVED! (*Song*)
PEDRO: Don't buy Californian grapes!
CHAVEZ: Brothers and sisters! We are here to fight for what we
believe in. That we should have better facilities for working in,
and something to protect our skin from the pesticides. We are
asking you to boycott Californian grapes!

Tony Smith, Shillinder Singh, Ted John

But for other children, sitting and working in the classroom, the sympathies and understanding for the real life
struggle of a victimised and caricatured people was
emerging. These voices of chicano people are from East
London, Jamaica and Ghana. And just as we had sent
off the work on Desmond Trotter to the man himself in
Roseau Jail In Dominica, the work on Namibia to the
London office of the South West Africa People's
Organization, the work on South Africa to 'Sechaba' —
the journal of the African National Congress of South
Africa, and the work on Victor Jara to his wife, the
children's writing on the United Farm Workers was
dispatched to the 'Huelga' school for the children of
farm workers in California, where it was read and studied
as a fraternal contribution to their own campaign.

We're Not Living, Just Existing

My name is Juanita, I am a chicano of California. We all started to
have a union meeting against the growers and teamsters, and the
selling of the grapes, lettuce and turnips. The problem was the
money. Our sweat and our blood have fallen on this land to make
other men rich, but yet we still don't get enough money to feed
my eight starving kids. My husband's been beaten and had to go to
hospital for treatment. This shall not stop us fighting. We shall
fight, we shall win.

We carried on till they killed two men. They were Nagi Abdullah
and Juan de la Cruz. Juan was killed with five bullets, one in the
heart. At his funeral we sang a song called 'Deportee'; it was sung
by Joan Baez. But it still didn't stop us. We carried on till they
got teamsters to gang up on us. They gave the white Americans

more, and easier jobs. One of us Mexicans was caught by the police spray and collapsed. Another man was killed a couple of days after. Nagi, an Arab, was beaten to death. We all believed in striking for better conditions and contracts, and not just travelling on from farm to farm. The teamsters believe in only getting their own members to work and getting them money. But we shall go on, and we shall all still go on!

Juerline Ingram

Grape Strike

The strike started in nineteen seventy three,
When from a grape field came a plea —
The chicano people want more pay,
They are still fighting to this day.

They want better conditions
And to work till they die,
But can they trust the grape farmers?
Or will they always lie?

Then the people formed a union group,
'The United Farm Workers' was their scoop.
Cesar Chavez was their chief —
The farmers were angry, oh good grief!

The film cameras moved on the farms
And they were pushed away by the farmers' arms.
'Go away reporters, you make me red!
You'd better go away or you'll get a punch in the head.'

The U.F.W.s were not violent,
They wanted no bloody fights.
They wanted a peaceful strike —
They had plenty of rights.

The teamsters stopped in to break up the strike,
This wasn't what the chicanos would like.
Then the police started beating the chicano men,
Kicked them all like stuffed, feathered hens.

Two men were shot, killed by the whites,
But they had to go on without starting fights.
'VIVA LA HUELGA!' that's what we say,
We'll go on striking till they give us our way.

Philip Stanley

138

Viva La Huelga!

'Viva la huelga', shout the chicanos, marching along,
With their red flag happily high, and singing their song.

Deportees, Migrants — call us either one
From farm to farm we go working on
With poor conditions, and we work in the blazing sun.

Teamsters come with guns, chains, stones and bats,
'Slap, bang, wallop' over our heads, face and stomach —
They just don't care and that's a fact.

Fitzsimmons pays his men to murder and mess us up,
The teamsters get sixty-five dollars a day
And the bosses are corrupt.

Stoop work we get, bending our backs to the limit,
And the bushes spring back and hit us like a pellet.

Andrew Ohene

On February 27th, 1973, two hundred Sioux indians
of the American Indian Movement began their occupation of the village of Wounded Knee in South Dakota,
U.S.A. By this action, they were occupying the very
spot, where, in 1890, 146 of their ancestors had been
mown down by the Hotchkiss guns of the U.S. 7th
Cavalry. The event, 'Wounded Knee Two', was an
organised and spectacular protest against the corruption
and injustice of the Bureau of Indian Affairs and the
Reservation system that had mismanaged, exploited and
underdeveloped American Indian life for over a century.
It was also a direct indictment of the genocidal treatment doled out to the Indian by the American Government over the previous two hundred years.

For our children, bred on the stereotyped and racist
idea that the American Indian was a whooping,
ululating savage who had consistently interfered with
the 'developing' and civilizing of the American West,
the occupation of Wounded Knee was a fundamental
and necessary antidote of knowledge. We had previously
worked hard in our classrooms at aspects of American
Indian history, informing the children of aspects of

Indian mythology, religion and culture, as well as emphasising the heroic resistance demonstrated through three centuries by Indian people. We completed this with a detailed study of the Battle of the Little Big Horn and the massacre at Wounded Knee in 1890.

Using passages from the book by Robert Burnette, Tribal Chairman of the Rosebud Sioux, *The Road to Wounded Knee,* we studied the repeated injustices meted out to the American Indian on the reservations: 40% unemployment; 42 years life expectancy compared to the 70 years of American whites; 42% 'drop-out' rate in reservation schools; one in six Indian children dying before the age of five. Accompanying this documentation of oppression, we told the children of the development of the American Indian Movement and its leaders, whose actions culminated in the events of Wounded Knee in 1973.

In one session, after hearing about this occupation, a St. Lucian boy, a Sikh, and a local white boy sat down together and wrote this short play:

Wounded Knee Two

The Sioux indians just took over the little village called Wounded Knee. They are in protest against the injustice done to their people. This is where 153 Sioux indians were murdered in 1890. They were these Indians' ancestors.

They are holding out in a small church, the Sacred Heart Church. Russell Means and Dennis Banks are in the church, talking to their fellow people.

RUSSELL MEANS: Fellow indians, brothers, sisters and races of all different colour. We thank you for the help you are giving us. As you know, we are protesting.against the way that the so-called Bureau of Indian Affairs are treating us Indians. We want better things for our people.

DENNIS BANKS: Now, you must keep calm, don't panic. When we run out of medical supplies you must not panic. We will get food from somewhere, and medical supplies.

(*Russell Means walks around the church, talking to some of the people*)

RUSSELL MEANS: Ha, what's your name?

ROCKY MADRID: My name's Rocky Madrid. I'm a chicano. The Americans treat us badly as well. I'm with you all the way.

FRANK CLEARWATER: The Army's arrived Mr Means.

RUSSELL MEANS: Right. Take up your positions.

(*The Indians had dug trenches around the church. After about ten minutes it went quiet. Suddenly they hear a helicopter. Bullets shatter the church.*)

INDIAN: That bloke's been shot through the head!

Everyone looked around. Frank Clearwater was lying on the ground. He had blood spurting out of his head. He was dead. Rocky Madrid had been shot through the leg.

Outside, Buddy LaMonte was in the trenches. An American soldier decided to throw a gas bomb at him. Buddy LaMonte was overcome by the fumes. He had asthma which he had picked up from the Vietnamese war when he was fighting for America! He got up and ran out of the trench. Then an American soldier shot him.

Russell Means later on signed a treaty with one of the American diplomats.

Philip Stanley, Tony Amable, Shillinder Singh

The story of Buddy LaMonte, an American-Indian Vietnamese War 'veteran' killed at Wounded Knee by the U.S. Army on April 27th 1973, as he escaped from a bunker to avoid the effects of C.S. gas, was full of insights and contradictions, and gave an additional narrative weight to the story of Wounded Knee. It caught the interest of several boys. Buddy LaMonte had finally been as much a victim of American racism and imperialism as those Vietnamese people whom he had been sent out to fight as a soldier of the U.S. Army. This fact penetrated through to these boys — one East Londoner, one Pakistani and one Ghanaian. They had stretched around the world and seen through the stereotype. They had shared in the life and death struggle of an American Indian in a way that undermined the 'popular' racist image and commercial, falsifying effects of half a century of Hollywood distortions.

Buddy LaMonte

Buddy LaMonte was a good man
He fought for his country in Vietnam.
Buddy LaMonte caught asthma there,
The sound of the guns filled him with fear.
When he got home, he heard their plea
To fight with the Sioux at Wounded Knee.
He said when he left, 'Bury me there with my people,
Bury me under the shadow of the steeple.'
He was in a bunker defending the church,
He was flushed out by C.S. Gas,
Then came the bullets in a great mass.
He died in pain, but he died not in vain —
The same soldiers who he was with in the war
Had shot him down, dead on the floor.

Tony Brown

I had been fighting in Vietnam for many years. Then when I came
back to my mother, I found out that my blood brothers were in
trouble. So I went straight to their aid. We weren't properly armed.
I had a shotgun — probably the only one on our side. I had asthma,
the terrible disease that puts you out of breath in excitement and
exercise.

We stayed in the bunkers, waiting for something to happen,
when I suddenly fell into deep thought about what I had said to
my mother when I left. I said, 'Mother, me go. Go save brothers.
If I die, bury me at Wounded Knee.'

I felt a bit regretful now, but still I wanted to help. My thoughts
are stopped by some movements in the distance, on the hill. I see
something being hurled into the air, and into our bunker. My deaf
ears didn't hear the thump, but I saw it fall. Soon smoke came
out, just like water flows in a stream. I was soon choking, but on
everyone else it had no such effect. The smell stinged my lungs and
windpipe, I lost my breath and started to hear the noises about. I
tried to stand it and couldn't. I'm gasping for air. Can't stand it.
I run out and BANG . . . BANG . . . I fall onto the ground, never
to move again.

Tariq Mahmood

Wounded Knee

I came back from Vietnam with asthma,
I came home to stay with my ma.

I heard of the Injustice done among my brothers,
At Wounded Knee the Army opened fire,
I heard children crying for their mothers.

I had fought with this army side by side,
But now when I see them, I'll have to hide.

My brothers were in the church sleeping
When bullets ripped through the roof.
One hit Frank Clearwater in the head
And his wife started weeping.

I was guarding a bunker when they threw in C.S. Gas,
I started choking, when my friend said, 'Don't fuss!'

I couldn't stand it, I had to get out of there,
My heart was beating fast as I reached the open air.

Now my heart was beating harder than ever,
I heard a shot, followed by gunfire.

Seconds later, I felt the ground beneath me.
I lay there still. My body was buried at Wounded Knee.

Andrew Ohene

South Africa

No subject exists as such a clear mirror of the most
terrible excesses of organised racism as South Africa. It
was a mirror into which we asked the children to look at
themselves and each other, in order to discover how
much life inside there reflected some of the vicious
racist ideas that were being passed around in their own
neighbourhood. Our own classroom mirrored the entire
world. Here, we worked together, with friendship,
argument and humour, sharing experience and reaction
to experience, living through and shaping to change the
same objective conditions. There, people were separated,
races and colours in permanent divorce. And yet the
same people were our brothers and sisters, cut off from

143

us by fascist barbarism and a racist stranglehold.

Our own children, at the bottom of the class hierarchy in Britain, did not find it a strain to go beyond race and nationalism to invest their empathy with the oppressed people of South Africa, whether they were labelled by any of the noxious terms of the South African reich.

There is a vast amount of documentation on the crimes of South Africa: work produced by the Anti-Apartheid organisation and the International Defence and Aid Fund of Southern Africa, including excellent pamphlets like Hilda Bernstein's *For Their Triumphs and For Their Tears,* an account of the women's struggle in South Africa, or *Forbidden Pastures* by Freda Troup, a study of Education under Apartheid. We used both of these in the classroom as background material, yet the written word by itself can never express the gross inhumanity that is Apartheid. After a basic introduction to some of the facts of South African life, we turned to Film. We showed *The End of the Dialogue* to the children, a film that strongly conveys the message of Apartheid, and followed that with a talk by one of our student teachers. She was from a South African Asian family, and had directly experienced the 'clearance' of her people from District Six of Cape Town, to make way for more city space for the whites. Her talk put South Africa directly into the pulses of the children.

As a direct response to *The End of the Dialogue,* two white children from different classes wrote these poems:

South Africa: A Black Man's Life

A black man's life in South Africa
Is sad and hard.
To pass time they sit on the
Pavement and play cards.

They get such little pay,
But work most of the day.
South Africa means 'Apartheid',
A black man is classed as dead.

White people have no respect
For black men's lives,
Black boys go to the city to carry
Baskets for white men's wives.

Boys cleaning shoes hard all day,
A couple of rands for pay.
Toilets are strictly split in two,
One for 'Whites' and one for 'Bantu'.

Arrested at night
If you're found in white cities —
You may have a family,
But you won't get no pity.

Karen Durrell

South Africa

South Africa is not for whites,
Let the black people live there, they have their rights!
At least let them work for better pay
And live in beautiful houses near the bay.

The blacks cannot drink in the bars,
They eat on the street out with the cars.
Vorster gave them their homelands,
But you can't grow food on heaps of sand.

The system of Apartheid has killed many men,
Does not let blacks out of their dens.
Blacks are poor through lack of pay,
But they'll get their country back one day.

Until blacks can live their way
Apartheid must be tackled every day.
They must fight for their future lives,
A lot depends on their husbands and wives.

Philip Stanley

These two poems were quickly duplicated, and
ploughed back to the other children at the beginning of
the following lessons. The children read the poems by
their classmates, and this brought back to their minds
the film and talk of the previous week. As a result, we
were flooded with creative work from the other children,
taking up incidents from *The End of the Dialogue* about

the Pass laws, Black child labour and the daily struggles of the majority of South African people. While the children were writing, we took out the record player and played them the music of Dudu Pukwana, Mongezi Feza, Louis Moholo and 'Spear'. The music of the South African townships was throbbing through the classroom as the children worked, and the children were writing with great conviction. Avia, a Jamaican girl, noticed that the 'Spear' long playing record was called, on the sleeve, 'In The Township'. As the music played, she wrote this:

I n Soweto
N othing goes right for the blacks!

T he whites criticise —
'H ey you blackie, shine my shoes!'
E ven the policemen criticise, or they don't do anything.

T ownship after township, blacks are treated like dirt.
'O h my black servant, she is incapable.'
'W oman, shine that goblet as if the sun's been on it!'
N othing they say is right,
S itting on the pavements, weeping for freedom.
H ouses are tumble-down shacks.
'I s your black baby all right?' the whites would say.
P eople, people black, black, — sometimes they wish they were
        white.

Avia Reid

Other children handed in eloquent and moving work. Of the pieces quoted, the authors' origins lie, in order, from East London, Jamaica, Jamaica, Jamaica, East London, India, Bangla Desh, Bangla Desh and Cyprus.

NEWSPAPER BOY: Extra, extra, come and get your paper!
(*A white boy, about 16 goes up to him*)
WHITE BOY: Ah nigger, give me a paper!
NEWSPAPER BOY: (*not taking any notice of him*) Extra, extra, come and get your paper!
WHITE BOY: Oh, go back to your own country!

NEWSPAPER BOY: Own country? O-W-N country? You damn
   white boys don't know the true facts.
(*The white boy goes to England on holiday. He goes to libraries
and finds many things out, about South Africa*)

Scene 2
(*The white boy finds the black boy*)
WHITE BOY: I'm sorry I said nasty things about you.
(*But a policeman had overheard*)
POLICEMAN: A white boy apologising to a black boy? Nigger,
   what did you do to him?
(*The black boy got put in prison. The white boy paid to get him
out, and they became very good friends.*)

Philip Stanley

It was a late Monday night when I was walking through the city of
Johannesburg, in South Africa. Seeing nothing about me but the
tall buildings with the lights on, looking like eyes, looking down on
me, and the headlights of the cars passing me like wild cats
screeching round the corners. I wasn't supposed to be in the city
without a pass, or for that matter at this time of night, or even in
the city at all. I just walked out of our labour camp, seeing what
it was like at night — no crowded streets, no black men sitting on
the pavements, no newspaper boys, no boot black boys.

I was alone out on the street, till I saw two or three policemen
coming up towards me. I tried to run but my legs gave way after
walking those 14 miles to the city. The police caught me, they told
me I should have my pass on me. I lifted my arm to reach for my
pass. The policeman caught hold of my arm and twisted it. I felt
hardly no pain, he had broken my arm. The other policeman
reached for my pass. He took it out and said, 'It's all right, he can
go.'

I was lying on the pavement with my broken arm as the
policemen went. They left me lying there.

Keith Randall

A Mother's Story

I was only five years old and I was having a bath. My mum came
and wrapped the towel round me and carried me into my little
nursery, and put my little night dress on. She tucked me into bed.
Then I said: 'Mum, tell me a bedtime story.'

She said, 'What one would you like?'

Then I said, 'Please tell me about Uncle going to South Africa.'
'You have heard that story so many times.'
'I don't care.'

My mum started with: 'Once upon a time there was fifteen and a half million blacks that were very poor, and they didn't have much to eat and their homes weren't much good either . . .'

'Wasn't their houses like ours Mummy?'

'No love. Come on, let's get back to the story.' So she did.

'Well, the black people had to catch the train to go to work in the city of Johannesburg. There were bootblack boys and paper boys and the ladies were servants to the white people. They were taken away from their husbands, and if the husbands went where their wives were they would be taken to the police station.' Then my mum said, 'That's all for tonight.'

'But mummy, you didn't finish it.'

'I'll finish it tomorrow night. Now go to sleep.'

My mum kissed me goodnight and turned the light off. 'Goodnight love, and sleep tight.'

Avia Reid

J ohannesburg is not a place for white,
O nly for black, and black it should be!
H aving hot pies and tea, that's all they need.
A long the wired roads they drive,
N ackered and starving, what more do they need?
N othing to keep them up at work,
E nslaved to whites I hate to say.
S hould this go on, I should swear —
B lack men are classed as dead.
U ntil blacks can live their way,
R acing to get a little pay,
G ave our soul to work for whites, and look what we get.

Juerline Ingram

Caught Without a Pass

I was on a platform at a station waiting for a train. The train soon came, but when it arrived at the station the black compartment was full up. As I was late for work, I took a great risk and sneaked in the white compartment. When the train arrived at the station I wanted, I sneaked off. I went upstairs and walked out of the station. Someone shouted, 'Oi you, stop!' It was a policeman. I stopped and waited for him to catch up. He said to me, 'A white person reported to me that you were in a white compartment on the train?' I said, 'No Sir, it wasn't me.' Then the policeman said,

148

'Let me see your pass,' and that's when I hit him, and after I saw
him hit the floor I ran off. Another policeman had seen this, and
before long there were about seven policemen after me. When I
turned round to look at them I ran straight into another policeman.
After that they caught me, and I was fined and put in jail.

Mark Riley

'A re you a black?' said a voice in the dark. 'Yes', I said.
'R ight, your pass or you'll be arrested, you black boy.
R ight, come on you wog, down the nick for you!'
E verybody in the nick was black or coloured.
'S am, what are you doing here boy?'
'T hey picked me up from the street and put me in this place.'
'E ither pay the fine, or one year in jail,' said the cop.
'D rop dead! I have only one rand, what do you want?'

Shillinder Singh

The Newspaper Boy

It was a normal day, and all the shoe shine boys and newspaper
boys were out in the street doing their usual daily jobs. But there's
one particular newspaper boy who was talking about something
interesting that would happen to him. As this boy was selling his
daily newspapers this white boy came up to him and said, 'Give
me a newspaper boy!'

'I'm sorry, I don't give newspapers before somebody shows
me the money,' and the white boy stood laughing. He said,

'Ha, you work from day to night but you still don't earn a
rand. We sleep in the sun all day and still get more than twenty
rands. Now, about that paper, boy.'

'Sorry, I still won't give my paper without the money for it.'
But the white boy still went on laughing, and the black boy
said,

'Whosoever laughs first, they laugh last!' But after about ten
minutes more laughter the white boy gave in, and as he put his
hand in his pocket for money, there wasn't any because he had
spent it all, and the black boy was laughing his head off.

When the white boy heard this he became very angry and he
said, 'Oy you nigger, stop laughing!' The black boy was still
laughing, he said, 'I can't, it's so funny! I've never heard of a
white boy out of cash.'

When the white boy heard it he hit the black boy. The black
boy put down his papers and started fighting. But luckily a
policeman saw it all and came running and took hold of the boys,

and took them to the station where they were fined, and luckily the white boy found the money in a pocket which he hadn't searched, and he paid the fine to the police. But the black boy didn't have any rand. The white boy, seeing this, paid for the black boy as well, and they became the very best of friends.

Ashfaq Kazi

Pass Laws

One day along a street, a man (Black) was walking. A few minutes later, a policeman came along and asked where is his pass? The man checked his pocket but he did not have it. The policeman said 'Come, I aint got all day, hurry up with your pass.' The man said to him, 'I must have left it home can I go and get it?' The policeman said, 'Try and trick me? are you going off to 16 miles to get a pass and never come back? No thanks, you are under arrest.' The man said 'But I have rights to . . .' The policeman said, 'Blacks have no rights in this country. As you are protesting I have right to give you some bashing up.' Then he called along another policeman and bashed the man up and took him along to the police station. The policeman told the sergeant what happened. He laughed first and ordered the policeman to bash him up again. Then when he recovered they said 'Pay the fine of 50 rand.' The man was scared and did not have much money on him, he said, 'I haven't got that much money.' They said, 'Well, you are staying in jail for five months, and the money you got on you,' he had 20 rand. They took that and kept him in jail for five months. He begged if he could be let off this time, and he would bring back another 30 rand, but they never believed him, and they again bashed him up. Every time they saw him talk or do something, a thing a bit wrong they kicked him, punched him, and give him a piece of bread and a glass of water to drink, and that was only two times in every twenty-four hours. He never had any peace in that five months, and it cost him another 40 rand for a new pass.

Ouhidur Choudry

Shoe Shine Boy

In the main street there were many bootblacks. One day, in the main street, I was cleaning a policeman's shoes when a man came up to me and hit me. As he was leaving I kicked the white man up the backside, and the policeman said, 'Why did you do that?'

'Because he hit me.'
'What do you mean?'
'I mean what I say.'

Then the policeman hit me.

'What was that for?'

'That was for being cheeky to a white person.'

Then he asked me for my pass. I knew it was out of date, but I hoped he would not find out, but he did.

'This pass is out of date,' he said, 'I will have to take you in.'

As we were walking along the main street he began to sing a black song. Then a thought came into my mind. I said to him,

'If you don't let me go I will report you for singing a black song, and for having your shoes cleaned on duty and not paying for it.' So he let me go.

A few minutes later, he and two other policemen were after me again. When they caught up with me, one of them was a sergeant and he said, 'This policeman said you were caught without a pass. You will go to court tomorrow.'

I went to court and I was fined ten rands. I said, 'But I haven't got that kind of money!'

Then the judge said, 'Six months as well, for Contempt of Court.'

Chris Elefteriou

Five second year boys wrote together and acted out a short play about Apartheid that made nonsense out of Apartheid. Two were Jamaicans, one English, one Bangla Deshi and the other's family was from Sierra Leone. Four continents: Europe, the Americas, Asia and Africa composed this piece in unity.

The Boot Black

Narrator *Ashfaq*
Policeman *Tony Ellis*
Shoe Shine Boy *Patrick Martin*
Judge *Raymond Brandon*
Englishman *Paul Woodford*

Scene 1
NARRATOR: In Main Street.
ENGLISHMAN: I want my shoes shining quickly!
S.S. BOY: I'm not shining it quickly, I'm taking my time.
ENGLISHMAN: You'd better watch your mouth sonny.
S.S. BOY: I'm not cleaning your shoes I will clean someone else's.
ENGLISHMAN: I'm getting the police. Hey you police, come over here.

Scene 2
NARRATOR: As the policeman came over to sort out the
    argument.
POLICE: What's wrong?
ENGLISHMAN: He refuses to clean my shoes!
S.S. BOY: If he asks me nicely I will clean his shoes.
ENGLISHMAN: I'll give you a clean shoe in a minute!
POLICEMAN: Why should an Englishman talk nicely to a bantu?
    Anyway, show me your pass.
S.S. BOY: I haven't got a pass.
POLICEMAN: Right, you'll have to come to the station with me.

Scene 3
NARRATOR: In the morning the bantu will appear in court.
JUDGE: Silence in court! Will the bantu stand up?
NARRATOR: In two weeks time he paid the money out of his
    wage and that's the end of our Play.

An English boy and a Jamaican boy wrote another
episode together:

Whites Before Blacks

Coloured Person *George*
Cashier *Darren*
Coloured Man's Friend *Andre*
Other White People
Copper *Chris*

The scene is set in a bank and the cashier is just about to serve a
white person.
CASHIER: Can I help you sir?
WHITE PERSON: I would like to send a cheque to England for
    £25.
CASHIER: O look, a kaffir's walked in. I wonder what he wants,
    I won't serve him.
(*to the white man*) That will be £25 plus £1 postage.
COLOURED MAN: How much is it for a licence for a radio?
(*Cashier takes no notice and serves a white person*)
COLOURED MAN: Hey man, why don't you serve me?
(*Cashier carries on talking to white people. Then the coloured man's
friend walks in*)
COLOURED MAN: (*to friend*) They won't serve me.
(*The friend pushes white people out of the way and a fight starts*)

152

POLICEMAN: Hello, hello, hello. What's all this then?
COLOURED PERSON'S FRIEND: They won't serve my friend, he's been waiting for one and a half hours.
CASHIER: These gentlemen were before these kaffirs. They started the fight.
POLICEMAN: Well you blacks started it, down to the station with you!

Darren Mills and George Small

And another couple in the same class, one English, one Guyanese, wrote this:

What a Life!

One day Mark and Andre are walking down the road when Andre says to Mark, 'Are you hungry?' Mark replied, 'Yessir, sure am! Let's go into the supermarket.'

We both walked in and went over to the fruit counter.

'I'm gonna steal some mangoes. First you keep him talking, then I'll stuff my pockets with 'em.'

'Mister, how much is them mangoes?'

'Half a rand, Kaffir.'

While Mark was doing this, Andre started stuffing his jacket with mangoes. They were both walking away when all of a sudden a mango dropped out of Andre's pocket. The man shouted at them.

'Oi, you black bastards!' They both started running. They ran as fast as they could, until they could run no more. Then they went down a side street and started to eat. All of a sudden they heard the pitter-patter of footsteps. The man approached them so they lifted up a mango each and pelted them at him.

'Squelch!' Then we ran. That night we slept in an old barn, as we had no mother or father. The next day, when we were walking we heard a man call, 'Help, police!' We looked behind us and saw the man who had chased us the other day. This time we weren't quick enough and two policemen caught us by the scruffs of our necks. We tried to struggle but it was no use, we just got booted and slapped. The next day we were to appear in court.

When blacks get caught and have to go to court, we never get found innocent, but with whites, they are never guilty. We were later put in Borstal for three years. What a life!

Andre Waterman and Mark Philips

153

One white boy, who had often expressed racist remarks, and yet who was very friendly with one particular Asian boy, seemed almost to savour the racism of Apartheid. He wrote a rhyming dialogue between a white man and his black servant. It was a powerful rhyme, and seemed to contain within its language much of the sexist violence of Apartheid, as well as of the violence of British racism. I read it out to the rest of the class, and asked them to consider it, and perhaps try their own dialogues.

The Servant

'Come here blackwoman, get this washing done!
Before you end up in hospital, 'cause I'll break your thumb.'

'Look here white man, why do you shout at me?'
'And you look here blackwoman, you're not too small to go across my knee.'

'In the end we blacks will get our way!'
'And if you carry on like this, you won't get no pay.'

'All you white men think you are the greatest!'
'You can't talk, you aren't fit to live with the natives.'

'Look blackwoman, I'll chuck you out on the street!!
Where all you niggers live who aint tasted meat.'

'I don't care, you can chuck me out!'
'Don't shout at me nigger, I'll give you a clout.'

'Go on blackwoman, get out of my way.
Go and find someone who'll give you more pay!'

Tony Smith

By the end of the same lesson, these three pieces had been written, the second by a Ghanaian boy, the other two by his white classmates:

Love Between the Colours

My Love and I met in the streets of Johannesburg, when she was sitting on the edge of the kerb. She was just sitting there, smiling. She's black, I'm white — all the colours should unite. South Africa won't let us be together, so how can we have a romance?

154

I don't know. She smiled at me, I looked into her eyes. I knew she liked me but I couldn't even say one word to her.

I couldn't stand it, so I walked down the street to hide my feelings towards the black girl. I wondered if she felt the same way towards me.

The next thing I knew, as I walked towards the bright lights city was the coloured girl following me. I didn't run, or tell her to go away, I started walking slowly. About three minutes later she had caught up with me. I knew I was taking a big risk, but that didn't bother me. Nothing could hide my love and deep affection for the coloured girl.

The Old Bill was on patrol in a squad car. We decided to take it calm, so we strode cautiously together towards the main city. The police still followed us strongly. Then suddenly the Old Bill sped up and jumped out after us. My coloured girlfriend, who I had just met, tripped. She cried in vain, 'My love, you keep on going, run till they can't keep up with you, use all your strength and courage to break away from them. Don't you worry, I'll remember you till my dying days! What your face looked like! What was your name?'

'Richie Brown.'

'I loved you, and by my words I will always remember you. Go on Richie, run for your life, don't let the bastards get you!'

'Shut up you nigger, you're not fit to live!'

The copper took out a revolver and shot Mandy. Richie looked in despair. She died a loved one by Richie, who escaped and disguised himself to this day to visit Mandy's grave.

Jon Smith

'It's getting dark, I have to go,'
'Right love, see you tomorrow.'
'Sally, until I knew you
I thought my heart was hollow.'

'But now when I am with you, all is forgotten,
I forget what the whites are doing to us
When I am with you —
They treat us rotten.'

(*when she got home*)
'Sally,' 'Yes Ma?'
Where in the Hell have you been?'
'I took a stroll in the park.'
'Don't you give me that Girl, who you been seeing?'

'It's not that nigger again,
If it is, I'll kill him!'
'He's the same as us only a different colour,'
'What's his name?' 'Jim'.

'Ma I love him,
And you won't spoil it for me!
I love him,
And that's how it's going to be!'

Andrew Ohene

The Boot Black

'Shine the boots boy!
You are black,
You'd better shine them clean
Or you'll get a big smack.

I am white, I rule over you,
You lot should be kept in the zoo —
You missed that speck on the rim,
You'd better clean it, or I'll make you dim!

You expect a rand for that job?
All I should give blacks is a couple of bob,
Go away Blackboy, you're not getting any money,
Go away and find your mummy.'

'Please give me some money
Mr rich white man,
I aint got no mummy
And my dad's a poor man.

I'll spit on your shoe
And you'll see the black gob,
I will spit in your face
If I only get half a bob.'

The white man kicked the bootblack into the road,
Then the police came out in a load.
The life of that black boy has come to an end,
Poor little boot boy, he has no friends.'

Philip Stanley

The children's response to South Africa had been so strong and full of insight, that we decided to continue the subject with another film: *Last Grave at Dimbaza.*

This film, with its skilful weaving of evocative visual images and startling information and statistics, provoked a strong response and lively argument. A St. Lucian boy, as soon as he had seen the film, wrote:

Last Grave at Dimbaza

It's the last grave,
Who will it be?

Some poor young innocent baby —
He hasn't done anything wrong.

He is just born,
Small, innocent, needy.

He needs to be fed,
He's hungry.

He'll die without food.
The poor baby, he's dead.

He's buried in his grave,
He was starved by the whites.

Bertram Williams

The children again took particular incidents from the film and worked from them. In one sequence, black dustmen are seen chasing through the back alleys of a white suburb with large skips of rubbish on their shoulders, running after the dustcart driven by a white driver who never stops, but makes the black dustmen work permanently on the double. A white boy and a Jamaican girl wrote stories, extending this incident from the film and filling it with their own plots, characters and insights.

Dustbinman .

Billy Ywanga was a dustbinman. He was not married, but had a brother called Felix, and Felix worked in the dustbin job too. Today was as usual work day and they were ready to go to their job. Six o'clock was the time. The driver, a white Englander, is a very bossy bloke who gets about £100 a week, and Billy and Felix are lucky if they get about £5 a week.

'Come on Felix!' shouts Billy as they walk out of their old shack. About a mile away are the white luxury estates with their rubbish just outside.

'Come on, hurry up. Right, that's a pound each taken off your wages.'

'Oh boy!' whispers Felix.

'Right, that's another pound off each your wages. Now get on the cart and we will start going.'

It does not take long before they are collecting rubbish at their first call.

'He's going faster today Felix,' said Billy.

'Yeh, but we better catch up to the cart, we don't want to lose any more wages.'

'Okay,' said Felix.

They come to a house where there is a pile of rubbish six feet high. This is too much. They cannot run back and forward like Steve Austin. They try anyway, but the dustcart is out of sight. The dustcart comes back.

'What do you think you are doing? You're sacked, both of you. Get lost!', the dustcartman went on at them.

In the weeks that went by the brothers had to scrounge for food, and Billy heard that his son, who lived in the township, had died from lack of food, lack of money. That broke Billy's heart and he died.

Philip Stanley

The Dustman

I am a South African girl and my father is a dustman. We live in a township very far from Cape Town. One morning, very early my father was up and getting ready to go to work. We were still in bed and we saw him go. He had to walk thirty miles to Cape Town. He also had to make sure that he had his pass on him, or he would be in great trouble.

When he reached the depot they all lined up behind their dust-carts, the white driver moved off, and they went round the back alleys and started emptying the rubbish. And then the horrible thing starts, the white driver doesn't stop, he carries on driving and the dustmen have to run for it. Well, my father would stop the job if he had the chance, but we need the money.

Then one day, as the dustmen were doing their usual work, one of the dustmen collapsed but the driver took no notice. But now my father couldn't stand it any longer. So he threw down his dustbin and went to help the man. But when he got there the man was dying, and my father stayed with him for a couple of

minutes. Then the man died in my father's arms. The dustcart
stopped moving and the white driver came out and walked towards
my father. And he hit my father but my father couldn't do nothing.
The white driver said 'You're sacked Kaffir! Get out of my sight!'

My father had to go, but he didn't care. He got his wages and
he walked thirty miles back home. And that meant that I had to
go out and work now, but I didn't care.

Avia Reid

The film ends on a shot of children's graves, ready to
be filled, in the black township of Dimbaza. The commentary adds that while the film has been projected,
sixty black children have died in South Africa of
malnutrition. Another Jamaican girl stretched herself to
Dimbaza, mourning for such a lost child.

My Child that Died

I live in a township called Dimbaza. I had twins, a girl and a boy.
They were two nice little ones with curly hair. My husband
worked night and day for us, and I will regret the day that he
left. Things weren't going all that good for me and my kids. I had
to take them to hospital three days every week. Today I had to
leave them at the hospital. The doctor said, 'I think you'd better
go home and get some rest now.'

I got home. I was hungry but I couldn't put a straw in my
mouth. Every time I went to put something in my mouth, my
mind ran up on my twins crying out for hunger. My husband was
going to stop in at the hospital on the way home from work. I
waited until six o'clock came. He still didn't come. I heard footsteps, I ran to the door. It opened. My husband walked in with
one girl, and in the other hand — a boy, dead. I took them and
held them close to my heart. My heart burned me. We buried it.
My husband said, 'I sweat, I bleed, and look what has happened.'

Juerline Ingram

In another sequence from the film, a black woman who
is a nanny to a white family in an all-white suburb, is
shown in hospital, about to have her own child. She
knows her child will be sent a thousand miles away from
her, to live on a Bantustan and brought up in poverty
and malnutrition. Two girls sitting next to each other,

one Jamaican, one white, were very affected by these sequences. The white girl's poem is one of the most terrifyingly honest pieces of work I have seen written in a classroom. Prompted by the dehumanising effects of poverty and racism, the black nanny's thoughts are driven towards infanticide. The force of empathy has been irresistible for her, even in its power to imagine the most horrific.

I wish I could see my child more often,
I wish I could live with her.
I've been working since I was fifteen years of age,
I know I am a nanny.

Usually I'm working twenty-four hours a day,
And I only get £2.20 a week.
I wish I was never created,
I wish I was in another country.

I wish that God could only help me,
And also change things.
If only I could see her,
I only want to be with her,
To see my child is all I want.

Jennifer Kandekore

The Nanny

Here I am feeding up my massa's baby son,
Making out I'm having fun.
Deep down inside I could kill this child,
For as far as I know
My own could be fading away,
Standing out there, miles away from me,
While I'm standing here feeding this fat little kid.
My own child could be wasting away
For I haven't seen him for so long.
My own flesh and blood is getting no more
Than a bowl of rice a day,
While this fat little kid
Just eats and eats away.
What can I do? There is nothing, I know.
I would kill off this kid
To get revenge for my own.

Cheryl Wakenell

160

Even the boy who had written the first dialogue between the black servant and the white master was clearly very moved by the film. It seemed to break down a wall behind which he hid his compassion. He now wrote:

Graveyard

Today a baby is born,
Not in a hospital, but maybe on the lawn.
She will be dead in a year or two,
One of the unlucky ones without any food.
There'll be lots of babies who will die this day,
Because their fathers don't bring home enough pay.
That's not all — sixty an hour or sometimes more
Because of their state, which is ever so poor.
So we leave the poor souls
Who haven't a chance to see the world,
Only their graveyard
That lies in Hell.

Tony Smith

By considering South Africa we had learned many lessons, and we had found a distorted reflection and stared at ourselves. But we had also joined with the oppressed people of another continent, shared their lives and struggles, and known them as *our* people. Tony, a St. Lucian boy, in the last lines of his poem, seemed to express the aims of our common classroom, and the aims of our future.

A Newspaper Boy (South African)

A newspaper boy, that's what I am,
We live on sand which they call our land.
We work all day, we work all night,
We work all the time for our rights.
They treat us like dirt
They treat us like pigs,
But we'll always stand up, 'Black is Right!'
They shout, 'Come here black boy,
Come and shine my shoes,
You might earn a couple of bob!'

We do their shopping
We clean their shoes,
They don't even let us swim in their bay.
We're human people, just like them,
We sweat our guts out, and £5 we get paid —
Some day or the other,
We'll live together like humans
In a Humanity's world.

Tony Amable

A few weeks after we had finished this work on South
Africa came the heroic events at Soweto in June 1976,
and the subsequent murder of one hundred and ninety
black South Africans there, and in the surrounding
townships. In Soweto, with its population of one million
black people (we found that the township was not
printed on the map of South Africa we had at school,
because of the colour of its inhabitants) schoolchildren
and youths had been organising school strikes and
demonstrations for many months. They had built their
campaign around objections to the compulsory use of
Afrikaans, their white masters' language, as the language
medium in their schools. But this in itself was only
another manifestation of an educational apartheid which
meant £17 yearly was spent on an African child's
education, compared to £320 a year on that of a white
child.

Our children, the same age as many of the children
who were shot down for peacefully marching in protest
against the use of the Afrikaans language in their schools
in Soweto, were seeing and reading about their contem-
poraries and peers in another country combining,
resisting and being brutally repressed by the armed forces
of a racist state. This lesson was eloquently emphasised
when Trevor Huddleston, now the local Bishop of
Stepney, visited the school shortly after the Soweto
murders, to speak to the children on South Africa in our

162

English lessons. He explained how, many years before, he had been a priest near Soweto, and how those children now dead were the sons and daughters of many of his old parishioners. The passion and directness of Father Huddleston's speech moved many of the children, as he told them of his own experiences of life in South Africa, and his active opposition to apartheid.

We followed his talk by quickly settling the children to writing about the events in Soweto. For the children whose work is quoted, Avia from Jamaica, Andrew from Ghana and Philip from East London — and for many others — the deaths of the South African children while fighting a battle over their own education in their own schools, was something very close. Philip's ballad-like poem was the last of many such pieces that he had written throughout the two years. We typed it out as a broadsheet and circulated it around to the other children. The huge social love that radiates from this poem by a white boy in a London working class classroom for black South African children in their struggle and agony, shows the massive potential links between imaginative power and political power, links that could span the world.

The apparent selflessness of the poem, the way in which the writer moves from the streets of Limehouse to the shanties of Soweto, and the force with which he projects himself directly within and amongst the South African children, shows in itself the human and political loyalties behind the consciousness of the poet. For although he is crossing continents and exchanging skins in words and imagination, he is still keeping within the context and power of his class and the ranks of the oppressed. That is where he is, and that is where the black South African children he writes about are. And from inside that bond and massiveness he is stating clearly and skilfully his need and ability to work towards, with all those others, its full emancipation all over the world.

163

No Afrikaans!

I go to a local school in Soweto with my big sisters and brothers.
The school is not like the whites' schools, it's like a shack. And
there's a lot of us in one class, we don't have good equipment
like the whites. They have paper, books — good books, they have
a good school building, they have a proper playground. We have
nothing like that — they even have a swimming bath, but we
have to swim in the river.

In the school we don't learn English, we learn the South
African language which is AFRIKAANS. But we don't like it, so
we decided to go on a march saying, 'We don't want no
Afrikaans!' The next day came and we decided to wait outside
the school — and then the march began. We were all carrying
banners with the words 'No Afrikaans!' We marched through the
city, and then to our surprise there was a row of police at the
other end. They had rifles and machine guns. They fired one shot
over our heads, but we still went on marching. Then they fired
again and my mates were dropping down. I stopped, and more
and more were dropping. Then we realised that they were shooting
us down. I couldn't believe it, I ran back to my best mate. I
started crying, I didn't know what to do next. I called out to
someone to help me carry my mate, so I could bury her. I did, and
I was still crying over her grave, until my mum came along and
said, 'Don't cry, she has gone to a better place than staying here
any longer.'

Avia Reid

No Afrikaans!

The language of the whites we don't want to know,
We want our language, but they won't let us do so.

English language is what we want, we don't learn it much,
So we're going to protest for our rights, we're going on a march.

So on we went, side by side —
The police opened fire on us, there's nowhere to hide.

Children fell to the ground like leaves from a tree,
The sight was unbelievable, you should have been there to see.

A hundred and ninety people died that day —
It looks like that language is here to stay.

We couldn't believe that people could be so cruel,
To live with these animals you must be a fool.

For what they've done, my heart will never forgive them,
They aint heard the last of us, next time we'll stand firm.

Andrew Ohene

On The March

The Afrikaans language we'll not stand,
They call us slaves, they work us to the ground,
We'll go on that march and tell the whites
'No Afrikaans! We have our rights!'

'No Afrikaans!' I can shout,
When shall we march all about?
We must arrange it to the best,
We can be brave and so can the rest.

I'll hold a banner
High in the air,
I'll stand next to Duma,
I'll bet he'll be there.

Tomorrow's the day, it's getting close,
Soon we'll have a right to really boast.
We have no equipment in our school,
We'll have no future when we are tall.

'No Afrikaans!' we shout into the ears
Of the white policemen with their growing fears.
A barricade the police have formed,
Their guns aloft in case they are stormed.

Suddenly we run towards the barricade,
We'll march on for ever, we're not afraid —
Then kids are falling, they're only young,
Still with lots of life to overcome.

'No Afrikaans!' we were shouting,
Then the police gave us a clouting,
Bullets they fired, never stopping —
All I could see were bloody people dropping.

One's been shot, he's dead, he's dead,
There's something coming out of him, its colour is red.
These are little boys who are being shot,
I've never seen a day like this, my memories will rot.

One boy was dead, his hand on a banner,
He'd done his work, he'd earned his tanner.
His mother and father weren't even here,
They were working in Johannesburg, but their hearts were near.

They shot at us though we're just boys —
It's not human, we aint just toys.
No money have our parents, their problems are clear.
No decent funeral for us, just a tear.

Philip Stanley

165

Namibia and Zimbabwe

To move on in our classes from South Africa to Namibia,
the neighbouring country it is illegally occupying, was
entirely logical. At the time that we were considering
Namibia, Aaron Mushimba and Hendrik Shikongo, two
leading members of the South West African People's
Organisation (S.W.A.P.O.), the liberation movement of
the Namibian people, were illegally sentenced to death
by a South African court, and there was a strong
campaign being waged on their behalf by the progressive
world.

We taught the children about the situation in Namibia
and its annexation by South Africa in the face of United
Nations verbal opposition. We used as background
information Randolph Vigne's booklet *A Dwelling Place
of our Own,* published by the International Defence and
Aid Fund. The facts were supplemented visually by the
Swedish film *Namibia: the Liberation Struggle.* This film
includes some evocative sequences of diamond extracting,
the beer halls of Windhoek and the history of the brutal
German colonisation and subsequent South African
occupation. It also shows the guerrilla soldiers of
S.W.A.P.O. at work on patrols, building schools, and
operating bush hospitals for rural Namibians and for
casualties of napalm bombs dropped in air attacks on
country villages. In another sequence, an old man called
Aaron tells of his torture by the South African security
forces and the murder of his family, who would not
reveal where the S.W.A.P.O. soldiers were. A white girl
wrote:

Aaron's Story

My name is Aaron. On November 25th, 1974, I was assaulted. I
was also suspected of supporting S.W.A.P.O. I was kicked in the
head four times, I was punched on the nose and my eyes were
pouring with blood. They tied a rope around me which cut into
my skin. They tried to make me tell them where the S.W.A.P.O.
people were, and what they were doing. I would not give in, so

they tied the rope so tight that it forced my skin to split like a piece of plastic.

They shouted and said, 'You tell me what they're doing this exact moment or God help you!' So they got a knife and slit my leg, and this is how I have so many scars. Here, look! My family's bones are buried here. They assaulted my children and raped my wife. There was nothing I could do except cry, and feel the pain they felt.

Carol Burton

We studied the speech made by a Namibian, Reuben Hauwanga, before the U.N. Council for Namibia in March 1976, which told of the brutality and torture employed by the South African security forces throughout the country.[17] We also discussed the way some British firms were making money out of the deaths of Namibian people, particularly the British company Marconi, which had sold the South African Government their sophisticated 'Troposcatter' telecommunication system for tracking down S.W.A.P.O. guerrillas. Two other white children followed this work up with these poems:

Namibia

Namibia is a country
Which is ruled by the whites,
But lurking in the jungle
The SWAPO lead a fight.

They work to live happily,
And not with White rule,
They want to live in buildings,
To live with colours all.

But SWAPO have a hard task,
Many doctors they aint got,
They must conquer napalm,
It's already killed a lot.

The British firms are selling whites their weapons
To insure themselves some money,
They don't know the situation in South Africa,
And it aint very funny.

Philip Stanley

Namibia

In Africa
There is a white army,
They are wicked,
They drive coloured people barmy.

They rape the women,
Old or young.
If they don't talk
They'll cut out their tongue.

The S.W.A.P.O. guerrillas
Are who they're after.
The white people
Are black people's masters.

So the torture goes on,
On and on,
It goes on
All day long.

But S.W.A.P.O.'s guerrillas fight back,
They are faithful friends,
They will not split on each other
If their life is coming to an end.

Lynn Torry

A West African boy transported himself back to become
a S.W.A.P.O. soldier, fighting ignorance and disease as
well as the South African occupation of his country.

S.W.A.P.O.

Our tactics are guerrilla warfare,
We bring medicine and education to the bush,
We don't charge for a check-up, we try to be fair.

We are always on the move,
They cannot track us with their troposcatter,
We clean our guns till they're smooth.

Our enemies use Napalm on us,
When it touches the ground it scatters about,
When it gets on you it sticks and burns through your skin,
When this happens it's best not to fuss.

168

We get our ammunition from our enemies,
If we are successful on our raids, we get their guns,
They don't pick on us, only our helpless families.

Two hundred miles we go, with medical supplies behind our back,
One day Namibia will be ours,
Then they will stop treating us like muck.

Andrew Ohene

Two other boys in another class, sitting next to each
other, the first from Barbados, the second half-Italian,
wrote about the terror of a napalm attack, this time not
in Vietnam but in Namibia.

Napalm

Maybe you have heard of napalm. But now here is what napalm
does from the eyes of a black person in Namibia.

A new day is born in Africa. The birds are singing, everything
is coming to life in the black village. Children are going out to
play just like nothing was going to happen. SWAPO came the day
before. They're coming back today, but people say they have seen
the South African army around here. So SWAPO have to come and
go before they come.

The men go out to get fire wood, the women are washing up,
children playing, the sun is high in the sky.

THEN!

a noise can be heard like a bee. It at first was just like a plane
going by. Soon we were to know it was a death plane. The plane
was over our village and dropped something. When it hit the
ground it blasted wide open and millions of red bits of napalm,
the red things, went through the skin like hot knives through
butter. Screaming could be heard for miles around. The playing
turned into a nightmare, people wishing they could die from the
red jelly. Children dead, all my friends and family dead. And all
in five minutes.

One hour later SWAPO came, and they helped them who did
not die. I was so angry I joined SWAPO, and I went with the hope
in my mind that I would kill hundreds of the white South
African army.

Louis Browne

Napalm!

We heard the planes coming over. We dashed for the shelters, the bombs were dropped. The bomb exploded and the jelly-like substance shot out. The napalm was burning everything in sight. A speck of the jelly landed on my face. It was burning and eating my flesh. I was screaming with pain. I got sand and stuffed it on my face. The burning stopped. The bombings stopped and the village was a mess.

The Government soldiers came back and questioned us. They chased me first. They laid me down on a table and said, 'Where are the SWAPO this moment?' I said nothing. They got a wired rope and put it around my neck, they asked me once again, I said nothing. They tightened it, I started coughing and choking. They took it off and slit my legs with a knife. I was screaming with pain. They sent me out of the room and moved out of the village.

After a couple of months the scars healed up. I went and joined the guerrillas. I wanted to get my own back on them. After I joined, I became a medical orderly at a bush hospital.

Chris Cattaneo

There was no doubt of the support of these children, black and white, for the right of the Namibian people to govern their own country. This was not a fairy story about an obscure people locked away in a far corner of the world: the oppressed were moving towards the oppressed. They had seen right through the South African occupation, and much of their response was public, unambiguous, campaigning support for a tyrannised but struggling people in Africa. Here are two of these voices, one from Ireland, one from the Caribbean.

N amibia we all love so very much!
A fter all, we are the supporters of our friends SWAPO.
M oney comes in from our European supporters.
I have scars and burns for life,
B ones, skulls, can still be found.
I have always said I would help to fight,
A fter all, we want our own community.

Jon Smith

170

N o one knows the pain we feel,
A rms broken, legs fractured, scars —
M arked for life, that is all we have to show.
I n the old days we were treated
B ad, but we have had enough.
I n a matter of time it will come,
A nd we shall rule our native land.

Ted John

'Rhodesia' had been a rallying point for racists and emerging fascist organisations in Britain ever since Ian Smith's white minority government had declared 'U.D.I.' in 1965. Andrew, from Ghana, soon showed his attitude to that historical event.

U.D.I.

Unilateral Declaration of Independence —
From the day that Smith took over
It's been 'Whites Rule' since.

He thinks that blacks can't rule a country well,
Black can rule as good as White.
When we ask for our country back
They say 'Go to Hell!'

Smith has no right to be in our lands —
One day we'll get our country back in our hands.

Andrew Ohene

But the 'kith and kin' arguments that appealed so strongly to the racists, and which they were peddling locally and nationally, were continually being reflected in the daily media. Our children, however, working class in London, soon recognised a different kind of kith and kin in the working people and peasants of Zimbabwe.

A chink appeared in the media's armour when the 'Daily Mirror' read by many of the children's parents, published an 'exclusive' story on February 27th, 1976 by a young white mercenary in Smith's Rhodesian Army, who had deserted and returned to England. We seized on this story as a useful base for work on Zimbabwe. Tom McCarthy was a twenty-two-year-old Londoner who had been lured by the military myths of glamour, manhood and excitement to Salisbury, where he joined the Rhodesian Light Infantry. He soon discovered the nature of Smith's army when his platoon was ordered to destroy an African village near the Mavuradonha Mountains, whose inhabitants had collected £1,000 for the Zimbabwe liberation soldiers. After destroying the village and massacring the sixty people who lived there, his platoon shared out the £1,000 and took £50 each. Later, appalled by what he had done, he deserted the Rhodesian Army, returned to Britain, and gave his story to the 'Daily Mirror'.

The incident was not to be tackled lightly in the classroom, for it brought alive, not only the present moment in Zimbabwe, but the mind of a mercenary and the nature of the 'professional' soldier. Mercenaries had been recruited previously in the year to fight with South Africa against the Angolan people, and had been totally discredited, even in the 'regular' media. But more importantly, the incident had much to say about army life, and the way in which the appearance of glamour and fulfilment of manhood hide repression and support for colonialism and injustice, whether in Rhodesia, Namibia or Ireland, and this particularly in a time of unemployment, when the Army recruiting officers fix an emphatic gaze on wageless working class youth. Soldiers like Tom McCarthy contrasted so hugely for the children with those men and women who fought for the freedom and independence of their people.

Massacre in a Village

The village is quiet, there's not a sound,
Except in the bushes where there's soldiers all around.
They've come to get one thousand pounds,
If they don't, they'll burn the village to the ground.

They attack just after dawn,
There's a mercenary there, his name is Sean,
The sergeant orders him to kill a child
Who's wounded, hurt, weak and mild.

Sean is wondering what to do,
The sergeant says 'You're only fit for the zoo!'
Then Sean hops it and runs away,
He's not feeling merry and gay.

The village is massacred and burned to the ground,
Now not one person is making a sound.
Five men are sent to find Sean or not,
They come back with him, he's tried, sentenced and shot.

Tony Power

Tom McCarthy's Story

I remember the day I flew out to Rhodesia to join Ian Smith's
army. I became a murderer. My job was to find the guerrillas
who were fighting to claim back their right to rule their land. We
were told that a thousand pounds was hidden in a nearby village,
and that the guerrillas were going to pick it up at some point. We
were all set, and then we burst into the village. We used fire bombs
to set the huts alight. Then the massacre began. People were shot
down as they were running away, I could hear their screams louder
than ever. Women were shot to the ground and the babies who
were on their backs were shot by machine guns. Then I was told
to shoot a wounded and unarmed boy. He lay there looking up at
me, I could not bear it. I was shaking with fear, my heart beat
fast. 'Shoot him!' shouted the army leader.

I turned my face and went to shoot him. I missed, by about a
foot. Once again the leader shouted and said, 'What's the matter,
you scared?' He pushed my face towards the wounded boy.
'SHOOT!' he ordered. I turned and pulled the trigger. I hit him
between the mouth and the nose, he was dead. 'Oh my God, what
am I doing here?' I said to myself.

Yet I did it, and all for fifty pounds. I fled from the army and
returned, back to England. My whole mind is scarred that I am a
murderer.

Dawn Tizzard

Three boys, one white, one from St. Lucia, and a Sikh boy from India, cooperated on a play about Zimbabwe which veered back and forth between comic-style fantasy and violent exaggeration, and realistic writing about heroic resistance. This clearly revealed the strange amalgam of contradictions in their minds, sometimes conceding to, sometimes resisting the influence of war comics and the dehumanising and profiteering industry of war-fantasy.

Life as a Guerrilla

The scene is set in the bush in Rhodesia. Three guerrillas, Mawapa, Bongo and Nkomo have just joined the guerrilla organisation ZAPU. The chief guerrilla, Colonel Mawba, is giving them a few details.

MAWBA: Have you ever experienced any kind of warfare?

BONGO: No sir.

NKOMO: No sir.

MAWAPA: No sir. All I have heard is a few rifle shots sir.

MAWBA: You will have to go to Mozambique for experienced training.

OTHERS: Yes sir.

End of Scene 1

Scene 2

They are on the way to Mozambique, when a jeep pulls out in front of them. Four white policemen get out of the jeep and they walk over to the bus. The black recruits recognise what the white policemen are doing, try to escape but they are all shot.

CAPTAIN JAKES: Search the bus for any more recruits.

(*He steps aboard the bus*)

PIGEON: Ha, you three get out.

(*As Nkomo walks off the bus, Pigeon kicks him down the step*)

CAPT. JAKES: You three work for ZAPU don't you?

BONGO: Pardon?

CAPT. JAKES: You heard.

BONGO: Pardon?

CAPT. JAKES: Why, you cheeky black bastard.

Jakes kicks Bongo hard in the cobblers and ruptures him. The policemen don't get any information out of the three men, so they take them to police headquarters for interrogation. They take them into a back room.

CAPT. JAKES: I bet you would like to know how we found out about your plans. Well, our little friend here Nakoco told us.

BONGO: Well, you're a traitor to your fellow blacks. You are a traitor!

CAPT. JAKES: Keep your mouth shut.

The first one they interrogate is Mawapa. They lay him on a table and chain him down. Nakoco takes a drill from the wall and drills through Mawapa's brain.

MAWAPA: Argh-h-h-h-h-h-h-h-h-h-h-h-h-h.

Mawapa is dead. They take Nkomo and chain him against the wall. Nakoco takes a chopper and chops Nkomo's right leg off.

CAPT. JAKES: Are you with ZAPU?

NKOMO: No.

Nakoco chops his head off. They take a rope and they tie the rope around a hanging light. They tie a loop and put it around Bongo's head. Bongo's body is pointing straight at a thick metal spike.

CAPT. JAMES: Are you with ZAPU?

BONGO: No. Why has Nakoco got to torture me? You white pigs have no courage. We will rid this country of people like you.

Nakoco pushes the hanging Bongo into the spike. The room fills up with blood. This is another day in the life of a ZAPU guerrilla.

Philip Stanley, Tony Amable, Shillinder Singh

We moved on to another press story about Zimbabwe, this time from the *Sunday Times.* Under the sub-headline 'SKULL BASHERS: Smith's Security men are driving young Africans into the Guerrilla ranks', an ex-teacher and Inspector of African schools in Rhodesia, Don Waters, wrote of Smith's soldiers machine-gunning and invading African schools, arresting, assaulting and detaining teachers and senior pupils, and wrecking class-rooms in their search for sympathisers of the Zimbabwe liberation soldiers. Three white girls, and Andrew, the Ghanaian boy who previously had written so passionately about S.W.A.P.O. and Smith's U.D.I., wrote pieces imagining themselves as teachers or soldiers involved in these attacks.

I Was a Soldier

I and other soldiers were ordered to massacre a village. We were also ordered to question teachers, torture them then kill them. As I and the other soldiers walked along the bombed-up streets of the village, I could see a man half wounded hiding behind a door. The door was hanging off its hinges. Although I was ordered to shoot to kill anyone looking or hiding suspiciously. I could shoot him. I felt sick, and anyway I was the only one who saw him. If any of the other soldiers had seen him they would have been sure to question him or kill him.

We walked a bit farther up the road, then stopped at a school. As the other soldiers barged into the classroom, they began to beat up the teacher. Other soldiers ordered me to take the children out for questioning. As I lead them out one by one, I thought, 'Why innocent children? Why question them?' As these thoughts passed through my mind, I could hear children crying. They were about 13 or 14 and in my mind I sympathised with them. As I questioned them my voice was shaky. I loved children, and I could not hurt them, or let anyone else. I thought of my wife and two children at home in England. My two years' service in the Rhodesian army was nearly up and then I would go home.

Sonia Quinn

Teacher's Story

I was teaching a class of forty, twenty less than usual because they were out in the yard. The remainder were doing history about the country, when suddenly the window smashed open, followed by gunfire. There were bullets everywhere, flying everywhere you turned. I told my pupils to take cover under the desks, which they did without any hesitation. As they went down they put their slates over their heads. All this time I was hiding behind the blackboard. Then someone kicked in the door. Four men in uniform came in and carried me off. They took me to the Hall, strapped me to the ground and ripped the shirt off my back. Then they got a branch shaped to a whip, and asked me, 'Do you know where the guerrillas are?'

When I replied no they started beating me, and in the process they asked me where the guerrillas were hiding. Half an hour later they left me there, with my back cut in slices and my face badly bruised.

Andrew Ohene

176

I remember that terrible day in school,
My classroom was right next to the Hall,
I stayed in school late that night,
That was when I got the terrible fright.

I was writing at the small desk
Then I sat back for a rest.
Then the nightmare had begun,
Bullets came flying from a machine gun.

I was so afraid, I jumped up quick,
The man saw me and threw a brick.
The man had gone, I screamed and cried,
A teacher came in and sat by my side.

I told him what had happened to me,
He said, 'Calm down, I'll get you some tea.'
I'll never forget it, as long as I live,
It sticks in my mind and it won't give.

Cheryl Wakenell

I am a teacher from a school in Rhodesia. I enjoyed teaching in the
school, but one day something terrible happened.

One day around breaktime the children went out to play, and
I was in the classroom marking the children's books. While I was
marking the books I happened to look towards the door of the
classroom. A bullet flew from one side of the room to the other,
it just missed me. That got me worried. I then piled the books
up on my desk and started to make my way to the door. I crept
out of the door into the corridor. There I saw a lot of men
coming towards me. I started to panic, and there they got me.
They asked me questions but I ignored them. So they beat me
up. My eyes went black and blue. From there they took me into
the nearest classroom. I recognised the men who had interrupted
my classroom. They were Smith's security men, his troops, I saw
them around a lot. From that day I have always been scared in the
class by myself.

So I gave up the job and now live on my own. My eyes are
still not healed and are still a bit blurred where I got beat up. I'll
never forget the day.

Theresa Braithwaite

Finally, the very name of a suppressed but emerging new nation — 'Zimbabwe', seemed to move the imaginations of some of the children. A Barbadian boy and a white girl wrote, inspired by the word itself, and the struggle behind its true realization.

Z oo, we live in a zoo to them. Fight,
I   say, fight. Ian Smith must go! Our
M ajority join the ranks, we will
B ombard their lines, hide by day
A nd kill by night. The
B lacks cry out for freedom!
W e will win, or else we will for
E ver be ruled by whites!

Louis Browne

Zimbabwe!

Zimbabwe is our country's name,
It's not what all the white men say.
Our country has an atmosphere
That's better than the whites.
We do not want 'Rhodesia'
To be our country's name,
For we are the ones that first lived here
Before the whites all came.
So surely friends we have the right
To call our country from the start
ZIMBABWE!

Dawn Tizzard

Part five

The Embrace of History

There is no doubt now, that despite colour and origins, our children, like their parents, belong to the British working class. Their present and future lie with the advances and organisation of that class, and the way it struggles and moves forward in response to the objective conditions that surround and pressure it. Though our children were only a small portion of the human vastness of that class all over the world, our work in the classroom had attempted to vindicate and sustain that feeling of belonging and oneness with oppressed humanity. And yet these children lived together in a particular country, a particular city and a particular neighbourhood. Their actual living relationships were fused with the streets, flats, canals and dockyards of East London, and their lives were taking place, moving forward and making sense in this particular concrete reality. These few streets and their extensions and activities threatened to circumscribe the daily lives of our children, whether they were Caribbean, Bangla Deshi, from Hong Kong, or born and bred in East London.

East London

East London is a dirty place,
It's untidy and smelly.
Every time a lorry comes past
You get dirty fumes in your belly.
You can't play football without getting stopped,
If you try to play on you'll get mopped.
They're building flyovers right through our city,
Oh what a nightmare
Oh what a pity.

Philip Stanley

Cottage Street

Down my way
There is nowhere to play,
All we have is the green
And that aint clean,
All we have is the square
And that aint fair.
We should have some playground
And that would be fair,
The cars go zooming down our street,
They knock you off your feet
Down Cottage Street.

Alan Elderton

The Mudchute

The Mudchute is a very nice place,
You can go over there and muck about
Without old people shouting out,
There's lots of birds that you can see
Nesting in their great big trees.
You can run with your friends and have a race
Up and down the hills at a steady pace.
But soon the Mudchute will be gone,
It will have council houses on.

Jackie Hart

East India Dock Road

There is a place near where I live
Called East India Dock Road.
The fumes of the lorries go all around,
The dirt and mud sticks to our shoes,
Old men passing, stinking of booze.
At night we all gather around
Going home looking like we've been under the ground,
What can we do, there's nowhere to go,
Only to walk to and fro.

Sharon Patten

These same streets, now hovered over by clouds of fumes and dust, pounded by articulated lorries, infected by lead poisoning, had seen massive and heroic acts in the past. Our school was pitched in the centre of an area of massive historical working class struggle and revolt. These streets which saw unemployed youths in desultory groups, and overlooked vast, vacant dockyards, had known strikes, marches, rallies, stirring speeches, and had been the site of great deeds over the previous two hundred years. Now, the experience and inspiration of that same history reached forward to our children with a wide embrace. It worked to enfold them, without exception, as it had eventually enfolded the Huguenots, the Flemish, the Irish, the Jewish. Now it was the newest immigrant groups, the West Indians, the Pakistanis, the Bangla Deshis. It was up to us, the teachers, to make history work for us and nourish our children, to interpret and present this knowledge and teaching to them for their benefit and advance. It was our task to transmit that consciousness and will to unite, organise and resist that had filled the past hearts and minds of East Enders.

Our own school building, itself nearly a century old, protruded from the rubble of Limehouse. It had seen thousands and thousands of East London children of all origins pass through its gates. It had lived through most of the events we were now asking the children to re-live in the classroom. In the very next street along, Dod Street, an event had taken place in 1885 of great importance for working people. The Social Democratic Federation, the first organised revolutionary socialist group in Britain, with its most famous member, the poet and craftsman William Morris, came down and spoke regularly on the corner of Dod Street and Burdett Road at street meetings, campaigning for the Socialist cause. In September 1885, when the government were doing their best to stifle such street meetings, the police violently broke up a meeting at Dod Street, arresting the leaders and seizing their banners and literature. This

183

event caused enormous indignation amongst the local trade unions, radical clubs and socialist groups. In order to uphold their right to free speech and street meetings, they organised an assembly of 30,000 to 50,000 people on the next Sunday, and the Sunday after when William Morris spoke and read his poems. This time the police kept their distance, awed by the multitude. As we went over this event in the classroom, only a street away from where it actually happened, and sang Morris' 'The March of the Workers'[18] as if we were on the terraces of Upton Park, History was reaching out to us, showing us the capability of our strength and unity, pressing us to go forward and tackle the unemployment, the closures of industry, the racism, and all the injustices around us. A St. Lucian boy, in an inspiring little acrostic, was right there, 'over the road', and so were many others:

D own in Dod Street
O ver the road,
D are you to hear what William told?

S tanding on the corner of Burdett Road
T rying to get Socialism,
R epresenting the Socialists,
E very Sunday we meet up
E very Sunday coppers break us up.
T housands and hundreds coming now — the coppers go away
    with a frown.

Ted John

It was a Sunday morning, the date was September 20th, 1885. I got up at nine, and at eleven o'clock I went around the corner to Dod Street. The speech was just about to start. There were about a thousand of us. The talk was by the Social Democratic Federation. They were trying to help the unemployed and were trying to make the poor as good as the rich, and trying to make more people join them. The time was about one, and a lot of people went to the pub and there were only 70 left. The police moved in to get rid of us and they took a lot away. They fined them and put them in prison. They done this so that we could not have free speech on the streets. Next Sunday came and there were about twenty or thirty thousand that Sunday and the police was frightened to go and move them out. That day we got free speech!

Darren Mills

Dod Street

It's Sunday morning in Dod Street,
Parlez-vous
William Morris is speaking there
Parlez-vous
There is a thousand there or more,
The coppers are lying on the floor,
Inky pinky parlez-vous.

It's one o'clock and the pubs are opening,
Parlez-vous
The crowd is slowly going away
Parlez-vous
The coppers decide to make the move,
There's only a hundred there to move,
Inky pinky parlez-vous.

A week has gone and the government's scared,
Parlez-vous
The coppers are hiding out of view
Parlez-vous
William Morris is there again,
The working class has won again,
Inky pinky parlez-vous.

Alan Elderton

William Morris (For England Alone)

William Morris is my idol,
He makes us feel like we're the heroes.
We will meet in Dod Street every Sunday,
But before we even start
There's something needed to be put straight.

The bobbies are our trouble,
They won't leave us alone —
So come on all ye people and help the workers' pride!
So stick up for our workers and ring out loud our marching song!
Because we are men, and men alone,
Because we will battle for the world and for the workers' right!
So go on marching on!

Tina Gilbert

The Dod Street Ballad

My story begins many years ago
In the heart of London Town,
How the aristocratic bourgeoisie
Were running this country down.

All the working class people believed
That they should have some say,
Of how this country should be run
And try to save the day.

To get their wish, vast meetings were held
In Dod Street safe and sound,
To hide away from hard police
Who sought them out like hounds.

In the end they won their fight
And free, fair speech was found,
And walking home through streets so bare,
Glad tidings without a sound.

Jackie Parkes

Dod Street had shown us History in the next street, and our children had re-lived it. We now embarked on a course of English which took as its theme incidents from the history of the area. We gathered poems, songs,[19] newspapers, prints, photographs and broadsheets that had been printed locally. In the local library we re-discovered files of old local working class journals like Sylvia Pankhurst's *Women's Dreadnought* and *Lansbury's Labour Weekly.* We sent home letters to parents asking them for any mementoes, photographs, or books from the past which might help us.

Firstly, we tried to encourage the children to re-experience the ordinary, working lives of Victorian children in the East End. A Jamaican boy and an Italian boy became chimney sweeps following a reading of Blake's 'The Chimney Sweeper':[20]

I was walking down the street with my brush and sticks, when one of the maids of a big house called me over to clear out their chimney. I didn't really want to go, but I had to keep the family alive. It was funny, it was like going to Heaven without being buried, but being buried in soot. I was just sweeping out the chimney when suddenly the master came shouting down the stairs and kicked me in the back and shouted, 'Get back to work you brat, or no money.'

So I got climbing. I got halfway, when some bricks and soot gave way and nearly hit the master of the house. His face went red, and I heard one of the maids giggle and he sacked her where she stood. He turned to me and told me to hurry up, or no money. As I got higher, the soot blocked my nose and mouth. I started to choke and I nearly fell twice, but I still had to get the money for all the family, and as I got to the top it really did feel like Heaven. But that's all we are fit for. If you're living on the streets there's nothing to live for, so you've got to beg for food.

Keith Randall

One day, when I was a boy, I used to be a chimney sweep-boy. I was very small, they shaved my head. I'd scamper up the chimney and knock all the soot down. It made me short-sighted and it made me lose my breath. I could hardly breathe and I got weaker and weaker. All I got was a couple of pennies and that was usually taken off me by bigger kids, and they called me skinhead. I gradually didn't have anywhere to go. So in the end I had to go to the workhouse. Times were hard, we were having our dinner and a boy said, 'You can use your head for mopping up soup with because it's bald.' So I started fighting with him, and I got my bowl and stuck it over his head, and booted him in the gollies. Then some big men came and stuck us to the ground and repeated hitting us with sticks. After a year we gradually rotted away until we died.

Bobby Giurdano

And there were also mudlarks and toshers, workhouse girls and sackmakers, and the women who worked in the sweaters' dens of Whitechapel and Spitalfields. Some of these accounts were coming via Cyprus, Jamaica, Ireland:

A Mudlark

It was a nice hot day and I got up and walked down to the river. The tide had just gone out. Then I saw a big lump of coal stuck in the mud, so I took my shirt and shorts off and walked towards it. Then I put my feet on a piece of glass. So I walked back and got a piece of cloth which I found coming there, and I tied it around my foot. Then I walked back out there and I brought the lump of coal with me. Then I took the piece of coal home and sold it to the next door neighbour for sixpense. I went and bought a pie and a 1d worth of chips and I had 2d left and I saved that for later.

Then I went back to the river and the water was coming in and it brought in a big lump of fat, so me and two other boys had a race to get it. I got there first, and one of the boys found a bar of metal. Then I took the fat to the market and sold it for 4d. By then my foot was really hurting me, so I went to a shop and bought some stuff to put on it that cost me 3d. With the other 3d I got two apples and a bar of chocolate and when I had finished it, it was getting dark. So I went back to my one room with my mum, dad, two brothers and one sister.

Darren Mills

Workhouse

I am Loisa Crankshaw, aged eighteen and I am in the workhouse, dressed in a grey uniform. I'm eighteen and I have got to work in the workhouse. You can't see any boys and boys can't see girls. We are all dressed in baggy uniforms.

My boyfriend is outside and I can't stand the workhouse. I am gonna rip my baggy uniform up. I know I shouldn't rip it up but I want to go out and meet the boy that is outside. He is the only boy I have ever fallen for. I am going to be bad, bad, bad. I'll rip up my uniform because I have got to see him. I have not nice clothes. All I have to do is to stay in the workhouse.

Christine Victorin

Tosher

It was about half nine at night, the street lamps were burning brightly, the moon was in the sky and I was all alone. Ned's me name, Ned Harris, and this was my last night of life. I walked down toward London Bridge. All I had on was a pair of ripped trousers and a thin shirt. The wind was calm but I stared at the clouds which were brewing up a storm down the side of the river. I saw this big sewer pipe. Luck was with me, the tide was out. I ran down onto the beach on broken bottles, sharp stones and mud. My feet were bleeding rapidly. I felt cold, alone, and most of all, frightened. I looked inside cautiously, all I saw was darkness, dim blackness. I wondered for a long time whether to venture along this tunnel. While I was thinking, I heard Big Ben striking twelve in the distance. I shivered, then I heard tugs and barges, floating along the bewildering Thames. Then I ran into the dark pipe, wondering what I might meet. I knew that if I wanted to live, this was the sort of thing I would have to do to get money for food. In the darkness I saw something glittering, shining. I picked it up and examined it carefully. I walked along and wondered what else I might find.

Then suddenly, in front of me, was this enormous rat, its skin black and brown, its eyes glittered with evil, its teeth gnashing, spitting fury, its tongue dropping. Then it ran at me. I froze for a moment, then turned to run. I ran and ran and ran until I was out of breath. I looked back at where I had run from and saw a whole pack of rats. I went to run and fell over a big boulder. I knew that the end was near so I just sat there. The rats surrounded me, their tongues lolloping, and all I heard as a rat came forward and sank his teeth into my stomach, was Big Ben striking half two, the necklace still in my hand, the outside world just a few paces away.

Paul Halfyard

A tosher is someone who goes into the sewers to look for bits and pieces. John Smith is one of those toshers. One day John was walking down a street when he came to a drain, and he looked down it. He saw a golden sovereign. He tried to put his hand down the drain, but his hand would not go through the slots in the drain. As he was a tosher anyway, he decided that he would have to actually go down into the sewerage pipe itself. He walked down to the beginning of the pipe. No one was about because of the smell, so he lifted up the drain and down he went. But he was a good four miles from the sovereign. He had forgotten that the tide was due in half an hour and that he needed about one hour to get to it at least.

He started on his way. When he had gone three and a half miles away from the entrance, he remembered the tide was due in. By that time he had about twenty minutes before the tide was going to come in. He hurried on his way and the tide was on its way through the pipe. He got to the sovereign. The tide was four minutes behind him. He tried lifting up the drain but it was stuck fast. By this time the tide was only one minute behind him. Then a horse and cart came along and stopped on the street above him. The tide had got to him. He tried to swim out of it but the current was too strong for him. He was a gonner.

Chris Elefteriou

189

Sacks

Sweating away
Sewing all day
Repairing holes
And tears

Sacks all around
In hundreds
They lie
Fingers sore
Swollen hard
Blisters big
I can't stand
No more

Sewing all day
Sit on the floor
More sacks
To sew
Hundreds more
No one to see
I close the door.

Kelly Connolly

The Sweaters' Den

What can be the matter mum,
Why do you look so sad?
My child,
My child it is hard to say,
Your father is dead there,
It's only you and me left
To try and live happy.
Years my child, will so pass,
And within those years
We shall live.

Debbie Walker

And there were the men who built the 'Great
Eastern', the nonpareil of iron ships, in Millwall, where
many of the children from the school lived. A girl
imagined herself as a child, suddenly seeing the huge ship

rising from the marshlands of the Isle of Dogs, and
Lynton, recently from St. Lucia, re-saw the 'Great
Eastern' with awe and wonder.

The Great Eastern

I am a kid, I live in Millwall.
One day when I went out to play,
I wandered a little too far away.
I went through fields and marshes bare
And to my amazement I did stare —
Standing high above the houses,
It looked like some kind of iron man.
I could see the people standing there,
Looking up to stare.
I asked a man who wasn't in a stare
What the iron was doing there.
'It's the Great Eastern,' he replied.
I said, 'Thank God, I thought it was a monster in disguise.'

Jackie Hart

I looked with wonder at this great mass of steel lying in the dock
like a great giant. A lot of thoughts went through my mind. One
which troubled me much was 'would it float, or would it sink?'
I saw men tipping molten iron with their bare hands with sweat
pouring from their bodies, other men with hammers the size of
themselves ringing and shaping red hot iron.

To my surprise there was hardly any wood, not as much as I
expected for a ship of this great size. Day by day I went to see the
progress of this great ship. One day I saw two great big wheels
go on the side of the ship — I had never seen such big wheels before.
There were six tall masts on deck, I heard they were for emergenc-
ies. The day came when this giant was to be woken up and launched.
It was a terrific day and thousands of people gathered to see this
great event. The ship was dropped into the Thames and it caused
a great tidal wave which had the whole area flooded for days and
a lot of people were soaked. The giant had a sad ending and to
think all these hard and dangerous jobs were to go to scrap after
a few years!

Lynton Popo

191

Up the road to the North, there still stood the Bryant and May match factory where the Matchgirls had organised their famous strike in 1888, one of the proto-type successful industrial actions by women organised at their own workplace. They struck against the appalling pay and working conditions which led to the horrifying industrial disease: 'phossy-jaw'. Also the statue of Gladstone in Bow Road, erected by the company with forced contributions from the Matchgirls' meagre wages, still stood, more as a memorial to the girls' fortitude than to Gladstone.

Phossy-Flossy

That's me, Flossy Jacobs!

When I was about fifteen, I got a job as a match girl at Bryant and May's.

On my first day, I didn't know much about the job and it seemed pretty good, but I soon learned to hate the job with a friend who also worked there. She helped me a lot at first, but we kept getting fined.

I was rarely late, but I was often fined for dropping matches or talking.

One day, I was eating my lunch, when my jaw began to ache painfully. I could barely eat my tiny luncheon. The next day my friend told me that my chin looked all baggy and shrivelled up. That afternoon I got the sack.

Every day, from then on, I tried to get work, but no one would take me. My jaw began to get worse and I got very hungry. In despair, I went out at night and searched for food. I seldom found any, but sometimes I found a small piece of stale bread or cheese.

After a while, I heard of a new danger, 'Jack the Ripper'. I sadly gave up all hope of life and returned to my bed of thorns to die. Now I am waiting my moment of freedom — Death.

Dawn Mitchell

The Matchgirls' Strike, 1888

We work all day
Without much pay,
We are the matchgirls of Bryant and May.
Many girls have phossy jaw,
They lose their money and end up poor.

So go on strike girls,
Though you won't get many pearls.
But for Bryant and May
it won't be funny —
But you will get more money.

Cheryl Wakenell

A Story About the Statue

We get tuppence farthing for making a gross of matches and out of
that we've been asked to give one penny to pay for the statue. We
didn't want it in the first place but the manager got it. We have to
work for our wages and then give it to him. He should pay for it
himself, as he's got more money than all of us put together. All he
knows is 'work yourselves to death and pay for my statue'. I bet he
goes home to a nice, warm, comfortable house while we go home
to a cold, dirty flat what's running alive with beetles and mice.
While we have bread and jam and a cup of cold water, he sits down
to a big roast dinner and a bottle of champagne to celebrate for us
paying for his statue. He's got a cheek taking money out of our
wages. I'd kill him if I had a chance. He sits in that office and stuffs
his self till he can't move. Fat, lazy, good for nothing pig! It makes
my blood boil to think of him.

Ann Reeves

And a West Indian boy crossed the lines of sex and race
when he wrote this:

Phosphorus

I've got an onion
With my bread,

I know what
I've got in my bread —
PHOSPHORUS!

Every day we eat it
Every day the same.

We don't have to buy it,
Every day it comes free.
But not long now for me,
I've bought a brand new oak tree.

Goodbye mum, goodbye dad,
What do you know?
Getting buried tomorrow.

Trevor Clarke

In *The Link,* a radical contemporary paper which had
helped the Matchgirls' cause, we found a poem — the
words of which seemed to echo the cause of the work in
our classroom. This was copied out in poster-size writing,
and hung across the classroom wall for the rest of the
year.

Our Union

(A song for the Matchmakers)

Three cheers for our Union! It shall knit us soul to soul,
For 'tis Love seals the compact — Love, which makes the ages roll;
We'll stand to each other, ay! in spite of friend or foe,
And all the world the reason for our Union shall know.

Marching on! marching on!
We'll fear no foe and our rights hold dear.
Marching on! marching on!
Let our chorus ring out clear.

Now we've linked hand in hand and are marching side by side,
We'll be true to each other whatsoever may betide,
For we live by honest labor and we scorn the tyrant's frown,
And we'll help the world grow better ere Life's sun goes down.

By the wrongs we have suffered and the rights that we have won,
We swear we will help all to do as we have done;
The Right hand of fellowship we ever will extend,
And every homeless outcast aye shall find in each a friend.

Marching on! marching on!
Fighting our way thro' the stress of the day
Marching on! marching on!
While our chorus rings out clear.

In the streets around our school, we were learning
that the 'New' trade unionism of the late nineteenth
century had had its birthplace and its first testing ground.

194

Following the Matchgirls were the Gasworkers in 1889, organising in Beckton Gasworks, two miles to our east, and winning the first eight-hour day.

At Beckton Gasworks

The time was 5 a.m., and I got up and put me clothes on and walked around the corner to the gasworks and that's where I work. When I get in there I get this bog shovel which weighs 89 lbs., and that's without coal. I work thirteen hours a day and get 5d an hour. We was so near the flames which burned the coal that it touched our backs. One day we was shovelling coal and one of my friends lost his balance and fell back in the fire. So I pulled his leg and he came out with his face and back burnt. So I told someone else and he helped me to take him to hospital. I lost 15d that day just because I helped a friend. Then the winter came and we had to work like mad. Then a man called Will Thorne made up a union to have eight hours a day. The manager of Beckton heard this and gave us eight hours a day. But we had to do twice as much work then. But the union got stronger and the manager said, 'All right, you will only have eight hours a day.'

Darren Mills

Michael Maloney

One day I went to work at 5 a.m. I first dried my clothes, still wet from the other night, to put on, and started work at 6 a.m. I worked until after 10 p.m. I struggled my guts out, with no food or nothing, just water and oatmeal. I was feeling ill and half dying, working in front of that retort, flames coming to my face, burning me. I felt half dead in myself. Men were watching me work. I couldn't stand on my own two feet where the flames were catching me, and I had severe pains at the back of my head. My companion helped me in my labour. I couldn't stand no longer. At 10.20 I fell to the floor in front of the retort, unconscious. I couldn't remember nothing else from that day on. But I always remember my friends.

Theresa Braithwaite

Most important for us, living and learning during a period of dock closures, when this great industry which had sustained the East End for generations was being strangled — was the Great Docks Strike of 1889. Dockers, supported by other riverside workers — most of them predominantly of Irish extraction — held their massive stoppage in 1889 for the guaranteed wage of 6d an hour — the 'Dockers' Tanner', and four hours regular work a day. We duplicated contemporary newspaper accounts of the strike, sung together the dockers' 'anthem' of the time — 'Strike Boys Strike for Better Wages',[21] which was sung by 120,000 strikers as they marched down Commercial Road and through the City to Hyde Park, and rolled off a poem by a striking docker that had been printed in the *East End News* during the course of the strike.

On the Stones

How many thousands do not know
The hardships of a docker's life;
What hours and days he has to wait
For work to keep his home and wife.
Oft' days and weeks he strives to hear
The ganger call the name he owns.
How hard he struggles to the front;
But still is left 'upon the stones'.

At any hour the calls are made,
And oh! how patiently he waits
Until at last his name is called,
And he may enter through those gates.
His long privations make him weak;
Yet well he stifles down his moans,
And struggles hard to work his best;
But in the morn he's 'on the stones'.

We know that some are well employed
Who are possessed of youth and power;
Yet, after working hard all day,
They only get five pence per hour.
But after youth and strength have gone,
When age and work affect his bones,
Although long service he can prove,
He's calmly left 'upon the stones'.

Ah! who can wonder that he strives
To gain an increase to his wage;
To cry against abuses great
That fill his heart with grief and rage.
And, by the great concessions made,
The Dock Committee surely owns
The docker had some grievous wrongs
That keep him out 'upon the stones'.

All points are granted now, we know,
Except the time at which to start;
And, now they can so far agree,
Why, surely each can give a part.
November's shorter days are near,
At which the docker truly groans;
So start the winter with the rise,
And take them all from 'off the stones'.

An Irish girl and a local boy wrote stirring poems:

Strike for a Penny

Strike for a penny, a penny, no more,
Sixpence an hour, a penny, no more.
We're not leaving until we're paid
We're not being driven to the lower grade.
So strike for a penny, a penny, no more,
Sixpence an hour, a penny, no more.
We struggle for food and our rent,
We can't pay back the money we lent.
So strike for a penny, a penny, no more,
Sixpence an hour is all we're asking for!

Kelly Connelly

197

The March

We are on a march today,
To see if we can get some pay.
All we need is sixpence an hour,
But the bosses think they have all the power.
We are only going to work four hours a day,
Then we'll get much more pay.
We're going to march to Hyde park,
The bosses think, 'O what a lark!'
The Australians sent us a few thousand quid a week —
The bosses felt very bleak.
In the end we got our penny,
We had done a good turn,
Me, John and Kenny.

Tony Smith

The solidarity of Australian dockers with their London comrades was re-echoed by Dawn, whose family had emigrated to Australia, where she had formerly been educated, but who had now returned with her family to Poplar:

The Cage

My name's Billy Mann and I'm an East End docker. I've a family of eight to feed and clothe, so I need work. The bosses only pick you if you're strong or always buy them a beer or give them money, so I buy the boss a pint every night and give him about a shilling.

On Sunday, I gave the boss a pint of beer and gave him a shilling under the table. In the morning I rushed to work early and fought my way towards the front of the crowd. Then the gates were opened, and hundreds of men rushed into the cage to be picked out like cattle. I struggled and fought my hardest to get to the front and get picked out. The cage was a long, wide shed with rusty iron bars at each end. The crush of the hungry crowd was too much for old Ben Rogers, and he was suffocated beneath the struggle.

Five gangers stood in the cage on Monday, so there was a better chance of being chosen. The first was a short, stout man with white hair and a goatie beard. He wore a bowler hat, which looked far too small for him.

The second was much taller and rather slim, with dark brown hair and sharp, staring eyes. He was dressed in dark green and wore no hat. The third, a tall, well-built man with a grey pencil moustache, wore mostly buff, with a bright red waist-coat. The fourth was very fat and quite short. He had small beady eyes and wore spectacles. The fifth was very similar to the first, but he had light brown curly hair. He chose me, with about seven other men. But how much work would we do that day? And how often would we get picked from hundreds of men, each fighting and bribing the bosses, to be picked out, like farmers buying cattle, or auctioneers buying jewels? When you grow old you won't get any work, and with no work — no money, and with no money — no food and with no food you'll die!

Dawn Mitchell

The same spirit of internationalism was underlined as some of the children wrote speeches, imagining themselves as the strike leaders, exhorting their workmates to keep up the pressure. Ben Tillett was particularly popular as a subject as we had his great-great-grandson Harry in one of our classes. Kaushik was a Ugandan Asian boy and Sandria was from Jamaica. Now they are absolutely a part of the British working class, using its history which now enfolds them:

I, Ben Tillett, the Chairman of the Dockers' Committee, want to say that you people, the dockers, work not more than four times a week or about ten or less hours. You don't get enough money and it is up to you if you want more money and at least four hours work every day. If we get what we want then you should get at least 24p a day, that's nearly twice what you get now. And if you don't do anything about it, you people will go on working like this for ever and lose your lives early!

I can't imagine how you can support your families, and I am sure that no one here spends more than a few hours with his wife and kids — you have all these problems, but what do the bosses do? Nothing, they don't have problems like yours, and how much profit do they get? £10,000 a year. We are entitled to some of this money and the profit should be divided between all the dockers. And these middle men so called, should lose their jobs. They pick only the strong men who can work much harder and quicker, so that they can get more money. They pick whom they know and if you are one of those, just think about the others and come and support the dockers. Tell your friends and neighbours to join the march on Sunday. We will begin from here early in the morning and walk to Hyde Park.

Lastly, I would like to thank all the people who have helped to organize the strike and who have contributed money for those who are on strike, and particularly our fellow dockers in Australia who have sent us £250 to help with the strike. DON'T FORGET SUNDAY.

Kaushik Ondhia

Fellow dockers, haven't we been sitting down long enough? What about your wives and children starving to death without a morsel of food? We feel that we should go on strike and fight for our rights. This five pence an hour is not enough. We should not get pushed around or ordered about just for the sake of five pence an hour. Do you think that five pence will do for the whole family? What about that £10,000 they make for profit, and we get only five pence an hour. I don't think that's fair at all to us or the family. Even if we stop for a little rest we get whipped, just because we stop. So I say we fight for six pence an hour and more money if we work overtime. So let us fight for better wages and if they keep bullying us, then we'll go on strike for more money, and this time everybody will come too, and we'll stay on strike for as long as it takes!

Agreed? Yes.

Sandria Bruce

We had tried to completely cut across the vertical bars of Race and Sex. Our unity was Class, and time and again the children were demonstrating the force of that oneness. A twelve-year-old girl showed us the spirit of collective action against historical injustice that we knew impinged directly on the present lives and future of our children:

Stopping the Train Full of Blacklegs

BEN: My name is Ben Tillett, and I am the one who arranged the strike. When we all come out we will go on a march.

(*A call comes from the docks*)

JOHN: They're all out!

BEN: Well done.

JOHN: Are we going on the march then?

BEN: Yes. Round up the men and tell them no fighting or shouting. It is going to be a peaceful march, and post some of the men as pickets, so no men can get in through the gates.

200

JOHN: Yes sir. Where shall I bring them then?
BEN: Right here, in this field.

On the March.
BEN: You're doing fine lads. Hold up your banners and sing our
   song.
ALL: Strike boys, strike for better wages,
   Strike boys, strike for better pay.
   Go on fighting at the docks
   Stick it out like fighting cocks,
   Go on fighting till the bosses they give way.
BEN: Come on Jim, hold that banner up.
JIM: I am.
DAN: Ben, Ben, I won't be able to go on any further.
BEN: Do you want your money and your work?
DAN: Yes.
BEN: Well, get a move on.
After they had walked a few miles and were at the gates of the
docks, they heard one of the pickets shouting, 'There's going to be
a train full of blacklegs coming in!'
BEN: Quick lads, get into the docks and stop them!
ALL: Yes sir.
So they all rushed off into the docks. There they could see that
the train was coming, and they all stood in the middle of the rails
so that the train would come no further.
BEN: The train has stopped. Good lads — now do you want this
   strike to go on?
ALL: Yes!
BEN: Well, get this train back where it came from!
So all the strikers push the train all the way back.

Tina Gilbert

As we moved on into the twentieth century, we found
it impossible to leave the dockers' struggles completely.
Theresa, a twelve-year-old girl, re-lived a school strike of
1911, when, from Hull to London, schoolchildren had
'come out' in solidarity with their striking docker fathers,
then realised the power they had themselves.[22] Our
school had certainly lived through that event:

Our Strike in 1911

My name is Willy Brown, I live in an old house. My mum died
when I was born, and my dad works in the docks. One day I had

to start my new school. So my dad said, 'You'll be better off at Farrance Street.' I went there and I got in. So the next day I tripped to school. In those days I had to go by foot. Everyone looks at me and laughs. I went into school and I was put in a class. There were some very bossy boys in there. They asked me questions, so I didn't take no notice, just carried on working all by myself. When it was time to go home, I went by the school gates and I walked home. When I got in my father asked me if I liked it at school. I said, 'Yes, not bad. Dad, why ain't you at work?' He said, 'I'm on strike, because I want more money to feed and look after you better. I can't manage with the money I get.'

I agreed with my father, so the next day I told all my friends of my dad going on strike. So one boy said, 'Your dad's right. Let us go on strike and stick and stand by our fathers. They do need more money, I think so. My dad works all through the week, even on weekend days too.' We all went on strike with our dads and agreed. So all the school went on strike. We thought it was funny, so we played out. Then after a few days my dad got a letter through the post, and it was from the company he works at. They agreed to give my dad and the other dockers more money. So my dad went to work, and I went to school with all my new friends I had made friends with. Me and my dad then lived happily together, and we invited some of my friends to tea. Me and my friends said we won't get the cane much now, but if we do, I was going on strike again. I told my dad, and he told me to go on strike about caning and hitting. I went on strike, and was away from school for about two weeks, just me by myself. I got bored by myself, sitting at home. So I gave up and went back to school. All my friends were happy to see me back, so was my dad after a while. He was very pleased with me, and very proud he had a boy like me.

Theresa Braithwaite

The self-organisation of working women had been a recurrent feature of the history of our area. We had already seen that truth with the Matchgirls. The formation of the East London Federation of the Suffragettes in Bow and Poplar in the years before the 1914—18 war was another step forward. Their fight for the Vote and campaign against the imperialist war, was an enormous contribution to development of organisa- tion amongst working women. We had the magnificent

journalism of the *Women's Dreadnought,* edited by
Sylvia Pankhurst in that pre-war period, to inspire us,
and we used poems like this one by an anonymous
woman contributor in 1914, to move our own children
to write.[23]

A Lullaby

O hush thee my baby, thy sire was a slave,
Whom overwork thrust in the dark early grave;
The gloomy, grey streets from this den which we see,
Are hungrily waiting, dear baby, for thee,
O hush thee my baby.

O sleep whilst thou may, babe, by night and by day
Thy pale mother rests not, but stitches away;
There's no one to guard thee from hunger but she,
Her tears flowing silently all for thee.
O hush thee my baby.

O hush thee my baby through days dark and wild
Stream sun shafts of glory that can't be defiled;
The marching of myriads is borne to our ears,
And we will march with them, and sing through our tears,
O hush thee my baby.

And write they did, with great force. As soon as she had
read this 'lullaby', a twelve-year-old girl wrote:

My Little Baby

My little baby, you're not brought up right,
Mother has got to fight for her rights.
We haven't much money, we really are poor,
But if I can help it, it won't happen anymore.

We haven't much money, and none to buy food with,
But I would get some if I could.
I hate to see you lying so thin and so pale,
And thinking of your father out drinking light ale.

One day we'll become rich, and buy many things,
And then we'll tell people how it all begins.
We'll have plenty of food and have roast on a Sunday,
And not have to think how we'll eat on the Monday.

Karen Green

203

Another girl imagined herself as Sylvia, in jail at Holloway, a victim of the Liberal Government's 'Cat and Mouse Act', and enduring the torture of forced feeding:

Force Feeding

I was arrested on Saturday the 15th of July, and I was put into Holloway Prison. At first I slept in a tiny cell which was very dark and dingy and I only slept for a little while because I was so worried about what was going to happen to me tomorrow.

When morning came, I was taken into a room in which there were a table, a doctor holding a long tube, a large container filled with some hot liquid, and three wardresses.

I suddenly realised what was going to happen and struggled hard to get out, but I was overpowered by the wardresses and dragged to the table on which I was laid. I was held down by the wardresses while the doctor forced a long tube up my nose. I screamed, not only with pain, but also fright, for I thought that I would surely die if this pipe went any further. My nose was throbbing and bleeding very fast on the inside. Then the tube went high up to the top of my nose and down on into my throat. I heaved with sickly pain. I thought that I couldn't survive another minute of it. I could hardly breathe and I felt as though I was being strangled from the inside. Then the tube was shoved into my stomach. I was burning all over and my head was throbbing. I tried to vomit it up but it was shoved down still further. Then suddenly my inside burned so much that I half believed that boiling oil was being poured down into me. At last the liquid reached my stomach and my whole body shook so much that I thought my bones were going to whizz off and I thought that I would be glad because then there would be an end to this terrible pain. If I was about to die, then the prison would probably be in trouble for letting such a thing happen.

By this time one of the wardresses was crying, and I wondered if she was sorry for me.

As the red hot liquid kept pouring into me, and I kept vomiting it back up, I felt as though I was being tortured to death, for I did not believe for one minute that I would live through this terrible day, and as they dragged me out, I screamed for God to save me from this tremendous pain, and I hoped that I would die before the next feeding time came.

I was left in my filthy cell, in my bloody clothes, just lying

there feeling worse than I had ever felt before, in my whole life.
I could hear the screaming from the next cell as they dragged
Betty Clover into the force-feeding room. I could do nothing at all,
I didn't even have the strength to cry.

Dawn Mitchell

Another girl imagined the same incident, but added the
reaction of one of the Holloway wardresses:

Forcible Feeding

Cell doors banging, the keys clanging, footsteps getting nearer to
my cell. While force feeding is taking place screaming and shouting
going on. You could almost feel the gag opening your jaws wider
and wider and then the tube going down deeper and deeper. The
food trickles down the tube and then up again.

My own fight with the wardress begins. I try to get up but my
legs are weak like a new born calf. The wooden gag is put into my
mouth. I fight. Then the steel gag is used, my jaws cracking with
the force of it. I fight once more, the four wardresses holding me
down with a struggle. The doctor announces that the tube should
be placed up my nose and down into my stomach. The sound of
that made me vomit again and again. Because of this, the doctor
said it would have to take place tomorrow.

That twenty-four hours in the dark cell I was praying for the
world to stop still.

Derilyn Savage

I Was The Wardress

Tears of anger in her eyes, clenching fists that are trying to fight
the struggle and pain. Strapped to the bed with her head hung back
and the gag forced in her mouth. The tube forced painfully down
as far as it can go. I will never forget the shouts and screams that
echo still in the back of my mind.

Shadows appear on the walls
But they soon fade away
But I'll never forget those women
I have seen through night and day.

As I sit wondering aloud and remember that I was the wardress.

Derilyn Savage

And Tony, 12, empathised with equal power in his short poem, even though, at the time of the incident he writes about, his ancestors were living on the Rock of Gibraltar.

Force Feeding

Their feet came stamping on the stone floor,
Their feet banging like the sounds of war,
The pipe in my throat ripped and tore,
They left my cell, I fell to the floor.
I wish they wouldn't come any more,
They'll come tomorrow, it's their kind of law,
I wish they wouldn't come any more.

Tony Brown

Brian and Lynton, the latter from St. Lucia, stretched themselves back to the rent strikes that East London women had organised during the First World War. Men were learning too from the historical struggles of women.

Once there was a rent strike,
The people would not pay.
This the council did not like,
But the tenants had their way.

'Mr Landlord, you will get no rent
Until from the war our men are sent,
As you know, we all hate you,
So Mr Landlord, you know what you can do.

For the rent, us you will not catch —
So Mr Landlord, go and have a scratch!'

Brian Dillon

Fair Rent

While our men are fighting to keep your houses and us safe,
You fight us with the rent which you know we cannot pay.
Why don't you show some gratitude to the men so brave?
By lowering the rent for widows grieving.
But no, no, no, you say, things are bad for you
You have wives and kids, and don't know what to do.

We ask for a shilling off, is it but too much?
But no, no, no, you say, things are bad for you
You have wives and kids, and don't know what to do.
Now Mr Landlord, you leave us with no choice,
So please Mr Landlord, don't be offended —
Don't come for the rent until the war is ended!

Lynton Popo

We stayed with the Great War and studied its effect
on the domestic lives of East End people. The children's
compassion was clearly moved by the story of the
bombing of Upper North Street primary school in Poplar
in 1917. On a sunny few days in Spring we took our
classes to the local park, Poplar Park, and told the story
of the bomb attack next to the commemorative statue
with the names of the children who were killed carved
upon it. Some of the same names survived in our own
class registers. Juerline, from Jamaica, and Dawn again,
got to work in the classroom as soon as we had returned
to the school.

I was a pupil in White Polc School. It was in 1917 when the
bombing started. The school was having lessons. Just then there
was a big jerk, the whole school shook. The children started to
panic, big flames were shooting in. Our class was the hardest to
get out of the building. I was stuck, my legs got caught in a
broken desk. We were panicking more. The place rumbled, bricks
fell down. One of the pupils got killed, one was flooded in blood.
The whole place was going to collapse in a few minutes. We were
soon being pulled out. Some of us came out flooding blood, some
dead.

I of course, had to wait. I was worried about my mother and
father, I came out with two broken legs. Some of the boys and
girls had their's blown off. I reached the hospital. I was so sick to
see so many children crying and screaming. I was afraid to see if
my mum and dad were there, but there was no sign of them, if
they were dead or alive.

Juerline Ingram

The Day 'The Ceiling Fell In'

When I was five years old, I was sitting in the little classroom in Upper North Street School, being very bored with the maths lesson I was having, when all of a sudden there was a loud bang and the ceiling came crashing down on top of us. There was a great confusion and a huge wooden beam came crashing down on the girl next to me. I screamed and ran. The teachers were trying to achieve order in the playground as I ran past them, and a teacher called me back, but I was too frightened to listen, so I just kept on running and running. As I was rushing out of the class, I can faintly remember a boy trying to pull himself out from under a beam, and a sudden crash of the remaining pieces of the ceiling as it fell on top of him.

Eventually, I ran out of breath and had to stop, not knowing where I was, for, I'd run far away from my home. I sat down on a low brick wall and with my head in my hands, I sobbed and sobbed, very confused and extremely terrified until an old man came up to me and asked me what was wrong.

I was very excited and I couldn't speak at first. Then I told him about my friend, Rose Tuffin, and the boy, Alfred. He asked me where I lived, and when I told him, he took me home. When I got home, my mother thanked the man for bringing me, after she'd finished crying. I wondered why she was crying, because I was home then, so she should've been happy, I thought. I don't remember what else happened that day, just that William, my brother, never came home that night, and I was sent to bed early.

The next day, I asked my mother if I could go and play with my friend Rose Tuffin, but my mother told me that she'd 'gone away'. I asked her where to? My mother just said, to the good place, where angels go. I argued with mother, saying Rose was in school when the 'ceiling fell down'. Then I remembered where the angels were. I was very unhappy that day, and stayed at home for about a week, then I went out into the park where I met a friend of mine. She told me that eighteen children had been killed, and I knew then that my brother and Rose were two of them. We both sat down and cried for about three hours. Then she went home, and I saw a boy who was in my class.

He told me about the bomb and he said that my brother had been killed when a brick had knocked him out, and then the room had caved in. I moaned at the boy for making me get upset again. And then I went and sat on a swing and as I slowly swinged, I snivelled gently at the loss of my only brother and best friend. At lunchtime, I went home for lunch and my mother was sitting in the corner crying. I asked her what was the matter, even though I knew really. She told me that she was 'alright', and after lunch, I went back to the park.

Dawn Mitchell

From the papers and journals of the period, we had learned that when the soldiers returned from the trenches they were promised 'a land fit for heroes to live in'. They found unemployment, hardship and low wages, and the British Government involved in the wars of intervention against the young workers' republic in Russia. Quickly, a 'Hands Off Russia' movement began amongst British trade unionists, with the support of active socialist campaigners like George Lansbury, Harry Pollitt and Sylvia Pankhurst. In 1920, London dockers in the East India docks refused to load the munitions ship 'The Jolly George', which was bound for Poland to be used against the Russians in the wars of intervention. This was an event of inspiring Internationalism. Working people in one country were actively supporting those of another, linking with contemporary acts of international solidarity, such as Liverpool seamen refusing to crew ships bound for Chile in 1975. Jackie, a fourteen-year-old girl from the Isle of Dogs re-lived the 'Jolly George' event, becoming a docker in the East India Dock, now ironically enough, a container park. And from the Caribbean and Ghana, Lynton and Andrew took incidents from Pollitt's autobiography, *Serving My Time,* and re-charged them with their own imaginations.

The Jolly George

My name is Jack Smith and I work at the East India Dock. Me and my mates shovel coal onto the 'Jolly George', and without us this ship would not go. One day we were shovelling coal on board when we heard some men talking about a revolution. My mate and me tried to find out more about it, but nobody would tell us anything. I told my mate that my wife might know something about it because she sells newspapers, and she knows all what goes on in the world. We finished work at six o'clock. I ran straight home and told my wife what I had heard. She said there was a revolution in Russia and all the poor people had taken over from the rich snobs. I said, 'I wish it could happen here.' My wife said, 'No change, the government are already trying to stop the one in Russia, so that not too many people hear about it.' 'How are they going to stop it?' I said. My wife told me that they were shipping guns, bullets, clothes and other arms over to Poland so that the Polish could fight the poor Russian people. When I got into work the next day I found out that they were using the 'Jolly George' to ship arms over to Poland. I told my mates who were also working on the 'Jolly George', and we all decided not to shovel coal onto the ship. And in the end the 'Jolly George' did not move.

Jackie Hart

The Ramming of the Neptune

We left the harbour as planned. The ship was beginning to gather steam when I called a few of the crew. As I spoke to some men, more and more men came to hear what I was saying, and it was not long before there was a bit commotion going on deck. The Captain came down to hear what was going on. The story was put before him and the argument grew hotter and hotter. Soon all the crew were up on deck to make a decision.

Something the crew did not know was that they had no choice about going to Poland to supply munitions to fight against their fellow workers in Russia, because as the argument was going on the ship was unmanned and was careering all over the place.

In the end, another ship collided with the 'Neptune' and half sank her. She was towed to port and there she stayed. This was one step forward to helping the Russian Revolution.

Lynton Popo

Hands Off Russia!

HARRY POLLITT: I am not loading these for the Polish!

MANAGER: You're sacked Pollitt. Now get out of my sight before I throw you out.

HARRY POLLITT: You just try it Mister, and see what you get manager.

1st WORKER: Poor Pollitt, he was such a good worker.

2nd WORKER: And a good friend to have around.

One day Pollitt went to Speakers' Corner at Hyde Park. As he is making a speech —

HARRY POLLITT: Do you want to be knocked about by your foremen and managers, who are trying to smuggle arms to the Polish soldiers to be used against ordinary working men like yourselves with wives and kids in Russia?

Andrew Ohene

In 1921 the Poplar Labour Council had refused to put up the local rates because of the enormous hardship faced by the people who had elected them into office. Inspired by their most senior councillor, the pioneer socialist George Lansbury, they were summoned to the High Court. Yet they still refused to levy the increase. The entire Council was subsequently imprisoned, the men in Brixton Prison, the women in Holloway.[24] This 'Poplarism' of the council in standing by their principles, created a huge campaign for their release. After they were freed from jail by the force of public pressure, the burden of the rates was more equitably levied all over the London boroughs. Dawn wrote a particularly strong poem about Lansbury:

George Lansbury

George Lansbury made speeches
Through the prison bars,
Although he was a councillor,
He did not drive posh cars.

For he was just a working man,
And upper class he hates,
For he was put into a cell
For preventing rising rates.

He spoke to many people
Although he was in jail.
He told them not to worry,
For they would never fail.

He said, quite soon the government
Would have to set them free,
For they had many people
And public sympathy.

Just as George predicted,
The Government gave in,
And George and all his councillors
Were 'forgiven' for their 'sin'!

He said they had a meeting room,
And keys to their own cells,
As everybody listened
To what he had to tell.

He said to many people
That he was not ashamed —
The man proud to be guilty,
George Lansbury he was named.

Dawn Mitchell

And other pieces came via St. Lucia, Pakistan and Jamaica:

P eople of Poplar, we are not going to raise the rates
O r let the Government come through the gates!
P olitics is our game.
L et the governors try to raise it, we'll not collect.
A nother thing we have to say,
R apping our troubles away,
I am going to court today —
S o goodbye, I may be there to stay,
M ake an effort to visit us, and we'll keep them all at bay!

Ted John

George Lansbury's Speech from Brixton Prison

Welcome my fellow friends. We men have demanded to have our own cell doors unlocked and unlocked they will be. Why should we be treated like criminals? We are only innocent men. We know what we have in our hearts is good and not evil and good cannot mix with evil like water will not mix with dirt.

We shall again breathe the freshness of freedom like all others. We are not different. After this imprisonment we are again going to fight for our equal rights. Why should we pay for what we have already paid? We shall protest against the government and win we shall my loyal friends. Now go home and make ready my friends, we shall meet soon.

Shahbaz Rana

George Lansbury's Speech from Brixton Prison Windows
(Arrested September 1st, 1921)

Greetings, my people of Poplar, brothers and sisters.

I have justly demanded for us to be treated as normal people, not criminals, but people who have been unjustly wronged, cheated out of trying to reduce the rates of poor, homeless people.

All of you who are here this day have no fear of us being badly treated. We have open cells, a cell to discuss our problems in, and we have exercises in the yard. We are staying put in this prison for the unemployed people who are being forced to pay nearly all their wages for the keep of their homes. That's why we took this step and we are not going to purge our contempt.

We thank all of you for your loyal support, and for trying to prevent any more arrests, but we can deal with these for ourselves. Try to keep up your faith and courage for as long as you can hold.

We have constant visits from the Town Hall officials, with forms to sign and discuss. We soon will be released.

So go home people, and we will go further into details tomorrow.

Cherie Brown

Finally, Rita, from a Greek Cypriot family, and Jackie again, wrote imagining themselves as two of the women councillors: Nellie Cressall, who went to jail despite her advanced pregnancy, and Minnie Lansbury, who still went to jail even though she knew she was dying.

Nellie Cressall's Story

My name is Nellie Cressall, and I am a Poplar councillor. My husband's name is Joe, and he is also a councillor. We were summoned to the High Court on July 29th, 1921, with a load of other councillors. We were summoned to go to court because we had refused to put up the rates, and the judges called it contempt of court. They said we would have to go to prison until we put the rates up. I knew that I was going to have a baby but I still went to prison. On the day they took the women councillors to Holloway Prison there were enormous crowds. There was also a band. Next day 15,000 people marched to Holloway Prison to cheer us for going to prison. There was one woman councillor who I thought was very brave, because she did not have long to live. Her name was Minnie Lansbury. Minnie and I were released on an earlier date than the rest of the prisoners because I was going to have a

213

baby, and Minnie was nearly dying. The other councillors still did not raise the rates, and the authorities were no nearer to getting their money. The longer the councillors stayed in prison the more public sympathy they got. In the end, the councillors got out of prison and they did not raise the rates. I was glad that it was all over and that I could have my baby in comfort with my husband. I knew the risks I took going into prison. Because with all that excitement I could have had a miscarriage. But I still went to prison.

Jackie Hart

A Letter from Minnie Lansbury to her Father-in-law

Dearest Father,

As you well know father dear, I am writing to you from Holloway Prison. With me in the prison is Nellie Cressall, who is about to have a child. Father dear, I have not told anyone yet of my serious illness — Father I am going to die. That is why I will not surrender our cause. I gave a speech yesterday saying that we should not give in. Why should the people of Poplar pay more rates? The government cannot hurt me or tell me to behave or make me do as they want, for I will die soon. I am sorry I have not told you sooner. I cannot tell Edgar as I cannot bear to leave him. I have never been happier than I have been with your son, even though I have not and never can give him a child. During my last few months I will try to help in this fight which we have undertaken. Father, when I die, please carry on with what you are doing for a good as ours. We must win. I will never forget you or Edgar. Please tell him of my illness as I most probably will not see you again. Remember me as I will always remember you, dearest Father, the best father-in-law any woman could ever have.

All my love,
Minnie

Rita Elefteriou

When we came to the General Strike of 1926,[25] we were lucky enough to have, as one of the teachers in our team, a man who had lived through the nine days, and had supported the strike as a schoolboy. Bill, the teacher, spoke about the event with a lively and authentic use of anecdote and recollection. He told how he, and all his friends, had gone to school on the first day of the strike

with red ties to show their solidarity with the strikers —
and how they had all been sent home for wearing
improper school uniforms! As soon as he had finished
his talk, we got a quick and very enthusiastic response:

My Childhood in 1926

It was on May 4th, 1926. It was a lovely sunny morning. I woke up
at about 6 o'clock. I could not hear the milkman rattling his
bottles, so I went and looked out of the window. I could not see
any people at the baker's. There was no buses rushing past. Instead,
all you could hear was the birds singing in the trees. I got dressed
and went downstairs. No one was up yet, so I went into the
kitchen. My dad's coat was on the door and his sandwiches still on
the table. I went back upstairs to see if my mum was awake. I went
into my parents' room. My mum was still asleep but my dad was
sitting by the table.

'What is it dad, what's up?' I said.

'Everybody's on strike. Everybody. The milkman, the baker, the
postman and me,' he said.

'Are you going on a march,' I said.

'Yes, when I've told your mother we're on strike,' he said.

'Will I still have to go to school?' I said.

'Yes,' he said.

I went downstairs and had my breakfast and got ready for
school. My father told me to wear something red to show that I
belonged to a striker's family. So I put red ribbons in my hair. It
was now half-past eight, so I went and knocked for my mate. She
was also wearing red ribbons in her hair, and so were all the other
girls. We all bought a copy of the 'British Worker', which cost us
one penny. When we got into school we all got told off and had to
go and see the headmaster. He said he would not have any of this
silliness and wasting of money in his school, and he sent us home.
When I got home and told my father, he was very proud of me. In
the afternoon my mates and I went up to London. (We hitch-hiked
all the way to Mile End.) The traffic was piling up all along Mile
End Road. All the office workers who worked up the City were
trying to get to work, but they could not. The strike lasted for nine
days, and I did not have any fresh bread or milk for nine days.

Jackie Hart

215

Playing Truant

I woke up in the morning,
Everything was bare.
I went to get my breakfast
And to comb my scruffy hair.

I looked out the window,
I could not see a moving thing,
Not even a big dirty dog
Clattering on a tin.

I put on my school clothes
And a red tie,
It dangles all about
From my neck down to my flies.

Then I hear my mate coming,
Walking in the road.
He knocks at the door, I let him in,
And he shouts at my pet toad.

We set off on our way
To try and hitch a lift,
Then a coach of posh people going —
Oh what a whiff!

They stop and pick us up
And then we move again.
We come to Gardiner's Corner
Where there's not a single moving tram.

Then we see hundreds of people
And they won't let us pass.
They try to rock the coach —
So we get off it fast.

Then one posh person gets off the coach,
'Let us get to work, you stinking filthy dummy.
You pigs may be striking
But we want to earn some money.'

Then a big strong worker
Whose muscles are like steam-rollers,
Stretches the man's hat over his head
And made it five bits of a bowler!

Philip Stanley

Stopping the Blacklegs (1926)

Two big lines of policemen were waiting for the fight,
We said, 'We'll stop the blacklegs, we'll try with all our might.
They won't work in these docks and break up our strike.
And soon the messenger boy will come round on his bike,
I hope he hurries up, the lazy little tyke.'
And now the boy approaches, shouting long and loud,
'They're coming, they're coming, a great big crowd!'
We fight and we struggle and drive them away,
We have won a victory, the crowd all cheer, 'HOORAY!'

Tony Brown

The East End dockers' resistance to blackleg labour
during the General Strike is well dramatised in Mervyn
Jones' novel, *Holding On.* We read the section in the
book where a striker's daughter is taken out for dinner
by a blackleg bus conductor in the City. A Jamaican girl
wrote her own version of the incident.

A Meal With a Blackleg

Walking down the road, thinking what to do,
When I saw an 86 and jumped on it.
I saw a blackleg on the bus,
And he started to chat me up.
I couldn't tell him to go away,
I was too afraid.

He asked me out, I couldn't shout,
I couldn't refuse.
We went down the cafe,
His name was Geoff,
He was a blackleg,
What would my parents say?
We were poor,
But we had to work hard.

He could afford a lot of money
But I couldn't take it.
He told the waitress to bring out the tray —
He brought me strawberries and trifle,
I felt like a fool.

I threw down the trifle
I threw down the strawberries
I walked out the cafe
Without looking round.
I had to leave him
For I didn't love him
So why go with him?

I saw my dad,
I think he saw me.
I started to run.
I never saw that blackleg again.

Jennifer Kandekore

In another class, a local white boy and a black boy
born in St. Vincent were sitting together, each of them
writing about the General Strike. The white boy
composed this song to the tune of 'Bye Bye Blackbird':

The Blackleg (1926)

There was a scab who was no good,
He drove a bus, he thought he was good —
Bye, bye blackleg.

He saw a girl one day,
He thought she was a bit okay,
Bye, bye blackleg.

He took her to one of those posh places,
She thought she was in one of those oases.
The waiter comes in with the bill,
She tells the blackleg to go to Hell —
Blackleg, bye bye.

Alan Elderton

The Vincentian boy however, objected to the use of the
word 'blackleg'. He saw no reason why a man who
betrays his workmates in a strike should be labelled
'black'. He asked if 'scabber' could be used instead of the
word 'blackleg', and wrote this song, which he sung out
defiantly and smilingly at his friend:

218

The General Strike Scabbers

Nice one Charlie
Nice one son
Nice one Charlie
That copper's on the run.
Come on dockers
Come on sons
Come on dockers
Let's take them both at once.

Scabbers are chickens
Scabbers run
Scabbers I've looked for
But scabbers are gone!

Well done dockers
They're all gone
We'll keep striking
Till Justice is done.
Dad's gone striking
Mum's gone too
Brother's going,
I'm going too . . .
When we get them scabbers
We'll stick 'em in the zoo!

Freddie Franklin

With the current growth of organised racism in the
neighbourhood, it was imperative for us, as teachers, to
evoke the East End's inspiring anti-fascist history. Many
would say that this had culminated in 1936 at Cable
Street, when thousands of local people: Jewish,
unemployed and local trade unionists, had united to
prevent Sir Oswald Mosley's fascist blackshirts from
marching through a predominantly Jewish area.[26] We
discovered an anonymous ballad which had been printed
as a broadsheet years before our time, and had been sold
in thousands and passed around the local community as
a celebration of the events of 1936. We duplicated this
poem, and read it with the children:

The Battle of Cable Street

You ask me how I got like this, Sir,
Well I don't care to say,
But I will tell you a little story
Of when I was in a big fray.

I'm not very well in my old age,
And as I sits drinking my broth,
My mind goes back to 1936,
That Sunday, October the fourth.

I was walking down Bethnal Green Road, Sir,
Just walking about at my ease,
When the strains of a famous old song, Sir,
Came floating to me on the breeze.

I stopped, I looked and I listened,
Now where have I heard that old song?
Then I dashed to the Salmon and Ball, Sir
I knew I wouldn't go wrong.

It was the Internationale they were singing,
They were singing it with a defiant blast,
And holding up a big red banner
With these words: 'THEY SHALL NOT PASS'.

We then marched on to the East End,
We were five thousand of us, I am sure.
And when we got to the Aldgate,
We were met by three hundred thousand more.

'Red Front! Red Front!' these workers cried,
It was a sight I wouldn't have missed
To see these thousands of defiant workers
Holding up their Mighty Clenched Fist.

The police said 'Now move along, please,
This is all we ask',
But we said 'No, not for those Blackshirts,
Those rotters, THEY SHALL NOT PASS'.

We then marched on to Stepney Green, Sir,
You could see that this fight was no sham,
For there were thousands and thousands of workers
Marching from Limehouse, Poplar, Stratford and East Ham.

You could see that Mosley wouldn't get through, Sir,
That our slogan that day was no boast,
And I shouted 'Hip, hip hurrah',
As I saw our flag being tied to a lamp-post.

The children shouted from the windows 'O, golly',
For Mosley no-one seemed sorry,
But someone had had the goodness
To lend us their two-ton lorry.

We got it over on its side, Sir,
It wasn't much of a strain,
But the police kept knocking our barricade down
So we built the damn thing up again.

The police said we worked mighty fast,
As with a hanky their faces they mopped,
So we got out our big red banner,
And stuck it right on the top.

The police then charged with their truncheons.
They charged us, the working class,
But they couldn't pinch our red banner
With these words THEY SHALL NOT PASS.

I wish you had been there to see it,
You would have said it was a ruddy fine feat,
How we kept that old Red Flag flying
On those barricades of Cable Street.

So this is the end of my story
And I must get back to my broth,
But I hope you will never forget, Sir,
It was Sunday, October the fourth.

The Tramp Poet

One girl imagined herself as a Jewish child, suddenly
caught in the conflict:

Behind the Barricades

One day my mum sent me down the shop, to get a cheese cake.
On the way back there was a big fight going on. People were
hiding behind barricades, breaking windows, nicking fruit and
throwing it. From where I was, it looked a bad sight. I saw a man
with his head split open in half. I ran behind a barricade and hid, I
got too scared.

Then along came the police, there were about 5,000 police
there, 3,000 fascists and 500,000 people. The street was packed
out, you couldn't even move. Then all of a sudden I heard an
ambulance speed round the corner. There were so many
ambulances because there were so many people hurt. Over the
other side I saw banners rising up in the air with this written on

221

them: 'THEY SHALL NOT PASS'. Then the policemen went and gave in. Sir Oswald Mosley thought that the blackshirts would get through, but they didn't. Sir Oswald Mosley's men couldn't get through so they went away. It seemed like it went on for ever. When everyone went home, the place was in a terrible mess.

Theresa Braithwaite

And two other girls, with simple profundity, expressed in their poems the power of determination that had stopped the blackshirts:

Memories of Cable Street

They blamed it onto the Jews,
They said, 'Put them into the zoos.'
They were fighting in Cable Street
And a little Jewish kid got beat.
The working men would not let them in,
They said that Mosley should be put in the dustbin.
They made a fuss,
They turned over a bus.
They kept the blackshirts away,
And that was how they won that day.

Cheryl Wakenell

They Shall Not Pass

They shall not pass, I swear to God.
They shall not pass 'cause Mosley
Thinks he's the great dictator,
While Mosley lives with his blackshirt army.

They shall not pass, we'll not let them —
For all they've done, so why should we let them?

They shall not pass
We also have an army,
But our army has a difference,
We fight for the Jews and our families.

We're going to win, I know we shall,
Because Good has power over the Bad.

Christine Duffy

222

Andrew, from Ghana, gave an impressive sense of witness in his acrostic:

B obbies, workers, — Mosley and his men
A ttempt to overcome the Jews.
T runcheons, bodies flying about,
T rampling, shouting, that's what they do —
L eading to be the British Hitler, that's Mosley.
E ast End people would not accept this!

O ther men went off with their banners,
F earless men kicking and pushing the others.

C able Street like a rubbish dump,
A rrested men struggling to get away,
B odies lying about, people bleeding,
L ow-paid workers being clubbed,
E ven ladies and children throwing things.

S treets, pavements being dug up for shields.
T he traffic was blocked, cars smashed —
R eally some of the workers' heads were split open.
E arlier that day the streets were ruined.
E ast End looked like it was being bombed,
T errible things happened that day!

Andrew Ohene

And Allison, a white girl, contemporized the struggle for all of us, black, brown and white, working in the same classroom:

Our Black Brothers

Brown, black, white or red
We must all go to work to earn our bread,
Either day in a factory
Or night in a train
In a boiling hot sun or a freezing cold rain

We can't afford to make a fuss
Who works on our roads or drives a bus,
Cause if we do
They'll all go back
And England will be useless, and that's a fact.

223

England called, and thank God it did,
Cause they've helped our country to earn a few quid,
In East End and West End
And Country too
The black man's our hero, who made our towns new.

Allison Ayres

We finished our work on local history by thinking and writing about the Blitz. We read one boy's grandfather's account of the bombing of the East India Dock in 1940, when he had been an air-raid warden. He described how the bombs had damaged Poplar Hospital, opposite the dock gates.[27] A Jamaican girl, Cherie, imagined herself as a patient at the time in the hospital — now closed down by Government 'economies'. It was strange to us that a local hospital which had withstood nazi bombs, was now being killed off by a British 'Labour' government. Again, Cherie's 'eyewitness' strength seems hugely authentic:

The Terrifying Experience When I Was in Poplar Hospital When The Blitz Was On

Years ago, when the Blitz was on, the daily raids occurred. I had been badly injured, and as a result, I was sent to Poplar Hospital. The whistle of the flying bombs, the horrid deafening sound of violence, destruction, disaster to all mankind.

This is how I felt at the time. I was terrified, thinking of a day when a bomb would hit the hospital. This happened just a few hours after thinking this thought. Blood and fire everywhere, dead and injured bodies lying on the floor, glass and rubble flying everywhere. I was screaming. Then I was hit by a piece of wood and knocked unconscious.

Hours afterwards I had awoken, still I saw agony and pain surrounding me. In the shelters I could still hear the bomb raids. My best pal's leg had been blown off, and I had seen this happen with my own two eyes! 'Oh God!' what a sight! Those fires were terrifying, especially to me, lying in a hospital, helpless.

Nothing much happened to me — I lost a hand, that's all. How people suffered then! It could never happen again like that.

Cherie Brown

And Tony, from St. Lucia, followed with another
acrostic:

T he bombs are falling
H eaven is where some of the people are going.
E veryone gets shocked, and everyone gets frightened.

B ombing is something terrible,
O ver every house they come
M ore and more they bomb and bomb,
B ombs get far, bombs get near,
S ometimes they get right on the spot.

A ll the people running to the shelters,
R eturn to their homes after the bombing has stopped,
E veryone's in danger, they never get any sleep.

F athers are all gone to the war,
A ll their sons are following them there,
L eaving their homes because they haven't got any,
L eaving their children to go somewhere else.
I n London it was a terrible place,
N ever was it so terrible in all the days
G o away Hitler, and let our country be!

Tony Amable

'Our country', he says, his childhood spent in Laborie,
St. Lucia, and now living in Bow, London, E.3. His
family were living on a small island in the Caribbean
when the events in London he writes about took place.
And his country it is, and the country of all our
children, no matter their origins or colour. As much as
local, white East London children had proved their
willingness and ability to extend their knowledge,
feelings and sense of witness to Oman, Chile, Wounded
Knee, Johannesburg, Namibia, Zimbabwe or Dominica,
so children from all over the world were being enfolded
by the history of the area which was now dominating
their lives and becoming their home. They were being
introduced to the heroes of their now local history – the
working people of East London, like themselves and their
families.

225

When these events, which they had studied, re-lived and shared in through their English lessons were actually happening, their parents and forebears were living and working in Jamaica, St. Lucia, Cyprus, Karachi, Dacca, Dublin, Ghana and Uganda. And yet through the power of their own social love and empathy they had reciprocated the embrace of history. And out of that embrace is created the knowledge, which if applied and dynamized, leads towards freedom. We had seen that knowledge and humanity are dialectical. They cannot exist, and cannot move forward without each other. As teachers and students we push them forward together, interlocking with each other at every step, thrusting aside the mystifications and forces that try to divert us or break us apart. For us, nothing smaller than the world is our classroom, and nothing less than humanity will be our class.

We were not defining ourselves merely by race or geographical origin. It was not enough to be white or black — that definition was divisive, incomplete, absurd. It was our acceptance of *class* that was welding us together and giving us new learning muscles, and our gathering knowledge of belonging to the continuing struggles of working people of the past and present all over the world, for a more just and loving world.[28] Yet we had not stared at Utopia in our classrooms. We had surrounded ourselves with, and seen the reality, the suffering and courage that had caused other men and women to heave themselves forwards — not as individuals who scramble amongst each other and use each other's heads as rungs in a ladder — but as the oppressed, as a class, united and organised. Our classrooms had become crucibles in that process, creating new knowledge, new energy, new conviction, synthesising the experience and dynamism of a certain future: finally socialist, ultimately human.

Background notes

Contents

Note	Page		Note	Page
1	—	231	15	—	253
2	—	232	16	—	156
3	—	233	17	—	258
4	—	235	18	—	260
5	—	236	19	—	261
6	—	237	20	—	264
7	—	238	21	—	269
8	—	239	22	—	274
9	—	240	23	—	275
10	—	243	24	—	275
11	—	243	25	—	276
12	—	245	26	—	279
13	—	245	27	—	283
14	—	247	28	—	286

This appendix has been compiled with the purpose of giving a fuller picture of the resources we used to prompt and stimulate the children to write creatively.

We found that it was possible to tap countless resources already within the community: from the local History room in the Public Library with its past journals, newspapers, photographs and prints, to contemporary local and national papers, unpublished local poems and those in anthologies, writers and trade unionists in the neighbourhood, folk songs and singers, parents, brothers and sisters and grandparents of the children themselves, and the very buildings, streets and industrial monuments that still stood in the area.

In this way, as teachers and pupils we were becoming our own researchers and academics into the history and culture of the neighbourhood, taking from the hidden cultural richness of the streets that were our home, from the people who came before us and from the other peoples now with us or from all over the world with whom we empathised. We were creating our own curriculum, discovering and uncovering our own texts and literature, and applying them directly to our teaching method and practice with the children who were the true owners and inheritors of this knowledge.

1 The latest front page story of bigoted bitterness in the local paper, the *East London Advertiser* (20/8/76), reads as follows:

'WE WON'T BE FORCED OUT', SAY FAMILY.
ASIANS' HOME SET ON FIRE.

A young Asian family claim they are the victims of a race-hate campaign after their home was set alight on Monday evening. They say the attack came after they were warned they would be burnt out.

Mrs Sandra Karim said after the fire: 'We shall not be moved. No one is going to force us out of here because we are Asians . . . we will fight back.'

The family are squatting in a mobile home at Cranberry Street, Bethnal Green. They returned home late on Monday to find the building on fire. Debris had been piled round the building and ignited, paraffin poured through the letter box had been set on fire, burning the door and carpet.

Mrs Karim, 17, said: 'We got back just as the fire brigade were putting out the fire. We have had a lot of trouble and threats since we moved in two weeks ago. A man told us they are not having "Pakis" on the estate and they are going to burn us out. These people think that all Asians are meek and they won't fight back. But we are not going to be forced out . . . we are staying.

'I may be an Asian, but I was born and bred in the East End and I can fight too. There was an Asian family in this house before we came here . . . but they were forced out by threats and bitterness. They left after all the windows were smashed in. We have put up boards in the windows now. The place is smashed up a bit and just before the fire I was thinking of moving out. But I am not going to move out now and let them think they've won.'

Mrs Karim's son, Paul, aged 20 months, is being looked after by a relative. 'I can't have him here while all this trouble is going on, at any time bricks could be thrown in and he could be injured,' she said.

Mr Abdul Karim, 23, said threats of violence have also been made against a relative who lives nearby and another Asian family on the estate.

Mrs Karim's sister, Miriam Ruzzaman, 29, lives in Anglesea Street, a stone's throw from the burnt home. 'I had a parcel sent to me just after I moved here,' she said. 'I thought it could be a bomb so I called the police. When they opened it there was a piece of old carpet and a note which said, "I wish you a short life here." Then someone threw bricks at the windows as I was putting my daughter to bed . . . one just missed her.'

Bethnal Green Police are investigating the fire. A spokesman said: 'It was recorded as a fire in suspicious circumstances.'

2 A particularly strong example of the cynicism of the established media appears as I collate this appendix. From the 'T.V. Page' of the mass circulation newspaper, *The Sun,* (21/8/76) comes this story — a complete surrender to racism.

'SPIKE COPS OUT.' 'I'M ASHAMED OF MY NEW HIT SHOW' HE SAYS.

Spike Milligan has given up. Copped out. Dropped out of what he considered was his personal campaign against race-hate.

Milligan — mad comic, original Goon, friend of royalty — told me this week: 'I'm 58. Late middle-age. And I've had enough. I'm now convinced there'll never be racial toleration in Britain. Or integration. I believe there's going to be a racial explosion. I've done my best with my preaching. But I've failed.' So . . . what happens now?

Milligan has decided to demonstrate his sense of defeat by making a new comedy series. A series which could make him rich. A series which he claims to despise before it is ever shown. The new show, based on a Comedy Playhouse programme of a year ago, is called 'The Melting Pot' . . .

And Milligan, who became famous for being way-out and different, confessed: 'We have deliberately written a comedy series like all the other hit television comedy series . . . It's all there. References to niggers, wops and wogs. That's what gets the laughs today. I'm hating every minute of it. I'm contemptuous of myself. But that's what people want. I believe 'The Melting Pot' will be a great success. It may get into the Top 20. And I'll be ashamed. But I'm not going to end up on the dole at Finchley Labour Exchange.'

'The Melting Pot' is about two Pakistanis, illegal immigrants who live in an Irishman's boarding house. Other inmates include a Chinese cockney, an Arab with a Scots accent and a ghastly old Australian bigot — played by Australian-born Bill Kerr, 46. He is a worse racialist than Alf Garnett. Hates the blacks, the Irish, the Jews, the British poms, the police and his own mother.

'This series won't do a thing to improve race relations or make people more tolerant,' Milligan said. 'Nothing I can do or say will do that. Sometimes I make remarks like "nignogs" or "wogs" — just to see people's reactions. Generally their eyes light up. They say: "You're dead right. We don't want them here. Clear them out." '

The producer of 'The Melting Pot' is 50-year-old Ian MacNaughton . . . He said, 'I agree with Spike. Our aim in the series is to make people laugh . . .'

3 One of the teachers who had regularly supported these pickets wrote this poem, which was duplicated, handed round and read in class with the children. It is a much less forced activity for children to write poetry if they

know their teachers are writing it also, and are not afraid
to show and read it to them.

The Railway Tavern

Now friends of all races, of all coloured faces,
A story I have here to tell —
Of a man who was biased, whose prejudice tried us
And made us as angry as hell!

This man kept a tavern, 'The Railway Tavern'
In a street down in Mile End Old Town.
And heaven preserve us, the cad wouldn't serve us
If our faces were black, tan or brown.

We wouldn't take that, that was too much old hat,
We knew we just had to unite,
So we mounted our pickets because this wasn't cricket,
And stood by the pub in the night.

He tried to deter us, threw boiling water o'er us,
But that only steeled our resolve,
Because it is oft said, that black and white comrades
Together will break racist moulds.

And now he's gone from us, no longer among us
To give out his hate and his lies,
And sisters and brothers, black, white and others
Together our lesson we prize.

Don't let them deride us, or seek to divide us,
We're strong hand in hand, side by side.
We'll all make an arch, us, the great working class
And through a rainbow of races we'll ride.

A related story to the 'Railway Tavern' incident was
the 'Colour Bar Strike' in 1957 at Kings Cross locomotive
depot. Charlie Mayo, a fireman at the depot, wrote this
song shortly after the event, with cautionary lyrics
which warned us clearly of the dangers of racism growing
roots in the Trade Union movement:

The Colour-Bar Strike

My union badge shows two joined hands,
With a lighted flame in common fight,
But trouble's brewing in the sheds,
For both these working hands are white.

But working hands are white and black,
And the work they do is all the same;
But prejudice and fear come in,
To break the grip and dim the flame.

The shunters broke the grip one day,
The King's Cross goods-yard went on strike;
Not in a fight for better pay,
But a coloured man they did not like.

They didn't like the coloured man,
They wouldn't work with him they said,
In truth it touched their overtime
And to a colour bar it led.

The colour-bar strikers soon went back,
Jim Figgins led the N.U.R.,
And when they asked for his support,
He said, 'We'll have no colour-bar.'

Jim Figgins said: 'Get back to work
This is a strike we'll not support;
This is the kind of ignorance
The unions have always fought.'

But though the union won that fight,
The pressure's there and rising higher,
Smoke rises in the engine sheds,
And where there's smoke, there's always fire.

Man, don't let smoke get in your eyes,
Kindle that flame and keep it bright,
To proud traditions still be true
And make those joined hands black and white.

Charlie Mayo (Music: Ewan McColl)

4 The poet also read to the children a poem: 'About London'. The evocation of the 'common ground' of humanity sought by poetry was one reason why we attached such huge importance to it.

About London

London I love for Johnson lingered there
Donne preached and Blake saw God
While Milton pondered man and God his ways with man
Have you ever heard the morning sing
The morning sings with Blake

I may walk at ease with these
I shall walk in peace with these
For they were first and always men
Poets tireless to find some common ground where men could meet

This special image poets sought
In special vision Blake once wrought
To capture in simplicity
The simple truth in you and me

Peter Blackman

5 Ulfet's remembrances of Cyprus, her village, and the civil war which caused her to find refuge in England, were very strong. On another occasion, when the class were writing about dreams they had experienced, Ulfet wrote this:

My Dream

Last night I saw my village in my dream. I saw that I was in my home with my family and I was doing a clear up. When I finished clearing up I went to the kitchen to help my mother for cooking dinner. Later on my father came home, and after a minute we prepared the table for eating, I mean we put all the things on the table and it was ready for eating. At the same time there was a wedding party in my village and we wanted to go to that party. When we finished our dinner, I started washing the dishes and everything. As I was doing that, my mother was trying to get ready, until she gets ready I finished the washing up and I started to get ready for the wedding party too. In a short time we were ready for the wedding party and we went to that party. It was very nice party, I liked it very much because it was a really nice party. I was very happy when I went there, but my happiness didn't last long because after half an hour we heard a gun's noises come from the outside. When we heard that noise at once we jumped outside to see what was going on, and when we went outside we heard that somebody killed his friend. Everybody was crying and shouting and when his wife heard that somebody killed her husband, she started to cry and his children too. I was afraid very much when I saw that the man who was dead. He was in the middle of the road and he was covered with his blood. When I saw him like that I started to cry too, and I told my mother, 'Come on Mum, let's go home,' and we went home. But I was still crying.

The next morning my mum called me, 'Wake up and you are
going to be late.' When I wake up I was thinking about my dream.
So my dream is finished.

Ulfet Halil

6 Muhammed Haque, who told the story of his immigration into East London from Bangladesh, is also an
accomplished poet who writes in both English and
Bengali. Shortly after the attack on his council flat home
in the neighbourhood of the school, when his front door
was smashed in and he was cut by flying glass, he wrote
this poem.

How Do You Feel?

How is it, what is it like, asked the friend in his letter
I shall be delighted to hear about that, he added in a manner
That showed his profound faith and solemn hopes in the matter
So I wrote to him, first thing next morning, surviving the engine
    clatter

'It is like truth as I never tasted before
It's like the ultimate thing
That makes you not to ask for more
It is a feeling that has 'no' more.

Like an enforced wave which fades before the tide
It is like the traumatic agony, scrambling to hide
While you have conquered the lofty terrain of youth
And are hounded by the stony ghost of a minor truth.

It is like being demoted to the lowest nursery class
For your failure in keeping up with the aged perverse

Looking like a beggar in the pavement of Calcutta bazaar
While wearing the best available attire
It is like an infamous convict, released after ten years inside
For the severest crime committed against all the neighbourhood
It is a perpetual effort, a struggle within a life assumed
In the borrowed fantasy of humanity, subdued.

It is like being dead
Before the destined dread of death
Everyday
It is like breathing your last
While saving some breath.

237

Like an abused effigy of a hated caste
You appear alive, never to last.

For from all the rest of fellow beings
You are aware
You are undeniably different
You are an immigrant.'

Muhammed Haque

7 The *East London Advertiser* reported this grotesque
story as follows:

WIFE WATCHES IN HORROR AS THUGS WAYLAY HUSBAND
YOUTHS TRY TO SLIT MAN'S THROAT

Thugs have attacked a slightly-built Indian building worker in the
street near his home in Bow twice in the space of a fortnight.

In the second attack they tried to slit his throat with a knife as
his wife stood screaming in terror in a nearby doorway. But no one
would open their door to the terrified woman. Curtains stayed
tightly drawn as the thugs beat her husband with bottles, slashed
at his throat with a knife and kicked him senseless.

The man, Mr Rawal Singh, 47, was still suffering from the
effects of the first beating when he was attacked a second time.

The first attack just over a month ago in Eric Street, Bow, had
left him with damaged vision in one eye after the youths had
beaten him up in the street.

'I was walking home along Eric Street when a group of youths
started shouting and calling me names,' said Mr Singh. 'I tried to
walk on but they attacked me and knocked me down. I was badly
beaten on the head and face and was taken to hospital where five
stitches were put in a cut over my eye. I have been unable to work
since that attack.'

Ten days later he was walking home with his wife when they
attacked him again.

'It was in Bow Common Lane. I walked home that way to
avoid the place where they first attacked me,' he said. 'They
seemed to be waiting for me. They started throwing bottles at me,
then they punched and kicked me. I told my wife to run so that
she would be safe, and she ran crying to nearby houses for help.
As my wife stood crying in a doorway the men punched and
kicked me and then one of them thrust a knife at my throat.

'He tried to slide the knife sideways across my throat to cut it.

238

I pulled my head away but he managed to stab me in the throat.
Then police arrived. I don't know who called them. No one would
open the door to my wife when she was trying to get help, but I
think someone must have phoned for the police.

'They took me to hospital and I had stitches put in the cut in
my throat. My clothes were soaked in blood. The men who did it
were aged about 17 to 20 and were all white. I can think of no
good reason why they should attack me. I get on well with my
English neighbours. I am not able to work because of my injuries
and if I go out of my home I have to go by taxi so that I do not
walk in the street.'

A police spokesman said: 'We are conducting a full investigation.'

8 Two of these poems follow.

La Vida (Life)

Tell me what a tree is like.
Tell me how a river sings
when birds are lying on it.

Talk to me about the sea
and the open smell of fields.
Talk about the stars, the air.

Tell me of a wide horizon
without locks and without keys
like the cottage of a poor man

Tell me what a woman's kiss
is like. Find me the word for love:
I have forgotten it.

Are the nights still perfumed
with lovers shuddering
in passion under the moon?

Or is there just this pit,
the light of a tomb
and the song of the flagstones?

Twenty-two years . . . I am forgetting
the size of things,
their colour, their smell . . . I write

gropingly: 'the sea', 'the fields' . . .
I say 'woods' and I have lost
the true proportions of a tree.

I speak only to speak of things
that the years have worn away.

(I cannot go on: I hear
the warder's coming steps.)

Marcos Ana

Deseo (A Wish)

That son of Cain, let him have no more power
to loose his fury on the unfettered Spring
or deal death to the kiss.
Let hatred be restrained from flooding
the pristine margins of the air.
Let knives become
impotent against swallows, and the assassin
powerless to garotte the dawn.
May war never again
batter the skulls of newborn babies, or sever
the exultant arteries of a man.
Let poisoned fangs and pistols
and slavering jaws be done away,
and nevermore let frenzy lash us
with its insensate waves.

Let nothing remain but a love
as vast as all the oceans,
pouring like a cataract across the pupils
of our eyes, flooding the planets,
filling the songs of poets everywhere.

Vidal de Nicolas

9 Mike Rosen's poem *John Bull* begins to explain the
motives that led to slavery and imperialism in a short,
incisive satire easily understood in the classroom.

John Bull

John Bull was an Englishman,
John Bull was a thief,
John Bull sailed across the seas
and robbed an African chief.

John Bull sailed around the world
to look for land to seize —
he stole some islands in the west
and called them his West Indies.

Now, John Bull he loved sugar
but there was none in his bowl
so he looked for willing hands
to cut cane on the land he'd stole.

To Africa went guns and shirts
these were John Bull's bribes
to buy the men and women
to buy the skills of their tribes.

He went among these people
he picked them for their size
then he shipped them across the Atlantic
letting 'em die like flies.

They sowed and reaped the cane,
they ploughed the land he'd stole,
they loaded the boats they'd come in
so John could fill his bowl

Back came the sugar they'd grown
and the barrels of rum they'd made
into the docks he had built
to carry this glorious trade.

John Bull sat down in his great country house
and sipped his Jamaica rum
saying 'The price of one Jamaican slave
is one of my Birmingham guns.'

John Bull had money now
to build his ports and railways,
to finance the first steam engine,
and found a bank at Barclays.

You see, John Bull was a christian
and dearly loved his neighbours —
he had made his neighbours slaves,
and dearly loved their labours.

Of course his slaves are all free now
(to sow the crops *he* likes to reap)
or to come to good old England
where there's work he wants done cheap.

241

John Bull takes what others make
but covers up his tracks,
he goes among the people
saying 'Blame it on the blacks'.

Mike Rosen

Such a poem, however, needs to be explained carefully
so as the white British working class children do not feel
either the guilt or blame for slavery or imperialism.
History does not accuse them, and the crimes of British
imperialism and its continuing consequences were not
engineered by them or their forebears. John Bull was
never their symbol.

As Gladys McGee, a local poet and grandmother, writes,
the white working people were also John Bull's victims.

Compromise

I agree with the black man,
He's had a bad deal,
Some have been tortured
And others have been killed.
Some of us local people have suffered too,
We have been treated the same as you!
Our childhood was hard
And we were poorly paid —
But I always remember my teacher said
'Give what you can to Indian Aid'.
I don't mind giving my help,
But I wish the black man
Would not leave us poor people with guilt!
I am not prejudiced towards you,
I just want you to know that
Some of us are poor too.

Such unity of black and white working people through
class was an underlying feature of all our work with the
children. And as Debbie Carnegie, a local teenage nursery
nurse who came to school to read her poems, emphasised,
that unity also stood firm in childhood.

He looked at me defiantly.
'My mum says I mustn't play with blacks.'
And he ran off with his friend.
He's three years old.
His friend's Jamaican.
Was it defiance?
Or innocence?
My question was answered
later that day.
When he asked me
who was black.

Debbie Carnegie

10 Andrew's visit particularly pleased some of the Jamaican children. Juerline, for example, wrote this short acrostic which we sent to him.

A ndrew, what an active person!
N othing you could say to hurt me,
D etermined to tell what you know
R ight or wrong, it doesn't matter,
E xperienced may he be,
W eary may he be, but never out of speech.

S eeing interest in him
A nybody would see,
L isten carefully to what he says
K eeping our eyes open and clear,
E ngrossed
Y apping away!

Juerline Ingram

11 To help recreate this event, we used the Jamaican ballad by Alma Norman, 'Ballad of Sixty-Five'.

Ballad of Sixty-Five

The roads are rocky and the hills are steep,
The macca scratches and the gully's deep.
The town is far, news travels slow
And the mountain men have far to go.

Bogle took his cutlass at Stony Cut
And looked at the small heap of food he'd got
And he shook his head, and his thoughts were sad,
'You can wuk like a mule but de crop still bad.'

Bogle got his men and he led them down
Over the hills to Spanish Town.
They chopped their way and they made a track
To the Governor's house. But he sent them back.

As they trudged home to Stony Cut
Paul's spirit sank with each bush he cut,
For he thought of the hungry St. Thomas men
Who were waiting for the message he'd bring to them.

They couldn't believe that he would fail
And their anger rose when they heard his tale.
Then they told Paul Bogle of Morant Bay
And the poor man fined there yesterday.

Then Bogle thundered, 'This thing is wrong,
They think we weak, but we hill men strong.
Rouse up yourself. We'll march all night
To the vestry house, and we'll claim our right.'

The Monday morning was tropic clear
As the men from Stony Cut drew near,
Clenching their sticks in their farmers' hands
To claim their rights in their native land.

Oh many mourned and many were dead
That day when the vestry flames rose red.
There was chopping and shooting and when it done
Paul Bogle and his men knew they had to run.

They ran for the bush where they hoped to hide
But the soldiers poured in from Kingston side.
They took their prisoners to Morant Bay
Where they hanged them high in the early day.

Paul Bogle died but his spirit talks
Anywhere in Jamaica that freedom walks,
Where brave men gather and courage thrills
As it did those days in St. Thomas hills.

Alma Norman

244

12 Life for Trotter and his fellow prisoners in Dominica was illustrated by reading out a letter sent by him from his cell:

The cells, 6 ft. by 10 ft., are supposed to be *single* cells, yet officers force two or three men to sleep in one and often enough 4, 5 or even 7 men have been forced to sleep in one . . . In the association cells where the other brothers reside, bugs and pests of all nature are the controllers. Mosquitoes reign supreme during the night time both there and in the block. This always prevents Man from getting any rest at night time. These brothers, who usually number over 20, are forced to inhale the scent of their shit for the whole night. Their cell which measures 50 ft. by 20 ft. has only four portholes and a small strip of opening on the top and fully covered with a galvanize sheet. During the day it is an *oven,* at night time it is a *freezer!* In the Block, November to February marks the *ICE AGE*, while the rest of the year the *oven is on!* In the kitchen where our food is cooked, flies control the scene and there is nothing to control them, *flies* and other insects *daily* make up part of our meals. A *doctor or health inspector* has *never* seen in this jail for the last *2 years.*

This however is nothing compared to the *abuse, insults, beatings* and degradations that we as prisoners are forced to endure! At times, brothers whose nerves have been destroyed by the horrors of confinement are allowed to remain unattended, resulting in their playing in and eating their own shit, sleeping on wet concrete and subject to the worst barbarities.

The similarity of these contemporary events to the inhumanities of slavery and the terrors of the Middle Passage was not lost on the children.

13

Victor Jara of Chile

Victor Jara of Chile
Lived like a shooting star
He fought for the people of Chile
With his songs and his guitar
   and his hands were gentle
   and his hands were strong

Victor Jara was a peasant
Worked from a few years old
He sat upon his father's plough
And watched the earth unfold
    and his hands were gentle
    and his hands were strong

When the neighbours had a wedding
Or one of their children died
His mother sang all night for them
    and his hands were gentle
    and his hands were strong

He grew to be a fighter
Against the people's wrongs
He listened to their grief and joy
And turned them into songs
    and his hands were gentle
    and his hands were strong

He sang about the copper miners
And those who worked the land
He sang about the factory workers
And they knew he was their man
    and his hands were gentle
    and his hands were strong

He campaigned for Allende
working night and day
He sang: Take hold of your brother's hand
The future begins today
    and his hands were gentle
    and his hands were strong

The bloody generals seized Chile
They arrested Victor then
They caged him in a stadium
With five thousand frightened men
    and his hands were gentle
    and his hands were strong

Victor stood in the stadium
His voice was brave and strong
He sang for his fellow prisoners
Till the guards cut short his song
    and his hands were gentle
    and his hands were strong

They broke the bones in both his hands
They beat his lovely head
They tore him with electric shocks
After two long days of torture they shot him dead
    and his hands were gentle
    and his hands were strong

And now the generals rule Chile
And the British have their thanks
For they rule with Hawker Hunters
And they rule with Chieftain tanks
    and his hands were gentle
    and his hands were strong

Victor Jara of Chile
Lived like a shooting star
He fought for the people of Chile
With his songs and his guitar
    and his hands were gentle
    and his hands were strong

Adrian Mitchell

14 This is a transcript of her talk:

I remember you Amanda
When the streets were wet
Running to the factory
Where Manuel was working
With your wide smile
And the rain in your hair
Nothing else mattered
You were going to meet him

Five minutes only
All of your life in five minutes.
The siren is sounding.
Time to go back to work.
And, as you walk,
You light up everything.
Those five minutes
Have made you flower.

247

I remember you Amanda
When the streets were wet.
Nothing else mattered,
You were going to meet him.
With your wide smile
And the rain in your hair.
Nothing else mattered
You were going to meet him.

And he took to the mountains to fight
He had never hurt a fly,
But he took to the mountains,
And in five minutes
It was all wiped out.
The siren is sounding
Time to go back to work
Many will not go back
One of them is Manuel.

I remember you Amanda
When the streets were wet.
Nothing else mattered
You were going to meet him.

These are the words of a song by my husband, Victor Jara. I want
to tell you, as briefly as I can, something about his life and death.
He was born in the south of Chile. His father was a peasant. His
mother was a folk-singer. Victor used to accompany his father as
he ploughed the earth and his mother to the wedding parties,
funerals and harvests where she went to sing with her guitar. He
had Chilean folklore in his blood. It was part of him. His family
were extremely poor but by luck, hard work, exceptional talent
and great privation — against all the rules of the establishment —
in 1960 he qualified as a theatre producer in the University of
Chile. Immediately his work produced great impact, the plays he
produced were taken on tour in Latin America and the States, he
was invited to Great Britain by the British Council, he was shower-
ed with praise and prizes by the establishment in Chile. However,
folksong and his guitar were always close to him and, although he
never studied music, and could not write it, he went on investigating the folklore of his country, and this was a natural means of

expression for him. My husband was a very warm, loving and spontaneous person, with a great sense of humour. He began to convert into song his feelings, his love for his people, his identification with them and their struggle for social justice, began to fight against the 'potted' imported culture then invading Chile, establishing new values and accusing those who were guilty of maintaining misery and injustice. He committed the crime of becoming a popular singer, in spite of having the mass media practically closed to him.

In 1969 he was stoned in an upper class secondary school, where a priest had invited him to sing; and won the first prize in the festival of new Chilean song.

At the beginning of 1970 he left the theatre to give himself entirely to singing and composing and the cause of popular unity feeling that, given the cultural conditions in Chile at that date, he could thus reach more effectively and more directly the people with whom he wished to communicate — the peasants, the miners, factory workers, students, children, the under-privileged who have never entered the theatre. The hatred of the extreme right wing increased with his power of communication with the greater majority of the Chilean people. He was one of the leaders and principal creators of the new song movement, which became 'popular' song in the true sense of the word. It was taken to the heart of the people because they recognised it was their own. Its artists did not aspire to become idols, were not manufactured by commercial propaganda, but in spite of that their song touched the youth and workers of Chile and became part of their cultural and political expression.

With the growth of Popular Unity, Victor could find himself singing one day in a University, the next in a mine, the next in a demonstration of half a million people. He said: 'I am a man happy to exist at this moment. Happy because when one puts one's heart, reason and will to work at the service of the people, one feels the happiness of that which begins to be reborn.'

During the three years of Popular Government in Chile there was a sort of cultural flowering, or you could call it an explosion — a real and massive participation of the people who had always been starved of any sort of cultural activity. New song groups, dance groups, theatre groups began to flourish. Drab walls in the towns of Chile blossomed with colourful murals painted by the people.

Victor felt very strongly that an artist should live the experiences of his fellow workers. The songs he wrote about a shanty town were the result of his own experience and close contact with the people. These are the words of one of them. It is called 'Man is a Maker.'

Like lots of other children
I was taught to sweat
I didn't know what school was.
I didn't know how to play.
They dragged me out of bed
Early every morning
And alongside my Dad
I grew up as a worker.

Because I was pretty handy
I got by as a carpenter.
A plasterer, a bricklayer,
A plumber and a mechanic.
Hey! It would have been useful
To have had some sort of schooling.
That would have been one more thing to use —
Man is a maker.

I can build you a house,
I can lay down a road,
Make wine that tastes good
And keep a factory smoking.
I go down to the depths of the earth.
I conquer all the peaks.
I walk among the stars
And carve furrows all over the earth.

I learnt the language
Of my masters and bosses.
They killed me over and over
For daring to raise my voice
But I get up off the ground again
Helped by the hands of others.
For now I am not alone,
Now there are so many of us.

In 1973 when the threat of civil war or a military coup was
hanging over Chile, and the terrible face of fascism was showing
itself more and more openly, Victor felt that our happy family life
was coming to an end, but had unshaken faith in the Chilean
working class and felt that nothing could reverse the advance in
experience of the years of the Popular Unity Government.

On 11 September, Victor was due to sing at the opening of an
exhibition about the horrors of civil war and fascism — to take
place at the Technical University, where Allende was to have
spoken.

He heard on the radio of the military operations taking place,

heard of the bombing of the Popular Unity radios — heard Allende
making his last speech — but answering the urgent call for all
workers to assemble in their place of work, Victor left home to
go to the University less than two hours before the bombing of the
presidential palace. He phoned me twice that day — it was
impossible for him to come home again. I learnt much later that
the University was already surrounded the last time he spoke to
me — but he gave me courage and told me he loved me.

The Rector and several hundred professors and students were
trapped in the University building. The military fired against them
all night to prevent anyone escaping. Some who tried to get out
after nightfall were killed by machinegun fire. The next morning,
Wednesday 12 September at nine o'clock, the military moved into
the University — students and professors were taken prisoners —
Victor was immediately recognised and given 'special' treatment.
I have been told by many witnesses that he behaved with great
courage and was a source of moral strength to his fellow prisoners.
That he sang there in the boxing stadium, that they broke his
hands and after two days killed him with machineguns.

Meanwhile I waited for news of him at home with my children.
Two days after the coup I received a message from him, brought
to me by somebody who had been in the stadium with him and
had managed to get out. Then nothing more, until a week afterwards I found his body in the morgue. It was an anonymous body,
among hundreds of other Chilean workers, students, university
professors — battered, bloody, half-naked and riddled with
machinegun bullets. I was lucky to have been able to bury my
husband. Many disappeared into a common grave.

The news of Victor's murder spread rapidly. It was reported
on the television and in a newspaper (controlled, of course, by the
junta) as though it had been a natural death — now the official
version is that Victor was shot resisting arrest with a machinegun
in his hand. Since December it is forbidden to mention his name in
Chile. A few days after Victor's death somebody working in the
military controlled television channel risked his life to insert a
verse of the song you are about to hear over the sound track of an
American film. It is a song called 'Prayer to a Labourer' and had
become a symbol of the new Chilean song. It says:

Stand up
Look at the mountains
Source of the wind, the sun, the water
You who change the course of rivers
You who sow the flight of your soul.

251

Stand up
Look at your hands
Take your brother's hand so you can grow
We'll go together united by blood
The future can begin today.

Deliver us from the master who keeps us in misery,
Thy kingdom of justice and equality come
Blow, like the wind blows, the wild flower of the mountain pass
Clean the barrel of my gun like fire.
Thy will be done at last on earth
Give us your strength and courage to struggle.
Blow, like the wind blows, the wild flower of the mountain pass
Clean the barrel of my gun like fire.

Stand up
Look at your hands,
Take your brother's hand so you can grow
We'll go together, united by blood,
Now and in the hour of our death. AMEN.

I have told you Victor's story only because it is the symbol of what
is happening in Chile today — thousands of other Chileans have
suffered his fate, thousands of other Chilean families have suffered
our loss.

Why did they hate him so much? Was it because he was the son
of a Chilean peasant and proud of it? Was it because he showed the
moral courage that the Chilean people are showing under their
repression? Was it because through his songs he expressed the will
and ideas — the very identity of the Chilean people?

Today, two years after the military coup, the terrible persecution of the Chilean people continues. A fascist military dictatorship
has installed a highly sophisticated repressive machine based on
terror, torture and a computerised intelligence system to quell any
opposition.

Chile has been converted into a country of concentration camps
in which not even the church is free from persecution.

Victor had faith in song as a means of communication which
could surmount barriers of language and culture. Certainly today,
due to the enormous wave of solidarity with the Chilean people

which has swept over the world, his songs are being sung in every continent. His voice cannot be silenced because it contains the voices of all those who have been murdered in Chile and whose struggle was and still is his own.

15 One of these farmworkers' poems, translated from the Spanish, had a particularly strong effect:

Un Pensamiento (A Thought)

i am from
the lost roads
can't remember
where i came from
don't know
where i'm going

my father
with all his valor
decides
our destiny

cotton fields
in texas
treacherous and suffocating

apple groves
in washington
blankets never suffice
the cold never ignored
in california
the vegetable and onion
back breaking
stoop work

sombreros
cannot stop
the roasting sun
from scorching
our brown skin . . .
more brown

up north again
pick apricots
and cherries

my father . . .
que lastima
tired and worn
dying
from the wounds
inflicted
by the days
but never complaining
muy gustoso
he awaits the moment
when
marianita, jorge
miguel, santitos
and ricardo
jump on him
with all their carino

that's all he lives for

my father
can no longer
work
like he used to

his children starving
we received
a very small amount
of unemployment
called WELFARE

for this
the capitalist rich growers
call my father scavenger

trying
just to stay alive
my father
with all his regrets
takes his
pregnant wife
and eight children
to work
but yet
they brand us lazy

my older brother
dropped out of school
to help support
our poverty-stricken family

a month later
he was drafted

nine months hence
he was killed
in action

for his country???
what did it ever do
for us

they never lent
an extra
breast
to help feed
our young ones

they never gave us
a decent place
to live in
just houses of tin
in farm labor camps

freezing in
the cold climate
steaming
during the warm months

my father
not speaking english
doesn't understand
WHY
we are treated this way

i have heard
and read
that this
is the richest country
in the world

that there is
no poverty

i don't see
how
my padres
can take it

I CAN'T

i mustn't feel
this way

i'm asking
for too much

what
silly hopes . . .
a day dream

i'm trying hard
to be
like my padres
but
my conscience
bothers me

i feel
it's all wrong

ah
forget it

i'm just
another migrant

16 Woody Guthrie's song follows, together with 'The Grape Pickers' Tragedy'. Jack Warshaw, its writer, an American folksinger, came to the school and sang to the children later in the year. Both songs concern Mexican migrant workers rather than Chicanos, but the links were fundamental and obvious.

Deportee

The crops are all in and the peaches are rottin',
The oranges all piled in their creosote dumps,
They're flyin' 'em back to that Mexican border
It takes all their money to wade back again.

My father's own father he waded that river
They took all the money he made in his life.
My brothers and sisters all climbed the frail fruit trees
And they rode on that truck till they broke down and died.

Chorus:
Goodbye to my Juan, goodbye Rosalita,
Adios mis amigos, Jesus y Maria,
You won't have a name when you ride the big airplane
And all they will call you will be . . . deportees.

The sky plane caught fire over Los Gatos canyon,
A fireball of lightning it blazed through the sky.
Who are these dear friends who all scattered like dry leaves?
The radio says they are just . . . deportees.

We died in your forests, we died in your deserts,
We died in your valleys, we died in your plains.
We died in your orchards, and died in your vineyards,
Both sides of the river we died just the same.

Chorus:

Some of us are illegal, and some are not wanted,
Our work contract's out and we have to move on;
Six hundred miles to that Mexican border,
They chase us like outlaws, like rustlers, like thieves.

Is this the best way you can grow your green orchards?
Is this the best way you can grow your good fruit?
To scatter like dry leaves and rot on your topsoil
And be known by no name, except deportees.

Woody Guthrie

Grape Pickers' Tragedy

The night-time is hot and the city is sleeping,
Ramon Sanchez takes Maria, his wife, by the hand —
The American border's a mile down the highway,
The border they've got to cross over to work on the land.
   Cross over to work on the land.

Ramon and Maria just follow the footsteps,
To a place called The Hole a little ways over the line,
Ten thousand are begging for work in the vineyards,
Where fruitflies are thicker than dust, or the grapes on the vine,
   Than dust, or the grapes on the vine.

At four the bus starts on another day's journey,
At six, see the sun in the hills and the sky glowing red,
At eight they arrive, at nine they are weary,
At eleven the drone of the duster is heard overhead,
   the duster is heard overhead.

You work in a blizzard of fruitflies and hoppers,
You sweat and you choke and you bend and you bleed and you
   crawl,
Your lungs fill with dust and your body is broken,
The life of a picker, you know it aint no life at all,
   You know it aint no life at all.

The duster plane's loaded with tanks of spray poison,
To kill off the fruitflies and hoppers that wither the crop,
It's killed off the insects that feed on the fruitflies,
They're breeding unchecked and so fast that the dusting can't stop,
    So fast that the dusting can't stop.

The duster plane circled low over the vineyard,
Ramon knew the sound that means run for the trucks or the shed,
It came down like rain where Maria was working,
Maria worked on, but a few hours later fell dead,
    A few hours later fell dead.

'Ramon', said the grower, 'we're all mighty sorry —
She must have been sick long before she came up from the South;
The spray can't hurt people, and we don't want trouble
So here's your day's pay, and don't come back and don't open
    your mouth,
    Don't come back and don't open your mouth.

He threw down the money — walked out of the office;
Maria was taken to town and they gave him her things.
There's nowhere to go but over the border —
Adios mi Maria, it's their blood that the next harvest brings,
    It's their blood that the next harvest brings.

Jack Warshaw

17 The following is part of the text of Reuben Hauwanga's statement before the United Nations Council for Namibia in March, 1976.

When I was arrested on the early morning of August 17 1975, I was taken to the Regional Prison at Ondangua. A certain white warrant officer Petrus Johannes Jordaan, assaulted me with the aid of Tweihala Kamhulu with fists, kicks and with the butt of a rifle. That day I was locked up together with a mentally ill man, Paavo, who kept dancing, laughing and shouting the whole night.

The next morning, this same Jordaan, an ex-professional boxer, came again accompanied by three white police, Botha, Jan Hoffman and another whose name has unfortunately escaped me. Jordaan again started punching and kicking me, assisted by the third policeman. I started bleeding profusely from both my nose and mouth.

I was then ordered back into my cell and Jordaan gave me,

what I believe was a Karate chop. I lost balance and what else I remembered were kicks on my back and buttocks.

After that I believe I became unconscious since I only came to find myself alone, my face swollen, my legs clumsy and jaws heavy. During and between the punches, Jordaan kept asking me: 'Who killed Filemon Elifas? What are SWAPO's future plans? Where are SWAPO's guerrilla camps?'

Jordaan returned two weeks later bringing writing material for me to write down everything I knew concerning SWAPO, myself, Elifa's death, etc. I stayed for two more weeks to recuperate and was then taken to Oshikango, a South African police station in the northern part of Ovamboland, where interrogations were conducted under torture by colonel Skoon, assisted by Lieutenant Diepenaar, Captain Steyn and Warrant Officer Loafs.

At Oshikango we were suspended from the roof so that our feet just touched the floor and were not allowed to sleep. Should it become impossible for us to keep awake and we slumbered, a bucket of water was poured over us. A punch in the stomach or a kick or a slap in the face were common.

Hours merged into days and days into weeks. Colonel Skoon would come now and then with a question or two and went. Some days later one of my arms was freed and with the other still suspended I was ordered to write down the answers I gave to their questions.

Diepenaar was not satisfied with my statement and told his man to suspend me from my feet. In this condition I hanged for some three to four hours, feet up and head down.

Further interrogation took place at Ogongo with Colonel Skoon again. It is at Ogongo that my comrades and I experienced unspeakable agonies. When one morning I was locked up in a police van, I heard constant screams coming from an apartment. It was obvious that the victim was in extreme physical pain and agony: the voice was that of our National Organiser, Aaron Muchimba. Later, when I was subjected to electric shocks, I understood why my comrade was screaming.

I also saw how they grabbed my beloved comrade and friend, Sam Shivute, one of them on his hair and the other at his feet swinging him to and fro and finally throwing him on to a table. He was screaming loudly.

What happened to me is very little in comparison to what is happening to many of my comrades still in South African hands. It is indeed an unexplainable miracle that many of them do not die under such circumstances; it is conditions like these that Western allies of South Africa support, thus prolonging our suffering and dehumanisation. They must be told this story.

18 We had the first verse and chorus of Morris' 'The March of the Workers' painted in large letters on sheets of art paper. This was taped to the back wall of the classroom and hung there throughout the year:

What is this, the sound and rumour? What is this that all men hear,
Like the wind in hollow valleys when the storm is drawing near,
Like the rolling on of ocean in the eventide of fear?
'Tis the people marching on . . .

Chorus:
Hark the rolling of the thunder!
Lo the sun! and lo thereunder
Riseth wrath and hope and wonder,
And the host comes marching on.

We studied the extension of struggle for free speech after the Dod Street incident through to the unemployment marches of 1887. Alfred Linnell, an unemployed worker from Bow, was killed by police in Northumberland Avenue during a march of the unemployed through the West End in that year. His funeral became a massive demonstration, and thousands of working people followed his body as it was carried from Soho to Bow Cemetery, where it still lies. Over his grave Morris spoke these words, and followed by leading the singing of his 'Death Song'. In a time of such unemployment, and when racism was being used as a false answer to its causation, the story of Alfred Linnell was particularly important.

'Our friend who lies here has had a hard life, and met with a hard death: and if society had been differently constituted, his life might have been a delightful, a beautiful and a happy one. It is our business to begin to organise for the purpose of seeing that such things shall not happen; to try to make this earth a beautiful and happy place.'

We did not have to look far to see who the Alfred Linnells of our own time were. It was obvious that some of them wore black and brown skins.

A Death Song

What cometh here from west to east a-wending?
And who are these, the marchers stern and slow?
We bear the message that the rich are sending
Aback to those who bade them wake and know.
    Not one, not one, nor thousands must they slay.
    But one and all if they would dusk the day.

We asked them for a life of toilsome earnings,
They bade us bide their leisure for our bread;
We craved to speak to tell our woeful learning;
We come back speechless, bearing back our dead.
    Not one, not one, nor thousands must they slay.
    But one and all if they would dusk the day.

They will not learn; they have not ears to hearken.
They turn their faces from the eyes of fate;
Their gay-lit halls shut out the skies that darken.
But lo! This dead man knocking at the gate.
    Not one, not one, nor thousands must they slay.
    But one and all if they would dusk the day.

Here lies the sign that we shall break our prison;
Amidst the storm we won a prisoner's rest;
But in the cloudy dawn the sun arisen
Brings us our day of work to win the best.
    Not one, not one, but thousands must they slay.
    But one and all if they would dusk the day.

William Morris

19 The folk songs of the area bear strong witness to its maritime past. Here are two songs about sailors returning.

Ratcliffe Highway

As I was-a-walking down Lodon,
From Wapping to Ratcliffe Highway,
I chanced to pop into a gin-shop
To spend a long night and a day.

A young doxy came rolling up to me
And asked if I'd money to sport.
For a bottle of wine changed a guinea,
And she quickly replied: 'That's the sort.'

When the bottle was put on the table,
There were glasses for everyone.
When I asked for the change of my guinea,
She tipped me a verse of her song.

This lady flew into a passion,
And placed both hands on her hips,
Saying: 'Sailor, don't you know our fashion?
Do you think you're on board of your ship?'

'If this is your fashion to rob me,
Such a fashion I'll never abide,
So launch out the change of my guinea
Or else I'll give you a broadside.'

A gold watch hung over the mantle
So the change of my guinea I take,
And down the stairs I run nimbly
Saying: 'Darn my old boots, I'm well paid.'

The night being dark in my favour,
To the river I quickly did creep,
And I jumped on a boat bound for Deptford
And got safe aboard of my ship.

So come all you bold young sailors
That ramble down Ratcliffe Highway,
If you chance to drop into a gin-shop,
Beware lads, how long you do stay.

For the songs and the liquors invite you,
And your heart will be all in a rage;
If you give them a guinea for a bottle
You can go to the devil for change.

Outward Bound

At the Blackwall docks we bid adieu
To Kate and Polly and Sal and Sue,
Our anchor's weighed and our sails unfurled,
We're off halfway across the world.

Chorus:
Hurrah we're outward bound (Repeat)

The wind it blows from east north east,
Our ship she sails nine knots at least,
The girls stand on the docks and cry,
While there's grog we'll never say die.

Chorus:
Hurrah we're outward bound (Repeat)

At last our captain comes on board,
Our sails are bent, we're manned and stored,
The peter's hoisted at the fore,
Hurrah for the girls we'll see no more.

Chorus:
Hurrah we're outward bound (Repeat)

One day the man on the lookout,
'There's a sail to windward,' he will shout,
'She's a pilot standing off from land,
Up on deck goes every man.

Chorus:
Hurrah we're homeward bound (Repeat)

And when we get to the Blackwall docks
Then pretty young girls come down in flocks,
And one to another you'll hear them say
'Here comes Jack with his ten months pay.'

Chorus:
I see you're homeward bound (Repeat)

And when we get to the Dog and Bell
Where there's good poison there to sell,
In comes grouser with a smile
Saying 'Drink my lads, it's worth your while.'

Chorus:
For I see you're homeward bound (Repeat)

But when the money is all spent
And there's none to be borrowed and none to be lent,
In comes grouser with a frown
Saying 'Get up Jack, let John sit down.'

Chorus:
For I see you're outward bound (Repeat)

So poor old Jack must understand
There's ships in the docks all wanting hands,
So he humps his gear as he did before
And bids adieu to his native shore.

Chorus:
For he is outward bound (Repeat)

20 We tried hard to emphasise to the children that their area had not only been the arena of great acts of industrial struggle, but it had also formed the backcloth and imagery for great works of literature. From that store of writing we used Blake's 'London':

London

I wander thro' each chartered street,
Near where the chartered Thames does flow,
And mark in every face I meet,
Marks of weakness, marks of woe.

In every cry of every man,
In every infant's cry of fear,
In every voice in every ban,
The mind-forg'd manacles I hear.

How the chimney-sweeper's cry
Every black'ning church appals;
And the hapless soldier's sigh
Runs in blood down palace walls.

But most thro' midnight streets I hear
How the youthful harlot's curse
Blasts the new-born infant's tear
And blights with plagues the marriage hearse.

There was also Mayhew and Dickens, particularly the parts of *Our Mutual Friend* that were set in the neighbourhood of our school in 'Limehouse Hole', and of course the workhouse passages from *Oliver Twist*. Thomas Hood's 'The Song of the Shirt' gives a stark and terrifying impression of the East London sweatshops and the trials of women garment workers of the last century, and Arthur Morrison's novels *A Child of the Jago* and *The Hole in the Wall* give more insights into the crushing poverty that so many of the working people experienced. We also used such East End autobiographies as A.S. Jasper's *A Hoxton Childhood,* Grace Foakes' *Between High Walls* — the story of a dockland girlhood, and extracts from Jim Wolveridge's *Aint it Grand?*. Dorothy Scannell, who had written *Mother Knew Best,* an account of her early life in Poplar, visited the school and read passages from her book to the children. And of course, there was Jack London:

From *The People of the Abyss* by Jack London

We had long since left Mile End Road, and after traversing a gloomy maze of narrow, winding streets, we came to Poplar Workhouse. On a low stone wall we spread our handkerchiefs, and each in his handkerchief put all his worldly possessions, with the exception of the 'bit o' baccy' down his sock. And then, as the last light was fading from the drab-coloured sky, the wind blowing cheerless and cold, we stood, with our pitiful little bundles in our hands, a forlorn group at the workhouse door.

Three working girls came along, and one looked pityingly at me; as she passed I followed her with my eyes, and she still looked pityingly back at me. The old men she did not notice. Dear Christ, she pitied me, young and vigorous and strong, but she had no pity for the two old men who stood by my side! She was a young woman, and I was a young man, and what vague sex promptings impelled her to pity me put her sentiment on the lowest place. Pity for old men is an altruistic feeling, and besides, the workhouse door is the accustomed place for old men. So she showed no pity for them, only for me, who deserved it least or not at all. Not in honour do grey hairs go down to the grave in London Town.

On one side the door was a bell handle, on the other side a press button.

'Ring the bell,' said the Carter to me.

And just as I ordinarily would at anybody's door, I pulled out the handle and rang a peal.

'Oh! Oh!' they cried in one terrified voice. 'Not so 'ard!'

I let go, and they looked reproachfully at me, as though I had imperilled their chance for a bed and three parts of skilly. Nobody came, luckily, it was the wrong bell, and I felt better.

'Press the button,' I said to the Carpenter.

'No, no, wait a bit,' the Carter hurriedly interposted.

From all of which I drew the conclusion that a poorhouse porter, who commonly draws a yearly salary of from seven to nine pounds, is a very finicky and important personage, and cannot be treated too fastidiously by — paupers.

So we waited, ten times a decent interval, when the Carter stealthily advanced a timid forefinger to the button, and gave it the faintest, shortest possible push. I have looked at waiting men where life or death was in the issue; but anxious suspense showed less plainly on their faces than it showed on the faces of these two men as they waited on the coming of the porter.

He came. He barely looked at us. 'Full up,' he said and shut the door.

'Another night of it,' groaned the Carpenter. In the dim light the Carter looked wan and grey.

In this century, such poets as Wilfred Owen and Isaac Rosenberg, both victims of the First World War, have written about East London. We read Owen's haunting 'Shadwell Stair' with the children, a poem which evoked a sense of weirdness and ghostliness from the Thames:

Shadwell Stair

I am the ghost of Shadwell Stair.
Along the wharves by the water-house,
And through the cavernous slaughter-house,
I am the shadow that walks there.

Yet I have flesh both firm and cool,
As eyes tumultuous as the gems
Of moons and lamps in the full Thames
When dusk sails wavering down the pool.

Shuddering the purple street-arc burns
Where I watch always; from the banks
Dolorously the shipping clanks
And after me a strange tide turns.

I walk till the stars of London wane
And dawn creeps up on the Shadwell Stair.
But when the crowing syrens blare
I with another ghost am lain.

Isaac Rosenberg's 'A Ballad of Whitechapel' was written in highly metaphorical and visionary language, but the children could feel the sense of suffering and desperation that the young Jewish poet — himself living in considerable poverty and hardship — wrung through his meeting with the young girl, forced into prostitution through her family's distress.

266

A Ballad of Whitechapel

God's mercy shines,
And our full hearts must make record of this,
For grief that burst from out its dark confines
Into strange sunlit bliss.

I stood where glowed
The merry glare of golden whirring lights
Above the monstrous mass that seethed and flowed
Through one of London's nights.

I watched the gleams
Of jagged warm lights on shrunk faces pale.
I heard mad laughter as one hears in dreams,
Or Hell's harsh lurid tale.

The traffic rolled,
A gliding chaos populous of din.
A steaming wail at doom the Lord had scrawled
For perilous loads of sin.

And my soul thought,
'What fearful land have my steps wandered to?
God's love is everywhere, but here is naught
Save love His anger slew.'

And as I stood
Lost in promiscuous bewilderment,
Which to my mazed soul was wonder-food,
A girl in garments rent

Peered 'neath lids shamed,
And spoke to me and murmured to my blood.
My soul stopped dead, and all my horror flamed
At her forgot of God.

Her hungered eyes,
Craving and yet so sadly spiritual,
Shone like the unsmirched corner of a jewel
Where else foul blemish lies.

I walked with her
Because my heart thought, 'Here the soul is clean,
The fragrance of the frankincense and myrrh
Is lost in odours mean.'

She told me how
The shadow of black death had newly come
And touched her father, mother, even now
Grim-hovering in her home.

Where fevered lay
Her wasting brother in a cold bleak room,
Which theirs would be no longer than a day —
And then — the streets and doom.

Lord! Lord! dear Lord!
I knew that life was bitter, but my soul
Recoiled, as anguish-smitten by sharp sword,
Grieving such body's dole.

Then grief gave place
To a strange pulsing rapture as she spoke,
For I could catch the glimpse of God's grace,
And a desire awoke.

To take this trust,
And warm and gladden it with love's new fires,
Burning the past to ashes and to dust
Through purified desires.

We walked our way,
One way hewn for us from the birth of Time.
For we had wandered into Love's strange clime
Through ways sin waits to slay.

Love's euphony,
In Love's own temple that is our glad hearts,
Makes now long music wild deliciously,
Now Grief hath used his darts.

Love infinite,
Chastened by sorrow, hallowed by pure flame —
Not all the surging world can compass it.
Love — Love — O tremulous name.

God's mercy shines.
And my full heart hath made record of this,
Of grief that burst from out its dark confines
Into strange sunlit bliss.

Finally, we used this anonymous poem which came
from a small local anthology of East End poems published
in 1922, *West Ham Poems*. There is a freedom here
which shines right through oppression and city despair.

May-Time in Canning Town

The high wind speeds cloud-galleons o'er the sky,
    And sets the wherries dancing where the tide
    Rushes in sunlit splendour up the wide
And foam-flecked spaces of the estuary:
White washing flaps its sails in gardens gay:
    The Earth's a bride arrayed in streaming white:
    On hedgerow, blossoming tree and woodland height
Her banners wave, and all the world's at play.

And even in Canning Town, where no white tree
    Symbols the far-flung rapture of the spring,
      Some dream of beauty by the wind is stirred,
    Some envy of the careless birds that wing
      High o'er her smoke, some longing for a word
To break her evil spell and set her free.

21

Strike for Better Wages (1880)
(to the tune of 'Tramp, tramp, tramp, the boys are marching')

At the docks there is a strike that the company don't like
A tanner on the hour they'll have to pay:
Like slaves they'd have us work far more than any Turk
And make us sweat our lives out every day.

Chorus:
Strike, boys strike for better wages!
Strike, boys strike for better pay!
Go on fighting at the docks,
Stick it out like fighting cocks
Go on fighting till the bosses they give way.

Every morning there are flocks for employment at the docks,
Hard working men who scarce can get a meal;
With wives and children dear, it would make you shed a tear
If you only knew the hardship that they feel.

If its slavery that you seek, for about a quid a week,
They'll take you on as soon as you come near,
Sweat your guts out with a will, or they'll try your job to fill
But that won't wash with working men, it's clear.

We'll stand up for our rights and the company we will fight,
Supported by our brothers everywhere,
For we have friends galore — the good old stevedores,
And the seamen and the firemen they are there.

Starvation 'tis they bids to a man with seven kids,
When he brings home only fifteen pence a day,
For what can you get to eat on seven-and-six a week,
When it often takes it all the rent to pay.

Here's a health to Mr Burns, he's done us all a turn,
Ben Tillett, Mann and Mr Toomey too:
We won't give in a bit, for we've got 'em in a fit,
And we've put the old dock-company in a stew.

The Great Dock Strike of 1889 was typical of a local historical event that could be reconstructed for the children by use of song, poetry, and newspaper articles of the period. We found the two very graphic items of late nineteenth century journalism that follow in the local history room of the public library. Jack London's portrayal of Dan Cullen, the victimised docker, showed that the 1889 strike was only a transitory victory.

The Dock Labourers' Strike
(East End News: August 23rd 1889)

The dock labourers' strike appears to be growing more serious and extensive. The demonstration they made on Tuesday was a credit to themselves, and should undoubtedly be the subject of the gravest consideration for the dock directors. The men assembled at the dock-gates on Tuesday morning soon after six and held a meeting, at which speeches were delivered in the midst of a tremendous downpour of rain. The rain, however, as Mr. John Burns boasted later in the day, did not appear to damp their enthusiasm or impair the success of their meeting, though hundreds of them must have been drenched to the skin. After their meeting they formed in column, and with bands and banners they moved, some thousands strong, for miles through the neighbourhood of the docks, holding meetings and calling on the men who had not already come out to join them in urging what they all of them believe to be a just demand. This early demonstration was apparently intended more particularly for the laggards in the movement.

At eleven o'clock they mustered again at dock gates, and again tramped off with their society banners and two bands up the Commercial-road, through White Horse-street, Butcher-row, and Brook-street into Shadwell, and thence on by Leman-street into the City, passing through Leadenhall-street and Gracechurch-street, and then returned to the West India Dock gates. They reckoned they had 14,000 men in their ranks at the outset, and in the course of their march they were joined by other bodies at various points; and though many of the men, probably unable to continue the tramp, fell out here and there, their numbers throughout were imposing. They were all of them genuine working men of the dock labouring class, and their quiet, orderly, good-tempered but thoroughly resolute bearing could not but have impressed all who saw them. Great enthusiasm was evoked at one point by the display of a big square shovel lashed to a pole and displayed on the pan of the shovel, 'Coal porters on strike', written in chalk. An outburst of grim merriment was called forth again and again by various illustrations of 'dockers dinners'. One was a slice of bread and a saveloy hoisted on a pole. That saveloy somehow disappeared before the journey was finished, and, indeed, in the midst of those hungry-looking men it could hardly be expected to travel far. But by the time the procession drew towards the end of the journey one or two other poles were to be seen moving along dangling a haddock and an onion, or a hunch of bread and a herring.

'But mind ye,' said one lantern-jawed fellow, with a lick-round of his tongue, 'it ain't the 'addocks and the 'errin's us grumbles at.'

'No,' says another, 'nor the saveloys neither. It's when a chap's got to buckle in his belt, and rub his stomach for a dinner as give ye the 'ump.'

At the Free Trade Wharf, in Brook-street, a halt was made for an effort to draw out some of the men employed there. The gates were closed, and were guarded by a couple of policemen, who seemed to regard the demonstration with no unfriendly eye; and, by the way, it was noticeable throughout that an excellent feeling existed between the processionists and the police, many of whom were heard to express their sympathy with the men.

'What d'ye think of us, boss?' asked one of the demonstrators as he paused for a moment in front of a policeman.

'Hope you'll get your penny, old man,' replied the policeman cheerily.

'Good, old Copper!' was the appreciative response followed by a ringing cheer.

The Dock Labourers' Strike
(East End News: August 28th 1889)

'Well, how are things going? Do you expect to get this penny?' 'No sort of doubt about it,' was the ready response from the spokes-man of a group of dock labourers, and the reply seemed to be endorsed by them all. The whole group of six or seven men had their backs up against the front of a public-house, and presented an epitome of their class throughout the dock region. There was the man of Herculean frame and sinewy muscle, who looked as though he could lift a hogshead of sugar, and there was the feeble-looking pale-faced man, the lines of whose face told plainly of physical debility and mental suffering, and whose general appearance indicated some sedentary occupation in the past. There was the typical toper with the bleared eye and faintly suggestive purple in the nose, and there was the short, sturdy, stolid-looking man, who might at one time have been a farm labourer. One was a mere youth — gaunt, slim, and spiritless, and one was growing grisly and bent with years, his hard, weather-beaten face looking as though he had long grown past all the enthusiasm with which — strange as it may seem — the prospect of another penny an hour as the result of a hard struggle, lighted up more than one of those uncouth faces as they discussed the progress of the movement. 'There's nothing to hinder us getting it,' said the spokesman of the group. 'All the working-classes are going to hang together this journey, and the docks'll have to give in.' 'Don't you think they will, sir?' inquired another. 'Really, I should not like to express my opinion. But if, as you say, all the working classes are going together no doubt you will be able to make a good fight for it.' 'If the working classes hold together they can do just what they likes,' said a dark-eyed, curly-headed, dapper-looking young workman who came up at the moment. 'They've only got to hang together and they could cut off the Queen's head tomorrow.' 'Ah! and then no doubt you'd be sure of your penny. But what have you to do with it? You're not on strike.' The man carried his tools over his shoulder, and had evidently just come from his work . . . No; he wasn't on strike today, but he and his mates were coming out. They were ship's painters and were going to stand by the dock labourers on principle. A firebrand this, with a good deal to say on general principles. In the training of the volunteers and the drilling of the boys in Board schools he foresaw the time when working men were going to fight for their rights. But revolutionary opinions drew forth a chorus of disapproval. 'Better stow that sort of bosh, mate,' said one of the party, taking a little black pipe with about an inch of stem from his mouth. 'We mean to hang together, but we're goin' to keep quiet about it. Yes, sir; that's what Mr. Tillett said. He says, "You keep orderly and respectable, and you got the public with 'e." '

'There's nothing unreasonable in what we want,' said a quiet young fellow; 'sixpence an hour ain't unreasonable pay for such work as dock labourers gets, especially when you come to consider the waitin' you have to do for it. I myself have had three days' work in a month, and there's hundreds o' poor fellows as have got nothin' for it to-night but to tramp the streets or lie up in a doorway.'

He goes on in the same strain, but his story is drowned in a general outbreak from others all around who tell distressing tales of hunger and weariness, and hope deferred, and of the bitter hardship of waiting hour after hour, day after day, for a job at the dock gates, and of their getting taken on at eight in the morning and discharged again at nine. They are agitating for sixpence an hour, and demand that a man shall be engaged for not less than four hours.

From *The People of the Abyss* by Jack London

It is a brief little story, the story of Dan Cullen, but there is much to read between the lines. He was born lowly, in a city and land where lines of caste are tightly drawn. All his days he toiled hard with his body; and because he had opened the books, and been caught up by the fires of the spirit, and could 'write a letter like a lawyer', he had been selected by his fellows to toil hard for them with his brain. He became a leader of the fruit-porters, represented the dockers on the London Trades Council, and wrote trenchant articles for the labour journals.

He did not cringe to other men, even though they were his economic masters, and controlled the means whereby he lived, and he spoke his mind freely, and fought the good fight. In the 'Great Dock Strike' he was guilty of taking a leading part. And that was the end of Dan Cullen. From that day he was a marked man, and every day, for ten years and more, he was 'paid off' for what he had done.

A docker is a casual labourer. Work ebbs and flows, and he works or does not work according to the amount of goods on hand to be moved. Dan Cullen was discriminated against. While he was not absolutely turned away (which would have caused trouble, and which would certainly have been more merciful), he was called in by the foreman to do not more than two or three days' work per week. This is what is called being 'disciplined', or 'drilled'. It means being starved. There is no politer word. Ten years of it broke his heart, and broken-hearted men cannot live.

He took to his bed in his terrible den, which grew more terrible with his helplessness. He was without kith or kin, a lonely old man, embittered and pessimistic, fighting vermin the while and looking at Garibaldi, Engels, and Dan Burns gazing down at him from the blood-bespattered walls. No one came to see him in that crowded municipal barracks (he had made friends with none of them), and he was left to rot.

But from the far reaches of the East End came a cobbler and his son, his sole friends. They cleansed his room, brought fresh linen from home, and took from off his limbs the sheets, greyish-black with dirt. And they brought to him one of the Queen's Bounty nurses from Aldgate.

She washed his face, shook up his couch, and talked with him. It was interesting to talk with him — until he learned her name. Oh, yes, Blank was her name, she replied innocently, and Sir George Blank was her brother. Sir George Blank, eh? thundered old Dan Cullen on his death-bed; Sir George Blank, solicitor to the docks at Cardiff, who, more than any other man, had broken up the Dockers' Union of Cardiff, and was knighted? And she was his sister? Thereupon Dan Cullen sat up on his crazy couch and pronounced anathema upon her and all her breed; and she fled, to return no more, strongly impressed with the ungratefulness of the poor.

Dan Cullen's feet became swollen with dropsy. He sat up all day on the side of the bed (to keep the water out of his body), no mat on the floor, a thin blanket on his legs, and an old coat around his shoulders. A missionary brought him a pair of paper slippers, worth fourpence (I saw them), and proceeded to offer up fifty prayers or so for the good of Dan Cullen's soul. But Dan Cullen was the sort of man that wanted his soul left alone. He did not care to have Tom, Dick, or Harry, on the strength of fourpenny slippers, tampering with it. He asked the missionary kindly to open the window, so that he might toss the slippers out. And the missionary went away, to return no more, likewise impressed with the ungratefulness of the poor.

22 The story of the schools' strikes is told in Dave Marson's *Children's Strikes in 1911,* published by History Workshop. We also read with the children the script of *Fall in and Follow Me* (History Workshop, 1973), a play written by Billy Colvill and Dave Marson, based on the schools' strikes in East London. This was first performed at the Half Moon Theatre, Stepney in 1973. It is a sharp and spirited play that is much appreciated in the classroom.

23 We duplicated another fine poem from the *Women's Dreadnought,* written in August 1914, close to the outbreak of the war. Again, the writer was an anonymous woman.

Rebel Song

Be not afraid whate'er they say,
Tyrant and priest, and threatening gun
Thy father for one inch of the way
Died with his face towards the sun.

Fear not their chains, my little child,
None are so vile and strong as fear;
Hope guards the prisoned eagle wild,
Truth's voice from living tombs speaks clear.

The vultures on the lion feed
But let this be thine inmost stay,
There's heaven in hell for those who bleed
To win an inch of freedom's way,

24 Charlie Key, who had been one of the imprisoned councillors, wrote an account of the events in his book, published later by the Poplar Labour Party — *Red Poplar.* Extracts from this were duplicated and read with the children.

Red Poplar

At 4 o'clock on September 1st the Mayor and four councillors were arrested. Other arrests were made on succeeding days, and public feeling rose rapidly until on the day on which the five women members were taken the crowds in the streets had grown to enormous proportions. On the day following, 15,000 men and women, many carrying babies in their arms, marched from Poplar to Holloway to show by demonstrating outside the prison that they were determined to support councillors in the fight they were waging.

The treatment of the prisoners was at first bad, but by united and determined action the conditions were soon altered. As a result of interviews with the governor and letters to the Home Office, prison discipline was relaxed, the dietary modified, and the prisoners allowed to meet together in one of the prison cells.

On September 19th the Council Room of Brixton Prison was placed at their disposal for evening meetings. Here, with the Mayor in the chair and the Town Clerk in attendance, regular meetings of the Councillors were held at which were present not only Councillors who had not been arrested but also women members who were brought by the prison authorities in special motors from Holloway to Brixton to attend. Thus day by day the prisoners were kept in touch with the actions that were being taken by supporters outside, and themselves took an active part in directing the fight.

Outside things were moving rapidly. Within two or three weeks over 10,000 of the men and women of Poplar had enrolled themselves in a Tenants' Defence League and had pledged themselves, should the members in prison deem it necessary, to refuse to pay rent until their representatives had been released — a form of mass action which had considerable effect on the result of the struggle. Deputations to the Prime Minister and the Minister of Health on the part of the Labour Mayors of London resulted in proposals for a conference to consider the question of Poor Law Finance and the provision of money for Outdoor Relief. It was suggested that the imprisoned Councillors should select some of their number to attend, but to this they rightly refused to agree. 'We can only enter a conference,' they said, 'when we are all free.' But a conference was essential and, therefore, it soon began to be realised that in some way or another release must be effected.

25 We found some very strong workers' poetry written at the time of the General Strike in the locally-edited Journal of the period, *Lansbury's Labour Weekly.* These poems we duplicated and read with the children. Of the examples that follow, two are about London, two are about the miners — who bravely continued the strike after the betrayal of the T.U.C. leaders.

The Street

Gaunt and gray is the slimy street,
Where pain and penury, mournful meet;
Where hucksters coarse, 'neath naphta flares,
Display their cheap and nasty wares;
While Mrs Demos sadly spends
The paltry pelf the pawnshop lends;
Or, with a gesture regal, blues
The old man's dole in kiddies' shoes.

There Demos, helped by hop-less booze
Haggles for Mayfair's worn-out shoes:
Or 'blows his kite' with jellied eels
(Does Mayfair know such tasty meals?)
And youth its dirty finger dips
In greasy paper filled with chips,
Whilst 'neath the barrows urchins crush
For rotten fruit embalmed in slush.

O Christ! Why leave us in the lurch?
They make a lot of you in church.
How can we worship at thy shrine
Or link our lowly lots with thine?
Our lives are spent in squalid street
Which white-hot Hell can never beat —
Our puny souls, of Hope bereft,
Have faith alone — in Labour's 'Left'.
H. Lazenby

London Town

I left with joy the crowd, the heat,
The gay profusion of the street;
This way and that, and to and fro,
I saw the stream of pleasure flow,
Pomp, folly, idleness and sin
So smooth without, so sick within.

A corner turned, and what is here?
A sight to raise a cynic sneer,
A pinched and ragged multitude
That haggles for its sickening food,
Hardship and poverty and care
Stark desolation everywhere.

Yet not a stone's throw lies between
Yon glittering and this loathsome scene;
Squalor and squandering side by side
Our too unhappy world divide:
'Tis here the worker hides his head,
Who finds those drones their very bread.

Then can you wonder at a choice
That fain would lend these woes a voice,
Woes which, if passed in silence by,
The very stones must rise and cry?
Better with misery here to dwell
Than yonder in a gilded hell.
C.W. Beckett

Pit Fields

The face of Earth is smiling, pranked in state
With green of hope and garlands of the Spring,
Her breath unlaboured, scented, fills the air
With promise of her beauty fostering.
    A thousand feet below, the coal pit's core
    The jinny rings for more and yet for more.

Her smile will change to laughter with the joy
Of June's rich mirth of melody and praise:
Her glade and field, the haunts of bird and bee
Resound the revel of her richer days.
    A thousand feet below the keen picks swing
    And putters stripped to pelt both sweat and sing.

On summer eves the nightingale will thrill
The dusk in calling to the dew-moist rose.
The moon will mount her realm and argent light
Will make the Earth's night pageant full disclose.
    A thousand feet below the night shift strive
    To save a comrade, trapped in number five.

T.D. Coughlan

Miners' Wives

We have borne good sons to broken men
Nourished them on our milkless breast,
And given them to our masters when
Their day of life was at its best.

We have dried their clammy clothes by the fire,
Solaced them, cheered them, tended them well,
Watched the wheels raising from the mine,
Watched the wheels lowering them to hell.

We have prayed for them in a godless way
(We never could fathom the ways of God.)
We have sung with them on their wedding day,
And wept as they took the uncertain road.

We have stood thro' the naked night to watch
The silent wheels that raised the dead:
We have gone before to raise the latch
And lay the pillow under their head.

We have done all this for our masters' sake,
Done it in rags, and did not mind;
What more do they want? What more can they take?
Unless our eyes, and leave us blind.

Joe Corrie

26 The Battle of Cable Street evoked strong memories
for many local residents who had lived through it. Two
local writers, Jim Wolveridge, a borough cleansing
worker who had been a youth in 1936, and Stephen
Hicks, an ex-professional boxer and now an old age
pensioner, contributed these two pieces, which we
duplicated for the children.

I'd been aware that there was going to be trouble in Cable Street
for at least a week. At the time I worked for a buttonhole maker
in Cable Street and as I was making my deliveries round the area
I heard the tailors saying they were going to stop Mosley and
knock hell out of his blackshirts. I thought then that it was going
to be purely a local affair but I was wrong about that. The
Communist Party and the Young Labour Party were organising
an opposition on a vast scale; I didn't learn about this until later.
    I belonged to no particular party at the time and the C.P.
didn't take me into their confidence. I used to work overtime
Sunday mornings collecting the bosses' debts and my own tips.
I was going the rounds quite easily at first but by 10 o'clock I was
beginning to find it more difficult — the crowds began arriving
about then, Tower Hill and Royal Mint Street filled up first and
then the Minories. Whole armies seemed to be marching through
Leman St. and soon every street in the area, even small backwaters
like Gowers Walk, were jampacked. Newspapers the next day
estimated the crowds at half a million — it seemed more to me;
the whole of London seemed to be there. I got back to the
workshop at about 11 and by then Cable St. was almost full, and
then like a scene from a film someone called out 'the dockers are
coming' and they swarmed into the street in their hundreds. Many
of them carried pick-axes and they used them to pry up the
paving stones — some they broke into pieces to use as missiles and
some they used to build a barricade; they also had marbles to roll
under the feet of the policemen's horses and fireworks to scare
them. They built other barricades just beyond Back Church Lane.
They overturned a lorry and piled it high with girders they'd

pinched from a builder's yard. Cable St. looked like a disturbed Ant Hill. The mounted police arrived first and they were met by a shower of missiles, the woman who owned the fruit shop at No.11 had neglected to put up her shutters and the crowd pinched her fruit to use as ammunition. She didn't like it much but it was all in a good cause! One of the crowd threw a large pair of pliers at a policeman — it missed 'im and went through my guvernor's basement window. Old Feldman was such a slave driver and paid such low wages, I'd often felt like throwing things through his window myself — but it was a pity they missed the copper!

I'd like to say I played a heroic part in the battle myself, but I didn't, I was 16 at the time and was so small I could still travel on buses for half fare so I didn't think I'd of been of much use anyway, and there was such a great crowd in the street I couldn't get out of the door. So I watched the fight from an upstairs window with the Feldmans. Unfortunately the Feldmans were people of large circumference and they were hogging most of the space so I could only catch glimpses of the fighting but what I could see was pretty nasty. The police were hitting out like maniacs and the people in front of the crowds were taking a nasty beating. I saw one man sitting on the pavement with his head split wide open and there were plenty of other casualties. The ambulances seemed to be arriving in convoys but the police weren't having it all their own way. They'd clear a small space and then more people would be coming in from side streets to fill the gap. I don't know how long the fight went on but it seemed to last forever. But one thing was obvious — the police weren't going to get through; it would have taken the army to do that, so in the end the police gave up.

They didn't march away in formation and there were no victory roars from the crowd — the whole thing just seemed to peter out and everybody seemed away. I walked through Cable Street just afterwards and it really looked a wreck; it was littered with bricks which people had thrown from the roof and the remains of the barricades were scattered all over the road. Cable St. looked like it had been hit by a bomb. I went to Gardiners Corner a little later; there was still a great crowd in Commercial Road and it was just breaking up as I came along. None of the people at the back of the crowd knew what was going on but they knew the police and the blackshirts hadn't got through. When I read the newspaper the next day they said that Mosley's mob hadn't got past Tower Hill so the people had won a great victory; the people themselves weren't in a jubilant mood, they kept talking about the injuries and they swore that there'd been a number of deaths and that this was being hushed up — whether this was true or not I just don't know but from the injuries I saw it wouldn't have surprised me. Later in the week the depressed mood wore off and the people started talking about the victory they'd won — they'd stood together and defeated the entire Metropolitan Police Force — and it was a bigger victory than they knew — the Fascists never again attempted to march in force through the East End; they did make a small sneak attack on Whitechapel the next Sunday; they burnt a few cars and threw a small Jewish girl through a plate glass window.

Of course no fascists were arrested — they never are — but it was their last fling. They went into a slow decline; it took a long time but in the end Mosley retired and wrote his memoirs — I haven't read 'em yet!

They Shall Not Pass   1936

I remember the day alright
When Oswald Mosley showed his might
Near the Whitechapel Road.
But he got a bit dismayed
For not much progress had he made
As the opposition growed.
The opposition there to be
Was the Jewish community.

The plan was this — in Mosley's mind
No trouble would he ever find
To reach Whitechapel Road.
And so he mustered all his force,
It was against the law of course
As forward they all strode.
And Oswald muttered with a grin,
'My mob can get through anything.'

But how wrong his big head was,
For he got turned right back because
He found it kind of tough,
To beat the law and thousands more
Of Jewish people rich and poor
Made of heroic stuff,
And others who had felt quite sure
Of him they'd had enough.

In Commercial Road right at the top
By Gardiner's Corner he had to stop
No further could they get.
'Cause of the law, and what they saw,
For Whitechapel was packed galore
The greatest crowd I'd met
And they cried out 'They shall not pass,
They will not pass us yet.'

'Twas like a race run on a course
With feeble men against a horse,
The last declining hope.
But more shadows are overcast
While he is playing loose and fast
With those who cannot cope.
For now he's got another stung
Calling it 'The National Front'
Some more fascist soft soap.

But whatever he has in mind
Will not be good for us, I find,
We've heard it all before.
And it needs no-one to tell
That we can get on quite as well
Without him I am sure,
By handing out the option of
An ever CLOSING door.

Stephen Hicks

Finally, Jack Warshaw's song 'Red Lion Square'
contemporized the 1936 incident at Cable Street. Two
generations meet, moved on by the need for a
continuous struggle.

Red Lion Square

Oh father, oh father, look what I see,
There's a big demonstration on T.V.
There's one bunch waving their Union Jacks
And another group under police attack.

Oh father dear, the news just said,
There's a young man hurt, they think he's dead.
There's people there saw him go down
And saw his head smashed and his blood on the ground.

Oh son, oh son, the things you see
Bring back a long time memory.
For I was young in '36
When the fascists tried the same old tricks.

Those blackshirts marched through London too,
They swore they'd kill the reds and the Jews.
For they were just one step behind
What was going through Hitler's mind.

They had big friends and they had the dough,
And the cops said 'yes' but we said 'no',
In Cable Street we took our stand
But the cops gave them a helping hand.

Confusion there was all around,
Their horses charged to run us down.
Some were running if they could
And some were lying in their blood.

The blackshirts and the boys in blue
Thought they could split our ranks in two
The cry went up 'THEY SHALL NOT PASS!'
We fought together and we held fast.

Now son, I'll tell you what they said,
'The violence was caused by reds,
Those agitators deserved their fate',
And they praised the cops for their restraint.

You've heard the word 'appeasement', son,
It did not stop the fascist guns.
One hundred million souls did die
Before those guns did cease their fire.

And now they've banned their uniform
But the hateful blackshirts have returned.
So son, remember Red Lion Square,
For it could happen anywhere.

Jack Warshaw
(Tune: Traditional)

27

The war years in the East End had its funny as well as serious
moments. I was in the East End, Poplar in fact, where the raids
were particularly heavy. I was on vital war work at the time, so

spent every night in the thick of it. The night the East India Docks was bombed I was living within 200 yards of the docks. The trusses from the dock warehouses were thrown in the air, over the dock wall and landed in the grounds of Poplar Hospital. Some also crashed into the front of the hospital, injuring already sick patients.

Another time at the docks, August Bank Holiday in fact, there was a day raid which was very serious. Lots were killed and injured. I was standing outside a tailor's shop, speaking to a pal of mine, and as the explosion occurred my pal and I for some reason turned our backs towards the blast, of course thus facing the shop window. After the dust and confusion was over I looked at my pal and saw that his face was pitted with glass fragments, and his clothes torn. I was standing next to him yet all that happened to me was that I got hit on the knee by a piece of timber from the shop front, which I thought was uncanny. The funny thing about that incident was that the dock entrance was made up of three arches. Lorries used to use the middle arch whilst the police were always guarding the right hand arch where the dockers came out, so the police could search the men if necessary. The left hand side was always shut. But after that particular raid the policeman was still standing in the middle of the arch and he was smothered in dust from top to bottom, and he stood there as if nothing had happened.

Another incident, was one Sunday afternoon I had been out during lunchtime to have a drink, and after the pubs closed I made my way towards home when the air raid warning went. We had got so used to it that we tended to ignore them. Anyhow, I sat down and was enjoying my dinner, when I heard a bomb whistle down. It must have landed very close, as the next I knew was I looked up and could see through the ceiling, through the roof (what was), and I could not find my half-finished dinner for slates and bricks. I had what was left of the window frame around my neck like a garland, plus a few cuts and bruises. I think I lost my ceilings and roof about ten times, but to me the experience was terrific.

I am still alive and kicking (just about) and I am almost on my pension. Plenty more stories on request, sad or otherwise.

Tony's Grandad

We showed Humphrey Jennings' film made during the war about the Blitz, *I Was a Fireman.* This documents the heroism of East End firemen fighting the fires caused by Nazi incendiary bombs dropped onto the docks.

Tony's Grandad's piece had expressed the kind of

stamina and spirit that had seen local people through the Blitz. Eddie Baunton's sonorous poem also remembered the war, and like Tony's Grandad, he had also lived through it and seen its wastage and wreckage, not only in East London, but throughout the world. Just before he wrote this poem, Eddie had been attacked by fascists while putting up Labour party posters for a local election. His poem was a statement of struggle and tenacity which for all our children was both a warning, and an inspiration.

Have you read Mein Kampf?
You should, it tells you why
So many of the world's young men
Were marched, and forced to die.
They started with a slogan
'Our Nation First' it said.
Then 'Tainted blood must be cleansed'.
They left six million dead.

Not dead in patriot's honour,
Not dead in soldiers' fame,
Dead. Gassed in multitudes,
Of six million, not a name.
To purify the nation,
Secret searchers were installed.
They murdered Jew and Gentile,
The whole world was appalled.

A national front was unified,
Jubilant in their quest.
The pall of death lay heavily
All over Europe's west.
Swollen with their victories
Over the helpless and the small,
They marched beyond their boundaries
To purify us all.

At last the outside world took heed,
Their rifles made of wood,
Dummy guns, planeless skies,
Ready for battle stood.

One by one they were beaten down,
The blood of their souls ran red,
A conqueror had purified
Another million dead.

The burning house, the bleeding child,
Held as its mother died.
The legless man, the blinded boy,
These were the purified.
So many paid the final price,
Who wished to see men free.
They left their trust with us who lived,
Their folk, like you and me.

Eddie Baunton

28 As I complete these notes, I have been given the
following poem by a local mother and garment worker.
Its anger and understanding shows where the real
divisions are in our society, and over much of the world.
If there is a sense of despair here, there is also the
passion and knowledge that the 'coming generation'
are inheriting. And as the news of the continuous
resistance of the valiant children of South Africa reaches
us, how can despair ever fix its grip?

Man's Hell

Szzzsht! Szzzsht! The sound of steam
    Escaping.
Brrroom! Brrroom! The Hoffman Press
    Awakening.
Clank, clank, power released,
By the touch of a treadle.
Clang, clang, the top rises,
To expose the knife edge
Of a freshly pressed seam.

On the factory floor
Machines! are coming to life.
Squeak of unoiled engines,
The crash! as feet meet steel.
From the office
Phone bells ring,
Feet rush to and fro,
An unending string
Of energy,
Released by a clock.

On Earth, is this Hell?
The working class
Know too well,
To be ruled by a clock,
At dawn! to rise.
At night! shut out by lock.
Deafened! by the sound of noise,
While the pious sing
'All men on Earth rejoice.'

Of whose creation,
This civilisation?
All men! equal to one?
While! some just laze and relax.
Others! work is never done.
Perhaps some day it will be revealed,
Why birth alone should separate the classes.
Poverty! known only to the lower masses.

Just a few share the riches
Of man's sweat and labour.
The whole earth laid bare,
The fruits of work turn sour.
One has not the energy to spare
For relaxation.
The steam of labour pollutes the air,
God help the coming generation

If this is living
Where does Hell begin

Sally Flood